Using R for Principles of Econometrics

Second Edition

Constantin Colonescu

Title: "Using R for Principles of Econometrics." Second edition.

Author: Constantin Colonescu

Affiliation: MacEwan University

Edmonton, Alberta

Canada

The examples presented in this book follow Hill, C., Griffiths, W., and Lim, G. (2018). *Principles of Econometrics*, Fifth Edition. Wiley.

This book has been created using Xie, Y. (2016a). *bookdown: Authoring Books with R Markdown*. R package version 0.0.71.

R version: x86_64-w64-mingw32, x86_64, mingw32, x86_64, mingw32, , 3, 4.3, 2017, 11, 30, 73796, R, R version 3.4.3 (2017-11-30), Kite-Eating Tree

ISBN-13: 978-1983486562

ISBN-10: 1983486566

Contents

5 The Multiple Regression Model   73

6 Further Inference in Multiple Regression   93

7 Using Indicator Variables   117

8 Heteroskedasticity   139

Chapter 1

Introduction

```
rm(list=ls()) # Caution: this clears the Environment
library(bookdown)
library(POE5Rdata)
library(knitr)
library(xtable)
library(stargazer)
library(rmarkdown)
library(DescTools) #Only for the command 'some()'
library(PoEdata)
data(food, package="PoEdata")
```

This manual can be used as a supplementary resource for the "Principles of Econometrics" textbook by Carter Hill, William Griffiths, and Guay Lim, fifth edition (Hill et al., 2018).

The following list gives some of the R packages that are used in this book more frequently:

- devtools (Wickham and Chang, 2016a)
- POE5Rdata (Colonescu, 2017)
- knitr (Xie, 2017)
- bookdown (Xie, 2016)
- xtable (Dahl, 2016)
- stargazer (Hlavac, 2015)
- rmarkdown (Allaire et al., 2016)

The function install_github from the package devtools installs packages such as POE5Rdata from the GitHub web site. Here is the code that installs devtools and POE5Rdata:

```
# Install the following packages if they are not installed
install.packages("devtools")
devtools::install_github("ccolonescu/POE5Rdata")
```

The computing environment for using R (R Development Core Team, 2008) is RStudio (RStudio Team, 2015). You need to install on your computer the following resources:

- R (https://cloud.r-project.org/)
- RStudio (https://www.rstudio.com/products/rstudio/download/)
- POE5Rdata package (https://github.com/ccolonescu/POE5Rdata)

This brief introduction to R does not intend to be exhaustive, but to cover the minimum material used in this book. Please refer to the R documentation and to many other resources for additional information. For beginners, I would recommend (Lander, 2013).

1.1   The RStudio Screen

A typical RStudio Screen is divided in four quadrants. The NW quadrant is for writing your script in text format and for viewing data, the SW quadrant (the console) shows results of calculations, the NE one shows lists of variables and more, and the SE quadrant is for help, graphs, and the package list.

1.1.1   The Script, or data view window

Here are a few tips for writing and executing R script in the Script window:

- You may start your script with a comment showing a title and a brief description of what the script does. A "comment" line starts with the hash character (#). Comments can be inserted anywhere in the script, even in line with code, but what follows the hash character to the end of the line will be disregarded by R.
- Code lines may be continued on the next line with no special character to announce a line continuation. However, code will be continued on the next line only if the previous line ends in a way that requires continuation, for instance with a comma or unclosed brackets.
- When you want to run a certain line of code, place the cursor anywhere on the line and press Ctrl+Enter; if you want to run a sequence of several code lines, select the respective sequence and press Ctrl+Enter; you can even run only a part of a code line: just select the part you want to run and press Ctrl+Enter.

1.1.2 The `console`, or `output` window

While it is always advisable to work in the script mode because thus you can save and re-use your code for different data, sometimes you may need to run commands that are out of the script context. Such commands can be typed at the bottom of the console at the sign >. Pressing Enter executes such a command, and the up and down arrows allow re-activating and editing older lines of code that had been previously typed into the console.

1.2 How to Open a Data File

To open a data file for the *Principles of Econometrics* textbook (Hill et al., 2018), first check if the devtools package is installed. If it is not, run the following code:

```
install.packages("devtools") # if not installed
library(devtools)            # activates devtools
```

After having activated the devtools package you can install and activate the RPOE5data data package as follows:

```
install_github("ccolonescu/POE5Rdata")
library(POE5Rdata) # makes datasets ready to use
```

Now, we can load and inspect a particular dataset, for example *andy*. When the dataset is available, it should appear in the Environment window (look in the top-right quadrant of the RStudio screen). Here is an example of opening the file *andy* and showing some of the data by using the commands head and Some.

```
library(POE5Rdata)
data("andy")   # makes the data set "andy" ready to use
# ?andy        # shows information about the data set

# Show the head of the data set, with variables as column names.
head(andy)
```

```
##   sales price advert
## 1  73.2  5.69    1.3
## 2  71.8  6.49    2.9
## 3  62.4  5.63    0.8
## 4  67.4  6.22    0.7
## 5  89.3  5.02    1.5
## 6  70.3  6.41    1.3
```

```
# Show a few rows in dataset.
Some(andy) # In package DescTools. Use capital letter in 'Some'
```

```
##     sales price advert
## 17  70.7  5.89    1.5
## 20  71.2  6.37    0.5
## 37  83.8  4.94    0.9
## 46  84.2  5.08    2.8
## 50  81.2  5.83    1.8
## 58  85.9  5.34    1.8
```

If you wish to open a file that you have previously created, you need to provide R with the full path where the file is stored on your computer. Otherwise, R will look for the file in R's current working directory. You can use the code setwd() to set a desired working directory, and getwd() to see what is R's current working directory. You can also use the drop-down menu Session - Set Working Directory to choose a particular working directory.

1.2.1   Importing or loading a data file

Sometimes it is frustrating to read a csv file into R; an error message like No such file or directory is rather frequent, especially in Windows, where the complete location of a file is sometimes not obvious. Try copying the file itself with Ctrl+C and paste it into RStudio's script pane. The result is the complete location of the file, with some extra characters at the beginning. Delete these characters and type quotation marks around the file address.

Here is an example of importing a csv file. The ~ character replaces the *working directory* part of the file address.

```
andy <- read.csv(
  "~/RPOE5All/DataFilesDownloadedAll/andy/andy.csv")
```

To load an R data file (rdata or rda), use the function load(), but do not assign a name as I did above for the csv file, because load() assigns a name automatically. The following line does not work because a name is assigned to the dataset:

```
andy <- load("~/RPOE5All/DataFilesDownloadedAll/andy/andy.rdata")
```

This works (no name assigned):

```
load("~/RPOE5All/DataFilesDownloadedAll/andy/andy.rdata")
```

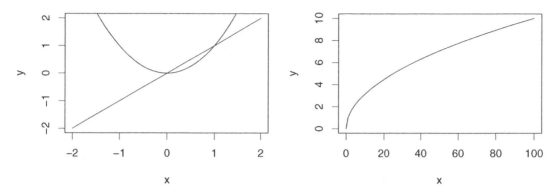

Figure 1.1 Examples of using the function curve()

1.3   Creating Graphs

The basic tools for graph creating are the following R functions:

The function plot(x, y, xlab="Income in $100s", ylab="Food Expenditure, in $", type="p"), where x and y stand for the variable names to be plotted, xlab and ylab are the labels you wish to see on the axes, and type refers to the style of the plot; type can be one of the following: "p" for points, "l" for lines, "b" for both points and lines, and "n" for no plot. The type value "n" creates an empty graph which serves other functions such as abline(), which is described below.

The function curve() plots a curve described by a mathematical function, say f, over a specified interval. When the argument add = TRUE is present, the function adds the curve to a previously plotted graph. The following code fragment and Figure 1.1 are examples.

```
par(cex=1.6,mar=c(4,4,1,1),lwd=1.6) #sets graphical parameters)
curve(x^1, from=-2, to=2, xlab="x", ylab="y" )
# Add another curve to the existing graph:
curve(x^2, add = TRUE)
curve(sqrt(x), from=0, to=100, xlab="x", ylab="y")
```

The function abline() adds a line defined by its intercept, a, and slope, b, to the current graph. For a sloping line, the arguments of the functions are the intercept, a=, and the slope, b=; for a horizontal line the argument is the ordinate of the line, h=; for a vertical line, the argument is the abscissa of the line, v=. The abline function can also take as its argument the name of a simple linear regression object, which includes the intercept and the slope of a regression line. The following code demonstrates the use of abline with both plot and curve; the results are displayed in Figure 1.2.

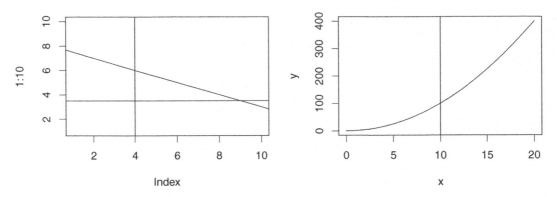

Figure 1.2 Examples of using the function 'abline()'

```
par(cex=1.6,mar=c(4,4,1,1),lwd=1.6)
plot(1:10, type="n") # creates an empty graph
# Add straight lines to graph:
abline(a=8, b=-0.5, h=3.5, v=4)
curve(x^2, from=0, to=20, ylab="y")
abline(v=10)
```

The function ggplot in package ggplot2 is a very flexible plotting tool. For instance, it can assign different colors to different levels of an indicator variable. A brilliant, yet concise presentation of the ggplot() system can be found in (Grolemund and Wickham, 2016), which I strongly recommend.

1.4   R Cheatsheets

There are plenty of materials about R that are freely available online. For instance, you can find a brief collection of the most popular R instructions here: https://cran.r-project.org/doc/contrib/Short-refcard.pdf

Here are some R commands used in this book:

lm(y~x, data = datafile) regresses y on x using the data in *datafile*

nrow(datafile) returns the number of observations (rows) in *datafile*

nobs(modelname) gives the number of observations used by a model. This may be different from the number of observation in the data file because of missing values or sub-sampling `set.seed(number)` sets the seed for the random number generator to make results reproducible. This is needed to construct random subsamples of data

`rm(list=ls())` removes all objects in the current `Environment` except those that have names starting with a dot (.)

`pdfetch` retrieves time series data from online sources such as the World Bank, Eurostat, European Central Bank, and Yahoo Finance

`WDI` retrieves data from the World Development Indicators database

`Quandl` retrieves financial and economic data from www.quandl.com

`quantmod` (Quantitative Financial Modelling Framework) retrieves fnancial data from various sources; moreover, it provides tools for developing quantitative trading models.

`eurostat` retrieves data from the rich databases maintained by Eurostat.

Chapter 2

The Simple Linear Regression Model

```
rm(list=ls()) # Caution: this clears the Environment
options(digits=4,signif=F)
library(POE5Rdata)
library(broom) #to create tidy tables
library(knitr) #cross-references for tables
library(ggplot2)
```

2.1 The General Model

A simple linear regression model assumes that a linear relationship exists between the conditional expectation of a dependent variable, y, and an independent variable, x. Sometimes, the independent variable is called *response*, or *response variable*, and the independent variable is called *regressor*. The assumed relationship in a linear regression model has the form

$$y_i = \beta_1 + \beta_2 x_i + e_i, \tag{2.1}$$

where

- y is the *dependent variable*
- x is the *independent variable*
- e is an *error term*

15

- σ^2 is the variance of the error term
- β_1 is the *intercept* parameter or coefficient
- β_2 is the *slope* parameter or coefficient
- i stands for the *i*-th observation in the data set, $i = 1, 2, ..., N$
- N is the number of observations in the data set

The *predicted*, or estimated value of y given x is given by Equation (2.2); in general, the *hat* symbol indicates an estimated or a predicted value. For the estimated β parameters, however, we are going to use the notation b instead of $\hat{\beta}$, though other works often use $\hat{\beta}$.

$$\hat{y} = b_1 + b_2 x \tag{2.2}$$

The subscript i in Equation (2.1) indicates that the relationship applies to each of the N observations. Thus, there must be specific values of y, x, and e for each observation.

The simple linear regression model assumes that y and x are random, *iid* (independently and identically distributed) variables and that x cannot be used to predict e (x is strictly *exogenous*); this latter assumption implies that the expected value of the error term for any value of x is zero and that the covariance between the error term and x is zero. Another assumption is one of *homoskedasticity*, which requires that the variance of the error term, σ^2, is the same for any level of x. When this is not the case, the error term is said to be *heteroskedastic*.

2.2   Example: Food Expenditure versus Income

The data for this example is stored in the R package POE5Rdata. To check if the package is installed, look in the Packages list in the bottom-right quadrant of RStudio. Table 2.1 displays the first few observations in the *food* data set.

```
data(food)
dta<-head(food)
kable(dta, caption="Head of the $food$ Data Set",
      col.names=c("Expenditure ($)","Income ($100)"))
```

It is always a good idea to inspect the data before using it in any analysis. One way to do so is to create a **descriptive statistics** table, as the one in Table 2.2.

```
dta<-tidy(food) #Calculates descriptive statistics
dta<-dta[,c(1:5,8,9,13)] # Selects the desired statistics
kable(dta,
```

Table 2.1: Head of the *food* Data Set

Expenditure ($)	Income ($100)
115.2	3.69
136.0	4.39
119.3	4.75
115.0	6.03
187.1	12.47
243.9	12.98

Table 2.2: Descriptive Statistics for the *food* Data Set

column	n	mean	sd	median	min	max	se
food_exp	40	283.6	112.68	264.48	109.71	587.7	17.82
income	40	19.6	6.85	20.03	3.69	33.4	1.08

```
caption="Descriptive Statistics for the $food$ Data Set",
digits=2)
```

Another way of inspecting the data is to visualize them in a **scatter plot**, which can be created in R using the function plot(). Figure 2.1 is a scatter diagram of food expenditure on income, suggesting that there is a positive relationship between income and food expenditure since food expenditure tends to be higher at higher incomes.

```
data("food")
par(cex=1.3)
plot(food$income, food$food_exp,
     ylim=c(0, max(food$food_exp)),
     xlim=c(0, max(food$income)),
     xlab="Weekly Income in $100",
     ylab="Weekly Food Expenditure in $",
     type = "p",pch=16)
```

2.3   Estimating a Linear Regression

The R function for estimating a linear regression model by the ordinary least squares (OLS) method is lm(y~x, data) which, used just by itself, does not show any output; It is useful to give the model a name, such as mod1, then show the results using summary(mod1). If you are interested in only some of the results of the regression, such as the estimated

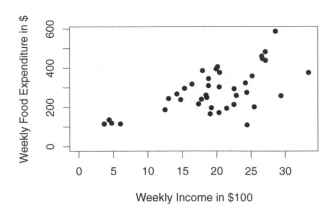

Figure 2.1 A Scatter Diagram for the *food* Model

coefficients, you can retrieve them using specific functions, such as the function coef().
For the food expenditure data, the regression model will be

$$food\_exp = \beta_1 + \beta_2 income + e \tag{2.3}$$

where the subscript i has been omitted for simplicity. The following code box demonstrates
the use of the lm() function on the *food* data set and shows the use of coef() to retrieve
the estimates for the coefficients β_1 and β_2.

```
mod1 <- lm(food_exp ~ income, data = food)
b1 <- coef(mod1)[[1]]
b2 <- coef(mod1)[[2]]
smod1 <- summary(mod1)
print(smod1, signif = F)


##
## Call:
## lm(formula = food_exp ~ income, data = food)
##
## Residuals:
##     Min      1Q  Median      3Q     Max
## -223.03  -50.82   -6.32   67.88  212.04
##
## Coefficients:
```

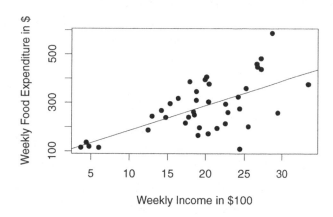

Figure 2.2 Scatter Diagram and Regression Line for the Food Expenditure Model

```
##               Estimate Std. Error t value Pr(>|t|)
## (Intercept)     83.42       43.41    1.92    0.062
## income          10.21        2.09    4.88  1.9e-05
##
## Residual standard error: 89.5 on 38 degrees of freedom
## Multiple R-squared:  0.385,  Adjusted R-squared:  0.369
## F-statistic: 23.8 on 1 and 38 DF,  p-value: 1.95e-05
```

The function coef() returns a list containing the estimated coefficients, where a specific coefficient can be accessed by its position in the list. For example, the estimated value of β_1 is b1 <- coef(mod1)[[1]], which is equal to 83.42, and the estimated value of β_2 is b2 <- coef(mod1)[[2]], which is equal to 10.21.

The intercept parameter, β_1, is usually of little importance in econometric models; we are mostly interested in the slope parameter, β_2. The estimated value of β_2 suggests that the food expenditure for an average family increases by \$10.21 when the family income increases by one unit, which in this case is \$100. The R function abline() adds the regression line to the previously plotted scatter diagram, as Figure 2.2 shows.

```
par(cex=1.3)
plot(food$income, food$food_exp,
    xlab="Weekly Income in $100",
    ylab="Weekly Food Expenditure in $",
    type = "p",pch=16)
abline(b1,b2)
```

How can one retrieve various regression results? These results exist in two R *objects*
produced by the lm() function: the regression object, such as mod1 in the above code
sequence, and the regression summary, which I denoted by smod1. The next code shows
how to list the names of all the results available in each object.

names(mod1)

```
##   [1] "coefficients"   "residuals"      "effects"        "rank"
##   [5] "fitted.values"  "assign"         "qr"             "df.residual"
##   [9] "xlevels"        "call"           "terms"          "model"
```

names(smod1)

```
##   [1] "call"           "terms"          "residuals"      "coefficients"
##   [5] "aliased"        "sigma"          "df"             "r.squared"
##   [9] "adj.r.squared"  "fstatistic"     "cov.unscaled"
```

To retrieve a particular result you just refer to it with the name of the object, which
in this example is mod1, followed by the $ sign and the name of the item you wish to
retrieve. For instance, if we want the vector of coefficients from mod1, we refer to it as
mod1$coefficients and smod1$coefficients:

mod1$coefficients

```
## (Intercept)      income
##       83.42       10.21
```

smod1$coefficients

```
##              Estimate Std. Error t value   Pr(>|t|)
## (Intercept)     83.42     43.410   1.922 0.06218242
## income          10.21      2.093   4.877 0.00001946
```

As we have seen before, however, some of these results can be retrieved using specific
functions, such as coef(mod1) for coefficients, resid(mod1) for residuals, fitted(mod1)
for the fitted values of the dependent variable, and vcov(mod1) for the coefficient variance-
covariance matrix that is discussed in the next chapters.

2.4   Prediction with the Linear Regression Model

The estimated regression parameters, b_1 and b_2, allow us to *predict* the expected food
expenditure for any given income. All we need to do is to plug the estimated parameter
values and the given income into an equation like Equation (2.2). For example, the expected

value of $food\_exp$ for an income of $2000 is calculated in Equation (2.4). (Remember to divide the income by 100, since the data for the variable $income$ is in hundreds of dollars.)

$$\widehat{food\_exp} = 83.42 + 10.21 \times 20 = \$287.61 \tag{2.4}$$

R, however, does this calculations for us with its function called `predict()`. Let us extend slightly the example to more than one income for which we predict food expenditure, say $income$ = \$2000, \$2500, and \$2700. The function `predict()` in R requires that the new values of the independent variables be organized under a particular form, called a data frame. Even when we want to predict food expenditure for only one value of income we need the data-frame structure. In R, a set of numbers is held together using the structure `c()`. The following sequence shows this example.

```
mod1 <- lm(food_exp~income, data=food)
newx <- data.frame(income = c(20, 25, 27))
yhat <- predict(mod1, newx)
names(yhat) <- c("income=$2000", "$2500", "$2700")
yhat   # prints the result
```

```
## income=$2000       $2500        $2700
##           287.6     338.7        359.1
```

2.5 Repeated Samples

The estimted regression coefficients, b_1 and b_2, are random variables because they depend on sample. Let us construct a number of random subsamples from the *food* data and re-calculate b_1 and b_2. A random subsample can be constructed using the function `sample()`, as the following example illustrates only for b_2.

```
N <- nrow(food) # `nrow()` = number of observations
C <- 100         # desired number of subsamples
S <- 39          # desired sample size

sumb2 <- 0 # sumb2 will store the sum of estimates of b2
for (i in 1:C){   # a loop over the number of subsamples
  set.seed(3*i)    # a different seed for each subsample
  subsample <- food[sample(1:N, size=S, replace=TRUE), ]
  mod2 <- lm(food_exp~income, data=subsample)
  #sum b2 for all subsamples:
  sumb2 <- sumb2 + coef(mod2)[[2]] # cumulative sum of b2
```

```
}
print(sumb2/C,digits=3) # calculates the average b2 and prints
```

[1] 9.84

The result, $b_2 = 9.84$, is the average of 100 estimates of b_2, with samples of size 39.

2.6   Variances and Covariance in Linear Regression

Many applications require estimates of the variances and covariances of the regression coefficients. R stores them in the matrix vcov():

```
# The variance-covariance matrix of the "food" model:
vcov(mod1)
```

```
##              (Intercept)  income
## (Intercept)      1884.4 -85.903
## income            -85.9   4.382
#
# Retrieving the variance of b1:
(varb1 <- vcov(mod1)[1, 1])
```

[1] 1884

```
#
# The variance of b2:
(varb2 <- vcov(mod1)[2, 2])
```

[1] 4.382

```
#
# The covariance of b1 and b2:
covb1b2 <- vcov(mod1)[1,2]
cat("Cov(b1,b2) = ", covb1b2)
```

Cov(b1,b2) =   -85.9

The **variance of the error term**, $\hat{\sigma}^2$, can be retrieved from the summary object, denoted above by smod1, which stores the standard error of the error term under the name of sigma. Thus, the estimated variance will be equal to squared sigma; the standard error of the dependent variable is calculated in R by the generic function sd().

```
sig2 <- smod1$sigma^2
sdy <- sd(food$food_exp)
cat(" Variance of the error term = ", sig2, "\n",
    "Standard error of food_exp = ", sdy)
```

```
## Variance of the error term = 8013
## Standard error of food_exp = 112.7
```

2.7 Non-Linear Relationships

Sometimes the scatter plot diagram or some theoretical considerations suggest a non-linear relationship between the dependent and the independent variables. The most popular non-linear relationships involve logarithms of the dependent or independent variables, as well as polynomial functions. An example of a polynomial relationship is the *quadratic* model, which requires the square of the independent variable. Equation (2.5) is an example of a quadratic model. Such models are still called linear regression models, although the relationship between the dependent and independent variables is non-linear; linear regressions are those that are linear in the regression coefficients.

$$y_i = \beta_1 + \beta_2 x_i^2 + e_i \tag{2.5}$$

In R, independent variables involving mathematical operators can be included in a regression equation by using the function I(). The following example uses the data set br from the package POE5Rdata, which includes the sale prices and the attributes of 1080 houses in Baton Rouge, LA. The variable price is the sale price in dollars, and sqft is the surface area of the house in square feet.

```
library(POE5Rdata)
data(br)
mod3 <- lm(price~I(sqft^2), data=br)
b1 <- coef(mod3)[[1]]
b2 <- coef(mod3)[[2]]
sqftx=c(2000, 4000, 6000) # given values for sqft
pricex=b1+b2*sqftx^2 # prices corresponding to given sqft
DpriceDsqft <- 2*b2*sqftx # marginal effect of sqft on price
elasticity=DpriceDsqft*sqftx/pricex
b1; b2; DpriceDsqft; elasticity # prints results
```

```
## [1] 55777
```

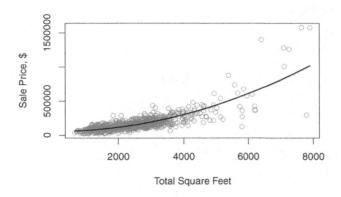

Figure 2.3 Fitting a Quadratic Model to the *br* Data Set

[1] 0.01542

[1]   61.69 123.37 185.06

[1] 1.050 1.631 1.817

We would like now to draw a scatter diagram and see how the quadratic function fits the data. The next chunk of code provides two alternatives for constructing such a graph. The first simply draws the quadratic function on the scatter diagram, using the R function curve(); the second uses the function lines, which requires ordering the data set in increasing values of sqft before the regression model is evaluated, such that the resulting fitted values will also come out in the same order.

```
mod31 <- lm(price~I(sqft^2), data=br)
par(cex=1.2)
plot(br$sqft, br$price, xlab="Total Square Feet",
    ylab="Sale Price, $", col="grey45")
#add the quadratic curve to the scatter plot:
curve(b1+b2*x^2, col="black", add=TRUE,lwd=2)
```

An alternative way to draw the fitted curve:

```
ordat <- br[order(br$sqft), ] #sorts the dataset after `sqft`
mod31 <- lm(price~I(sqft^2), data=ordat)
plot(br$sqft, br$price,
    xlab="Total Square Feet",
    ylab="Sale Price, $", col="grey45")
lines(fitted(mod31)~ordat$sqft, col="black",lwd=2)
```

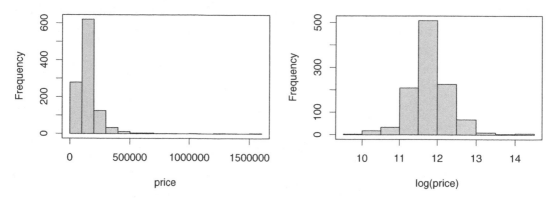

Figure 2.4 A Comparison Between the Histograms of $price$ and $log(price)$

A **log-linear** model regresses the log of the dependent variable on a linear expression of the independent variable (unless otherwise specified, the log notation stands for natural logarithm, following a usual convention in economics and the corresponding R function):

$$log(y_i) = \beta_1 + \beta_2 x_i + e_i \qquad (2.6)$$

One of the reasons to use the *log* of a dependent variable is to make its distribution closer to the normal distribution. Let us draw the histograms of price and log(price) to compare them (see Figure 2.4). It can be noticed that the log is closer to the normal distribution.

```
par(cex=1.5,mar=c(4,4,1,1),lwd=1.6)
hist(br$price, col='grey',main=NULL, xlab="price")
box(bty="o")
hist(log(br$price), col='grey',main=NULL,xlab="log(price)")
box(bty="o")
```

We are interested in estimating the coefficients and interpreting their values, in calculating the fitted values of price, and in determining the marginal effect of an increase in sqft on price.

```
library(POE5Rdata)
data("br")
mod4 <- lm(log(price)~sqft, data=br)
```

The coefficients of the log-linear model are $b_1 = 10.84$ and $b_2 = 4.1 \times 10^{-4}$, showing that an increase in the surface area (sqft) of an apartment by one unit (1 sqft) increases the price of the apartment by 0.041 percent. Thus, for a house price of $100,000, an increase of 100 sqft will increase the price by approximately 100×0.041 percent, which is equal to $4112.7. In general, the marginal effect of an increase in x on y in Equation (2.6) is

$$\frac{dy}{dx} = \beta_2 y, \tag{2.7}$$

and the elasticity is

$$\epsilon = \frac{dy}{dx}\frac{x}{y} = \beta_2 x. \tag{2.8}$$

Equation (2.9) shows how to calculate the fitted values in a log-linear model.

$$\hat{y} = exp(b_1 + b_2 x) \tag{2.9}$$

The next lines of code draw the fitted curve of the log-linear model and calculate the marginal effect and the elasticity of y with respect to x at the median price in the data set. Please note the use of the function `fitted()`, which extracts the fitted values from a regression model. Sorting the dataset for plotting is just one way of drawing the curve; another way is to create a vector of artificial values of x and re-calculate the fitted values for those values using Equation (2.9). Figure 2.5 shows the result.

```
ordat <- br[order(br$sqft), ] #orders the dataset
mod4 <- lm(log(price)~sqft, data=ordat)
par(cex=1.2) # graphical parameters for plot
plot(br$sqft, br$price, col="grey45",
    xlab="Sqft",ylab="Price")
lines(exp(fitted(mod4))~ordat$sqft,
    col="black",lwd=2)

pricex<- median(br$price) # median price
sqftx <- (log(pricex)-coef(mod4)[[1]])/coef(mod4)[[2]]
(DyDx <- pricex*coef(mod4)[[2]]) # marginal effect
```

```
## [1] 53.46495
```

```
(elasticity <- sqftx*coef(mod4)[[2]]) # elasticity
```

```
## [1] 0.9366934
```

R allows us to calculate the same quantities for several *(sqft, price)* pairs at a time, as shown in the following sequence:

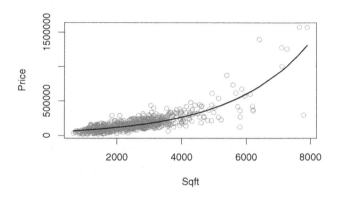

Figure 2.5 The Fitted Curve in the Log-Linear Model

```
b1 <- coef(mod4)[[1]]
b2 <- coef(mod4)[[2]]
#pick a few values for sqft:
sqftx <- c(2000, 3000, 4000)
#estimate prices for those and add one more:
pricex <- c(100000, exp(b1+b2*sqftx))
#re-calculate sqft for all prices:
sqftx <- (log(pricex)-b1)/b2
#calculate and print elasticities:
(elasticities <- b2*sqftx)
```

```
## [1] 0.6743 0.8225 1.2338 1.6451
```

2.8 Indicator Variables

An indicator, or binary variable marks the presence or the absence of some attribute of the observational unit, such as gender or race if the observational unit is an individual, or location if the observational unit is a house. In the data set utown, the variable utown is equal to 1 if a house is close to the university and equal to 0 otherwise. Here is a simple linear regression model that involves the variable utown.

$$price_i = \beta_1 + \beta_2 utown_i + e_i \tag{2.10}$$

The slope coefficient of such a variable in a simple linear model is equal to the difference between the average prices of the two categories, while the intercept coefficient is equal to the average price of the houses that are not close to university, as in Equation (2.10). To show this, let us first calculate the average prices for each category, which are denoted in the following sequence of code price0bar and price1bar:

```
data("utown", package="POE5Rdata")
price0bar <- mean(utown$price[which(utown$utown==0)])
price1bar <- mean(utown$price[which(utown$utown==1)])
```

The results are: $\overline{price} = 277.24$ for houses that are close to university, and $\overline{price} = 215.73$ for houses that are not close to university. I now show that the same result can be obtained just by retrieving the coefficients of the regression model in Equation (2.10).

```
mod5 <- lm(price~utown, data=utown)
b1 <- coef(mod5)[[1]]
b2 <- coef(mod5)[[2]]
```

The results are: $\overline{price} = b_1 = 215.73$ for non-university houses, and $\overline{price} = b_1 + b_2 = 277.24$ for university houses.

The function ggplot() in package ggplot2 (Wickham and Chang, 2016b) is a very powerful (though rather complex) tool for visualizing data. I illustrate its use on the utown data set to highlight the difference in prices between university and non-university houses (recall that utown is equal to 1 for houses close to university.) Figure 2.6 shows a scatter plot, and Figure 2.7 shows two fitted linear regression lines, one for each group (you may disregard, for the moment, the shaded areas around the lines; they represent confidence intervals, the object of a subsequent chapter.)

```
utown$utown<-as.factor(utown$utown)
ggplot(data=utown)+
  geom_point(mapping=aes(x=sqft,y=price,alpha=utown))+
  xlab("Square Feet")+
  ylab("Price")+
  theme(axis.text=element_text(size=14))+
  theme(axis.title=element_text(size=14))+
  theme(legend.text=element_text(size=14))+
  theme(legend.title = element_text(size = 14))

ggplot(data=utown)+
 geom_smooth(mapping=
      aes(x=sqft,y=price,linetype=utown),method="lm")+
  xlab("Square Feet")+
  ylab("Price")+
```

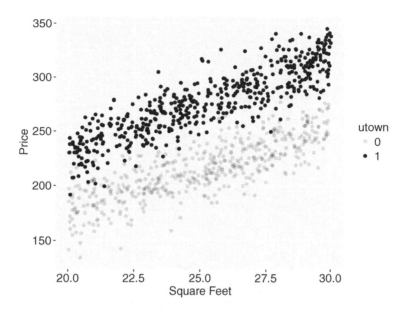

Figure 2.6 Scatter Plot by Group of Houses

```
theme(axis.text=element_text(size=14))+
theme(axis.title=element_text(size=14))+
theme(legend.text=element_text(size=14))+
theme(legend.title = element_text(size = 14))
```

2.9 Monte Carlo Simulation

A Monte Carlo simulation generates random values for the dependent variable when the regression coefficients and the distribution of the random term are given. The following example seeks to determine the distribution of the dependent variable in the food expenditure model in Equation (2.3).

```
N <- 40
x1 <- 10
x2 <- 20
b1 <- 100
b2 <- 10
mu <- 0
sig2e <- 2500
sde <- sqrt(sig2e)
```

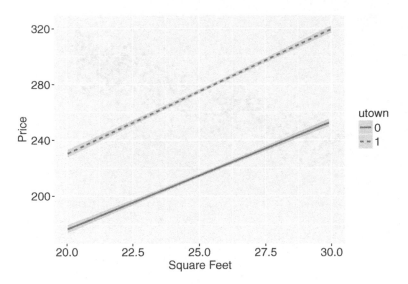

Figure 2.7 Fitted Curves by Group of Houses

```
yhat1 <- b1+b2*x1
yhat2 <- b1+b2*x2
par(cex=1.2,lwd=1.5)
curve(dnorm(x, mean=yhat1, sd=sde), 0, 500, col="blue",
      ylab="Density")
curve(dnorm(x, yhat2, sde), 0,500, add=TRUE, col="red")
abline(v=yhat1, col="blue", lty=2)
abline(v=yhat2, col="red", lty=2)
legend("topright", legend=c("f(y|x=10)", "f(y|x=20)"),
       lty=1,col=c("blue", "red"))
```

Next, we calculate the variance of b_2 and plot the corresponding density function.

$$var(b_2) = \frac{\sigma^2}{\sum(x_i - \bar{x})} \tag{2.11}$$

```
x <- c(rep(x1, N/2), rep(x2,N/2))
xbar <- mean(x)
sumx2 <- sum((x-xbar)^2)
varb2 <- sig2e/sumx2
sdb2 <- sqrt(varb2)
leftlim <- b2-3*sdb2
rightlim <- b2+3*sdb2
```

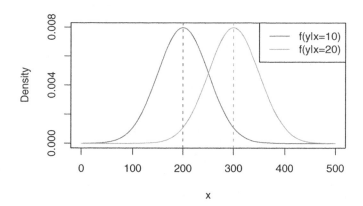

Figure 2.8 The theoretical (true) probability distributions of food expenditure, given two levels of income

```
par(cex=1.2,lwd=1.5)
curve(dnorm(x, mean=b2, sd=sdb2), leftlim, rightlim,
      ylab="Density")
abline(v=b2, lty=2)
```

Now, with the same values of b_1, b_2, and error standard deviation, we can generate a set of values for y, regress y on x, and calculate a set of estimated values for the coefficient b_2 and its standard error.

```
set.seed(12345)
y <- b1+b2*x+rnorm(N, mean=0, sd=sde)
mod6 <- lm(y~x)
b1hat <- coef(mod6)[[1]]
b2hat <- coef(mod6)[[2]]
mod6summary <- summary(mod6)#summary contains standard errors
seb2hat <- coef(mod6summary)[2,2]
```

The results are $b_2 = 11.64$ and $se(b_2) = 1.64$. The strength of a Monte Carlo simulation is, however, the possibility of repeating the estimation of the regression parameters for a large number of automatically generated samples. Thus, we can obtain a large number of values for a parameter, say b_2, and then determine its sampling characteristics. For instance, if the mean of these values is close to the initially assumed value $b_2 = 10$, we conclude that our estimator (the method of estimating the parameter) is unbiased.

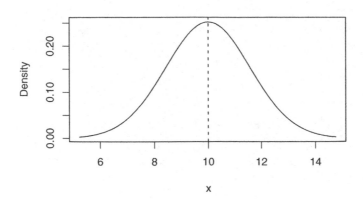

Figure 2.9 The theoretical (true) probability density function of b_2

We are going to use this time the values of x in the *food* data set, and generate y using the linear model with $b_1 = 100$ and $b_2 = 10$.

```
data("food")
N <- 40
sde <- 50
x <- food$income
nrsim <- 10000
b1 <- 100
b2 <- 10
vb2 <- numeric(nrsim) #stores the estimates of b2
for (i in 1:nrsim){
  set.seed(12345+10*i)
  y <- b1+b2*x+rnorm(N, mean=0, sd=sde)
  mod7 <- lm(y~x)
  vb2[i] <- coef(mod7)[[2]]
}
mb2 <- mean(vb2)
seb2 <- sd(vb2)
```

The mean and standard deviation of the estimated 40 values of b_2 are, respectively, 9.989 and 1.1607. Figure 2.10 shows the simulated distribution of b_2 and the theoretical one.

```
par(cex=1.2)
plot(density(vb2),ylim=c(0,0.4),
```

```
        zero.line=FALSE,lwd=1.8,lty=2,main="")
curve(dnorm(x, mb2, seb2), col="red", add=TRUE)
legend("topright", legend=c("true", "simulated"),
        col=c("red", "black"),lty=c(1,2),lwd=c(1.8,1.8))
hist(vb2, prob=TRUE, ylim=c(0,.4),main=NULL)
box(bty="o")
curve(dnorm(x, mean=mb2, sd=seb2), col="red", add=TRUE)
```

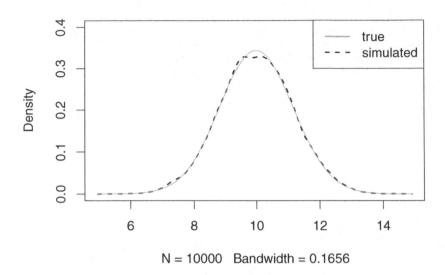

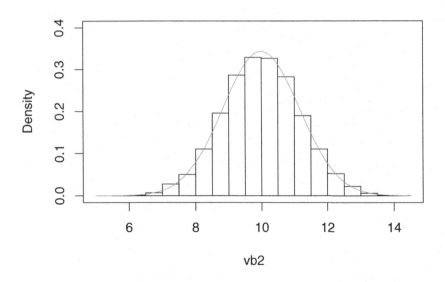

Figure 2.10 The simulated and theoretical distributions of b_2

Chapter 3

Interval Estimation and Hypothesis Testing

```
rm(list=ls()) # Caution: this clears the Environment
options(digits=3)
library(POE5Rdata)
library(broom) #to create tidy tables
library(knitr) #cross-references for tables
library(ggplot2) # data visualizing
library(stats)
library(xtable) # creates tables
library(car)
```

So far, we estimated only a number for a regression parameter such as β_2. This estimate, however, gives no indication of its reliability, since it is just a realization of the random variable b_2. An *interval estimate*, which is also known as a *confidence interval*, is an interval centered on an estimated value, which includes the true parameter with a given probability, say 95%. A coefficient of the linear regression model such as b_2 has a conditional normal distribution with mean equal to the population parameter β_2 and a variance that depends on the population variance σ^2 and the sample size. The following equation gives the distribution of the regression parameter estimator b_2:

$$
b_2 | x \sim N \left(\beta_2, \ \frac{\sigma^2}{\sum (x_i - \bar{x})^2} \right),
\tag{3.1}
$$

3.1   The Estimated Distribution of Regression Coefficients

Equation (3.1) gives the theoretical distribution of a linear regression coefficient; this distribution is not very useful, though, since it requires the unknown population variance, σ^2. If we replace σ^2 with an estimated variance $\hat{\sigma}^2$ given in Equation (3.2), the standardized distribution of b_2 becomes a t distribution with $N - 2$ degrees of freedom.

$$\hat{\sigma}^2 = \frac{\sum \hat{e}_i^2}{N - 2} \tag{3.2}$$

Equation (3.3) shows the *t-ratio*:

$$t = \frac{b_2 - \beta_2}{se(b_2)} \tag{3.3}$$

3.2   Confidence Interval in General

An interval estimate of b_2 based on the *t-ratio* is calculated in Equation (3.4), which we can consider as "an interval that includes the true parameter β_2 with a probability of $100(1 - \alpha)\%$." In this context, α is called *significance level*, and the interval is called, for example, *a 95% confidence interval estimate for* β_2. The critical value of the t-ratio, t_c, depends on the chosen significance level and on the number of degrees of freedom. In R, the function that returns critical values for the t distribution is $qt(1 - \frac{\alpha}{2}, df)$, where df is the number of degrees of freedom.

$$b_2 \pm t_c \times se(b_2) \tag{3.4}$$

A side note about using distributions in R. There are four types of functions related to distributions, each type's name beginning with one of the following four letters: p for the cumulative distribution function, d for density, r for a draw of a random number from the respective distribution, and q for quantile. This first letter is followed by a few letters suggesting what distribution we refer to, such as norm, t, f, and chisq. Now, if we put together the first letter and the distribution name, we get functions such as the following, where x and q stand for quantiles, p stands for probability, df is degree of freedom (of which the F distribution has two), n is the desired number of draws, and lower.tail can be TRUE (default) if probabilities are $P[X \le x]$ or FALSE if probabilities are $P[X > x]$:

- For the uniform distribution:
    - dunif(x, min = 0, max = 1)

- punif(q, min = 0, max = 1, lower.tail = TRUE)
- qunif(p, min = 0, max = 1, lower.tail = TRUE)
- runif(n, min = 0, max = 1)

- For the normal distribution:

  - dnorm(x, mean = 0, sd = 1)
  - pnorm(q, mean = 0, sd = 1, lower.tail = TRUE)
  - qnorm(p, mean = 0, sd = 1, lower.tail = TRUE)
  - rnorm(n, mean = 0, sd = 1)

- For the t distribution:

  - dt(x, df)
  - pt(q, df, lower.tail = TRUE)
  - qt(p, df, lower.tail = TRUE)
  - rt(n, df)

- For the F distribution:

  - df(x, df1, df2)
  - pf(q, df1, df2, lower.tail = TRUE)
  - qf(p, df1, df2, lower.tail = TRUE)
  - rf(n, df1, df2)

- For the χ^2 distribution:

  - dchisq(x, df)
  - pchisq(q, df, lower.tail = TRUE)
  - qchisq(p, df, lower.tail = TRUE)
  - rchisq(n, df)

3.3 Example: Confidence Intervals in the *food* Model

Let us calculate a 95% confidence interval for the coefficient on *income* in the food expenditure model. Besides calculating confidence intervals, the following lines of code demonstrate how to retrieve information such as standard errors of coefficients from the summary() output. The function summary contains the results of a linear regression model, some of which are not available directly from running the R function lm() itself.

```
data("food")
alpha <- 0.05 # chosen significance level
mod1 <- lm(food_exp~income, data=food)
b2 <- coef(mod1)[[2]]
```

```
df <- df.residual(mod1) # degrees of freedom
smod1 <- summary(mod1)
seb2 <- coef(smod1)[2,2] # se(b2)
tc <- qt(1-alpha/2, df)
lowb <- b2-tc*seb2   # lower bound
upb <- b2+tc*seb2    # upper bound
```

The resulting 95% confidence interval for the coefficient b_2 in the *food* simple regression model is $(5.97, 14.45)$.

R has a special function, confint(model), that can calculate confidence intervals taking as its argument the name of a regression model. The result of applying this function is a $K \times 2$ matrix with a confidence interval (two values: lower and upper bound) on each row and a number of rows equal to the number of parameters in the model (equal to 2 in the simple linear regression model). Compare the values from the next code to the ones from the previous to check that they are equal.

```
ci <- confint(mod1)
print(ci)


##               2.5 % 97.5 %
## (Intercept) -4.463 171.30
## income       5.972  14.45

lowb_b2 <- ci[2, 1] # lower bound
upb_b2 <- ci[2, 2]  # upper bound.
```

3.4   Confidence Intervals in Repeated Samples

```
data(table2_2)
alpha <- 0.05
mod1 <- lm(y1~x, data=table2_2) # just to determine df
df<-df.residual(mod1)
tc <- qt(1-alpha/2, df) # critical t

# Initiate four vectors that will store the results:
lowb1 <- rep(0, 10) # 'repeat 0 ten times'
upb1 <- rep(0, 10)  # (alternatively, 'numeric(10)')
lowb2 <- rep(0, 10)
upb2 <-rep(0, 10)
```

Table 3.1: Confidence Intervals for b_1 and b_2

lowb1	upb1	lowb2	upb2
29.404	157.9	5.141	11.34
28.116	155.1	5.840	11.96
29.437	224.1	1.901	11.29
-36.911	148.9	6.751	15.71
1.081	173.4	4.980	13.29
36.207	208.9	2.633	10.96
6.648	177.2	5.727	13.95
3.561	141.4	7.176	13.82
16.069	164.6	5.168	12.33
27.039	230.1	2.094	11.88

```
# One loop for each set of income:
for(i in 2:11){  # This curly bracket begins the loop
  dat <- data.frame(cbind(table2_2[,1], table2_2[,i]))
  names(dat) <- c("x", "y")
  mod1 <- lm(y~x, data=dat)
  smod1 <- summary(mod1)
  b1 <- coef(mod1)[[1]]
  b2 <- coef(mod1)[[2]]
  seb1 <- coef(smod1)[1,2]
  seb2 <- coef(smod1)[2,2]
  lowb1[i-1] <- b1-tc*seb1
  upb1[i-1] <- b1+tc*seb1
  lowb2[i-1] <- b2-tc*seb2
  upb2[i-1] <- b2+tc*seb2
} # This curly bracket ends the loop

table <- data.frame(lowb1, upb1, lowb2, upb2)
kable(table,
  caption="Confidence Intervals for $b_{1}$ and $b_{2}$",
  align="c")
```

Table 3.1 shows the lower and upper bounds of the confidence intervals of β_1 and β_2.

Table 3.2: Regression Output Showing the Coefficients

	Estimate	Std..Error	t.value	Pr...t..
(Intercept)	83.42	43.410	1.922	0.0622
income	10.21	2.093	4.877	0.0000

3.5 Hypothesis Testing

Hypothesis testing seeks to establish whether the data sample at hand provides sufficient evidence to support a certain conjecture (hypothesis) about a population parameter such as the intercept in a regression model, the slope, or some combination of them. Hypothesis testing requires three elements: the hypotheses (the *null* and the *alternative*), a test statistic, which in the case of the simple linear regression parameters is the *t*-ratio, and a significance level, α.

Suppose we believe that there is a significant relationship between a household's income and its expenditure on food, a conjecture which has led us to formulate the food expenditure model in the first place. Thus, we believe that the (population) parameter β_2 is different from zero and we would like to test this conjecture. Equation (3.5) shows the null and alternative hypotheses for such a test.

$$H_0 : \beta_2 = 0, \quad H_A : \beta_2 \neq 0 \tag{3.5}$$

In general, if a null hypothesis $H_0 : \beta_k = c$ is true, the t statistic (the *t*-ratio) is given by Equation (3.6) and has a t distribution with $N - 2$ degrees of freedom.

$$t = \frac{b_k - c}{se(b_k)} \sim t_{(N-2)} \tag{3.6}$$

For the *food* example, let us test the hypothesis in Equation (3.5), which makes $c = 0$ in Equation (3.6). Let $\alpha = 0.05$. Table 3.2 shows the regression output.

```
alpha <- 0.05
data("food")
mod1 <- lm(food_exp~income, data=food)
smod1 <- summary(mod1)
table <- data.frame(xtable(mod1))
kable(table,
   caption="Regression Output Showing the Coefficients")
```

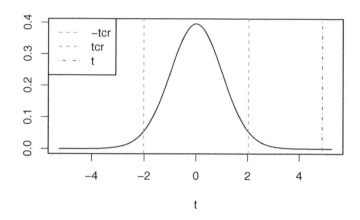

Figure 3.1 A Two-Tail Hypothesis Testing for b_2 in the *food* example

```
b2 <- coef(mod1)[["income"]] #coefficient on income
# or:
b2 <- coef(mod1)[[2]] # the coefficient on income
seb2 <- sqrt(vcov(mod1)[2,2]) #standard error of b2
df <- df.residual(mod1) # degrees of freedom
t <- b2/seb2
tcr <- qt(1-alpha/2, df)
```

The results $t = 4.88$ and $t_{cr} = 2.02$ show that $t > t_{cr}$, and therefore t falls in the rejection region (see Figure 3.1).

```
# Plot the density function and the values of t:
par(cex=1.2,lwd=1.5)
curve(dt(x, df), -2.5*seb2, 2.5*seb2, ylab=" ", xlab="t")
abline(v=c(-tcr, tcr, t), col=c("red", "red", "blue"),
       lty=c(2,2,4))
legend("topleft", legend=c("-tcr", "tcr", "t"), col=
       c("red", "red", "blue"), lty=c(2, 2, 4))
```

Suppose we want to determine if β_2 is greater than 5.5. This conjecture will go into the alternative hypothesis: $H_0 : \beta_2 \leq 5.5, \quad H_A : \beta_2 > 5.5$. The procedure is the same as for the two-tail test, but now the whole rejection region is to the right of the critical value t_{cr}.

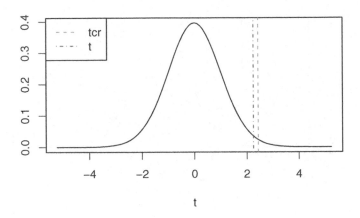

Figure 3.2 Right-Tail Test: the Rejection Region is to the Right of t_{cr}

```
c <- 5.5
alpha <- 0.01
t <- (b2-c)/seb2
tcr <- qt(1-alpha, df) # note: alpha is not divided by 2
par(cex=1.2,lwd=1.5)
curve(dt(x, df), -2.5*seb2, 2.5*seb2, ylab=" ", xlab="t")
abline(v=c(tcr, t), col=c("red", "blue"), lty=c(2, 4))
legend("topleft", legend=c("tcr", "t"),
       col=c("red", "blue"), lty=c(2, 4))
```

Figure 3.2 shows $t_{cr} = 2.4286$, $t = 2.2499$. Since t falls this time in the acceptance region, we cannot reject the null hypothesis $H_0 : \beta_2 \leq 0$.

A left-tail test is not different from the right-tail one, but of course the rejection region is to the left of t_{cr}. For example, if we are interested to determine if β_2 is less than 15, we place this conjecture in the alternative hypothesis: $H_0 : \beta_2 \geq 15$, $H_A : \beta_2 < 15$. The novelty here is how we use the qt() function to calculate t_{cr}: instead of qt(1-alpha, ...), we need to use qt(alpha, ...). Figure 3.3 illustrates this example, where the rejection region is, remember, to the left of t_{cr}.

```
c <- 15
alpha <- 0.05
t <- (b2-c)/seb2
tcr <- qt(alpha, df) # note: alpha is not divided by 2
```

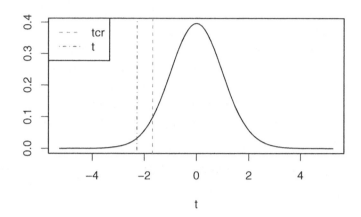

Figure 3.3 Left-Tail Test: the Rejection Region is to the Left of $t_{cr} =$

Table 3.3: Regression output for the 'food' model

	Estimate	Std..Error	t.value	Pr...t..
(Intercept)	83.42	43.410	1.922	0.062
income	10.21	2.093	4.877	0.000

```
par(cex=1.2,lwd=1.5)
curve(dt(x, df), -2.5*seb2, 2.5*seb2, ylab=" ", xlab="t")
abline(v=c(tcr, t), col=c("red", "blue"), lty=c(2, 4))
legend("topleft", legend=c("tcr", "t"),
      col=c("red", "blue"), lty=c(2, 4))
```

R does automatically a *test of significance*, which is indeed testing the hypothesis $H_0 :$ $\beta_2 = 0,\quad H_A : \beta_2 \neq 0$. The regression output shows the values of the t-ratio for all the regression coefficients.

```
data("food")
mod1 <- lm(food_exp ~ income, data = food)
table <- data.frame(round(xtable(summary(mod1)), 3))
kable(table, caption = "Regression output for the 'food' model")
```

Table 3.3 shows the regression output where the t-statistics of the coefficients can be observed.

3.6   The *p*-Value

In the context of a hypothesis test, the p-value is the area outside the calculated t-statistic; it is the probability that the t-ratio takes a value that is more extreme than the calculated one, under the assumption that the null hypothesis is true. For a right-tail test, the p-value is the area to the right of the calculated t; for a left-tail test it is the area to the left of the calculated t; for a two-tail test the p-value is split in two equal amounts: $p/2$ to the left and $p/2$ to the right. We reject the null hypothesis if the p-value is less than a chosen significance level, which is most econometric applications is equal to 0.05.

The p-values for the t-distribution are calculated in R by the function pt(t, df), where t is the calculated t-ratio and df is the number of degrees of freedom in the estimated model.

Right-tail test, $H_0 : \beta_2 \leq c, \quad H_A : \beta_2 > c$.

```
# Calculating the p-value for a right-tail test
c <- 5.5
t <- (b2-c)/seb2
p <- 1-pt(t, df) # pt() returns p-values;
```

The right-tail test shown in Figure 3.2 gives the p-value $p = 0.0152$.

Left-tail test, $H_0 : \beta_2 \geq c, \quad H_A : \beta_2 < c$.

```
# Calculating the p-value for a left-tail test
c <- 15
t <- (b2-c)/seb2
p <- pt(t, df)
```

The left-tail test shown in Figure 3.3 gives the p-value $p = 0.0139$.

Two-tail test, $H_0 : \beta_2 = c, \quad H_A : \beta_2 \neq c$.

```
# Calculating the p-value for a two-tail test
c <- 0
t <- (b2-c)/seb2
p <- 2*(1-pt(abs(t), df))

par(cex=1.2,lwd=1.5)
curve(dt(x, df), from=-2.5*seb2, to=2.5*seb2)
abline(v=c(-t, t), col=c("blue", "blue"), lty=c(2, 2))
legend("topright", legend=c("-t", "t"),
        bg="grey100",col=c("blue", "blue"), lty=c(2, 4))
```

The two-tail test shown in Figure 3.4 gives the p-value $p = 2 \times 10^{-5}$, for a t-ratio $t = 4.88$.

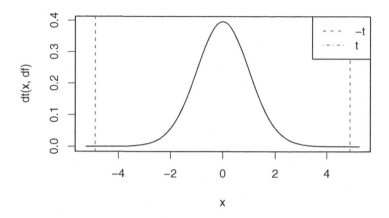

Figure 3.4 The p-Value in Two-Tail Hypothesis Testing

Table 3.4: Regression Output Showing p-Values

	Coefficients	Std. Error	t-Value	p-Value
(Intercept)	83.42	43.410	1.922	0.0622
income	10.21	2.093	4.877	0.0000

R gives the p-values in the standard regression output, which we can retrieve using the summary(model) function. These p-values test the two-tail hypotheses $H_0 : \beta_k = 0$, $H_A : \beta_k \neq 0$, where $k = 1, 2$.

Table 3.4 shows the output of the regression model, where the p-values can be observed; they indicate that the intercept coefficient, β_1, is not statistically significant at a 5% significance level (its p-value is greater than 0.05), but the slope coefficient is significantly different from zero. Since β_2 is significant, we conclude that the data support the conjecture of a significant relationship between food expenditure and income. Here is the code to build Table 3.4:

```
table <- data.frame(xtable(smod1))
knitr::kable(table,
    caption="Regression Output Showing $p$-Values",
    col.names=c("Coefficients","Std. Error","t-Value","p-Value"))
```

3.7   Testing Linear Combinations of Parameters

Sometimes we wish to estimate the expected value of the dependent variable, y, for a given value of x. For example, according to our *food* model, what is the expected expenditure on food among all households with an income of \$2000? We need to estimate the linear combination of the regression coefficients β_1 and β_2 given in Equation (3.7) (let us denote this linear combination by L).

$$L = E(food\_exp|income = 20) = \beta_1 + 20\beta_2 \tag{3.7}$$

Finding confidence intervals and testing hypotheses about the linear combination in Equation (3.7) requires calculating a t-statistic similar to the one for the regression coefficients we calculated before. However, estimating the standard error of the linear combination is not straightforward. In general, if X and Y are two random variables and a and b two constants, the variance of the linear combination $aX + bY$ is

$$var(aX + bY) = a^2 var(X) + b^2 var(Y) + 2\,a\,b\,cov(X, Y). \tag{3.8}$$

Now, by applying the formula in Equation (3.8) to the linear combination of β_1 and β_2 given by Equation (3.7), we obtain Equation (3.9), where the variances and the covariance are conditional on $income = 20$.

$$\widehat{var}(b_1 + 20b_2) = \widehat{var}(b_1) + 20^2 \widehat{var}(b_2) + 2 \times 20\,\widehat{cov}(b_1, b_2) \tag{3.9}$$

The following sequence of code determines an interval estimate for the expected value of food expenditure in a household earning \$2000 a week.

```
data("food")
alpha <- 0.05
x <- 20 # income is in 100s, remember?
m1 <- lm(food_exp~income, data=food)
tcr <- qt(1-alpha/2, df) # rejection region to the right of tcr.
df <- df.residual(m1)
b1 <- m1$coef[1]
b2 <- m1$coef[2]
varb1 <- vcov(m1)[1, 1]
varb2 <- vcov(m1)[2, 2]
covb1b2 <- vcov(m1)[1, 2]
L <- b1+b2*x   # estimated L
varL = varb1 + x^2 * varb2 + 2*x*covb1b2 # var(L)
```

```
seL <- sqrt(varL) # standard error of L
lowbL <- L-tcr*seL
upbL <- L+tcr*seL
```

The result is the confidence interval $(258.91, 316.31)$.

Next, we test hypotheses about the linear combination L defined in Equation (3.7), looking at the three types of hypotheses: two-tail, left-tail, and right-tail. Equations (3.10) − (3.12) show the test setups for a hypothesized value of food expenditure c.

$$H_0 : L = c, \quad H_A : L \neq c \tag{3.10}$$

$$H_0 : L \geq c, \quad H_A : L < c \tag{3.11}$$

$$H_0 : L \leq c, \quad H_A : L > c \tag{3.12}$$

One should use the function pt(t, df) carefully, because it may give wrong results when testing hypotheses using the p-value method with negative t-ratios. Therefore, the absolute value of t should be used. Figure 3.5 shows the p-values calculated with the formula 1-pt(t, df). When t is positive and the test is two-tail, doubling the p-value 1-pt(t, df) is correct; but when t is negative, the correct p-value is 2*pt(t, df). (This part uses the function shadenorm (Cookson, 2011).)

```
par(cex=1.4,mar=c(4,4,1,1),lwd=2)
.shadenorm(above=1.6, justabove=TRUE)
segments(1.6,0,1.6,0.2,col="black", lty=2,lwd=1.8)
legend("topleft", legend="t", col="black", lty=2,lwd=1.8)

.shadenorm(above=-1.6, justabove=TRUE)
segments(-1.6,0,-1.6,0.2,col="black", lty=2,lwd=1.8)
legend("topleft", legend="t", col="black", lty=2,lwd=1.8)
```

The next sequence uses the standard error of the linear combination already calculated, a hypothesized level of food expenditure c=$250, and an income of $2000; it tests the two-tail hypothesis in Equation (3.10) first using the "critical t" method, then using the p-value method.

```
c <- 250
alpha <- 0.05
t <- (L-c)/seL
```

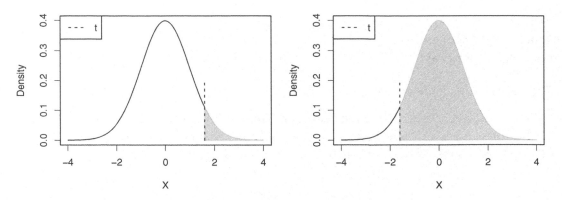

Figure 3.5 p–Values for Positive and Negative t in a Right-Tail Test

```
tcr <- qt(1-alpha/2, df)

# Or, we can calculate the p-value, as follows:
p_value <- 2*(1-pt(abs(t), df)) #p<alpha -> Reject Ho
```

The results are: $t = 2.65$, $t_{cr} = 2.02$, and $p = 0.0116$. Since $t > t_{cr}$, we reject the null hypothesis. The same result is given by the p-value method, where the p-value is twice the probability area determined by the calculated t.

One can use the function linearHypothesis from the package car (Fox and Weisberg, 2016) to test a two-tail linear hypothesis based on a previously run regression model, as follows:

```
hyp <- "(Intercept)+20*income = 250"
linearHypothesis(m1,hyp,test="F")
```

```
## Linear hypothesis test
##
## Hypothesis:
## (Intercept)  + 20 income = 250
##
## Model 1: restricted model
## Model 2: food_exp ~ income
##
##   Res.Df    RSS Df Sum of Sq    F Pr(>F)
## 1     39 360890
## 2     38 304505  1    56384 7.04  0.012 *
## ---
```

```
## Signif. codes:  0 '***' 0.001 '**' 0.01 '*' 0.05 '.' 0.1 ' ' 1
```

The test rejects the null hypothesis that the expected expenditure for an income of $2000 is equal to $250, a result that confirms our previous finding.

3.8   Simulation: Normally Distributed Errors

Assuming that the population parameters β_1, β_2, and σ^2 are known, we would like to know how close to these true values the least square estimates are. To do so, we construct a large number of samples that are consistent with the true parameters: we draw the error terms from a normal distribution having the same variance as the population variance and, for a number of arbitrary values of the independent variable, x, we calculate y. Then, we regress y on x and find the estimates b_1 and b_2. The next code does the simulation and Table 3.5 displays the results for just a few samples.

```
library(broom)
library(knitr)
M<-10000     #Number of samples
N=40         #Sample size
alpha<-0.05
x1<-10
x2<-20
b1<-100
b2<-10
vare<-2500
stde<-sqrt(vare)
tcr<-qt(1-alpha,N-2)
tcr1<-qt(1-alpha/2,N-2)
x<-c(rep(x1,N/2),rep(x2,N/2))

    sample<-rep(0,M)
    B2<-rep(0,M)
    SE<-rep(0,M)
    tstat<-rep(0,M)
    reject<-rep(0,M)
    lwb<-rep(0,M)
    upb<-rep(0,M)
    cover<-rep(0,M)
    rej<-0
    cvr<-0
```

Table 3.5: Monte Carlo Simulation with Normally-Distributed Errors

sample	B2	SE	tstat	reject	lwb	upb	cover
211	12.062	1.645	1.253	0	8.732	15.392	1
212	10.116	1.642	0.070	0	6.791	13.440	1
213	12.967	1.616	1.835	1	9.694	16.239	1
214	12.970	1.611	1.844	1	9.709	16.231	1
215	8.408	1.754	-0.907	0	4.857	11.959	1
216	7.544	1.914	-1.283	0	3.669	11.418	1
217	12.471	1.327	1.861	1	9.784	15.158	1
218	10.338	1.784	0.189	0	6.726	13.950	1
219	9.980	1.857	-0.011	0	6.220	13.739	1
220	10.011	1.855	0.006	0	6.257	13.766	1

```
for(j in 1:M){
  set.seed(j)
  e<-rnorm(N,0,stde)
  y<-b1+b2*x+e
  m1<-lm(y~x)
  b2hat<-tidy(m1)[2,2]
  seb2<-tidy(m1)[2,3]
  t2<-(b2hat-b2)/seb2
  ifelse(t2>tcr,rej<-1,rej<-0)
  ifelse(t2<tcr1 & t2>-tcr1,cvr<-1,cvr<-0)
  ci<-confint(m1)

  sample[j]<-j
  B2[j]<-b2hat
  SE[j]<-seb2
  tstat[j]<-t2
  reject[j]<-rej
  lwb[j]<-ci[2,1]
  upb[j]<-ci[2,2]
  cover[j]<-cvr
}
tab<-data.frame(sample,B2,SE,tstat,reject,lwb,upb,cover)
kable(tab[211:220,],digits=3,align="c",caption=
"Monte Carlo Simulation with Normally-Distributed Errors",
row.names=FALSE)
```

The average b_2 over all samples is 9.9954, quite close to 10, the true value.

Chapter 4

Prediction, R-squared, and Modeling

```
rm(list=ls()) # Caution: this clears the Environment
options(digits=3,scip=TRUE)
library(POE5Rdata)
library(xtable)
library(knitr)
```

A **prediction** is an estimate of the value of y for a given value of x, based on a regression model of the form shown in Equation (4.1). **Goodness-of-fit** is a measure of how well an estimated regression line approximates the data in a given sample. One such measure is the correlation coefficient between the predicted values of y for all x-s in the data file and the actual y-s. Goodness-of-fit, along with other diagnostic tests, helps determining the most suitable **functional form** of our regression equation, i.e., the most suitable mathematical relationship between y and x.

$$y_i = \beta_1 + \beta_2 x_i + e_i \tag{4.1}$$

4.1 Forecasting (Predicting a Particular Value)

Assuming that the expected values of the error term in Equation (4.1) is zero, Equation (4.2) gives $\hat{y}_0$, the predicted value of the conditional expectation of y for a particular value x_0, where b_1 and b_2 are the (least square) estimates of the regression parameters β_1 and β_2.

$$\hat{y}_0 = b_1 + b_2 x_0 \tag{4.2}$$

The predicted value $\hat{y}_0$ is a random variable, since it depends on the sample; therefore, we can calculate a confidence interval and test hypothesis about it, provided we can determine its distribution and variance.   The prediction has a normal distribution, being a linear combination of two normally distributed random variables, b_1 and b_2, and its variance is given by Equation (4.3). The variance in Equation (4.3) is not the same as the one in Equation (3.9); the latter is the variance of the estimated *expectation* of y, while the former is the variance of a particular occurrence of y. Let us call the former the variance of the forecast error. Not surprisingly, the variance of the forecast error is greater than the variance of the predicted expectation of y, $E(y|x)$.

As before, since we need to use an estimated variance, we use a t-distribution instead of a normal one. Equation (4.3) applies to any given x, say x_0, not only to those x-s in the data set.

$$\widehat{var}(f|\mathbf{x}) = \hat{\sigma}^2 \left[1 + \frac{1}{N} + \frac{(x_0 - \bar{x})^2}{\sum_{i=1}^{N} (x_i - \bar{x})^2} \right], \tag{4.3}$$

which can be reduced to

$$\widehat{var}(f|\mathbf{x}) = \hat{\sigma}^2 + \frac{\hat{\sigma}^2}{N} + (x_0 - \bar{x})^2 \widehat{var}(b_2|\mathbf{x}) \tag{4.4}$$

Let's determine a standard error for the *food* equation for a household earning an income of \$2000, using Equation (4.4); to do so, we need to retrieve $var(b_2)$ and $\hat{\sigma}$, the standard error of regression, from the regression output.

```
data("food")
alpha <- 0.05
x <- 20
xbar <- mean(food$income)
m1 <- lm(food_exp~income, data=food)
b1 <- coef(m1)[[1]]
b2 <- coef(m1)[[2]]
yhatx <- b1+b2*x
sm1 <- summary(m1)
df <- df.residual(m1)
tcr <- qt(1-alpha/2, df)
N <- nobs(m1)    #number of observations, N
```

```
N <- NROW(food) #another way to find N with no mising values
varb2 <- vcov(m1)[2, 2]
sighat2 <- sm1$sigma^2 # estimated variance
varf <- sighat2+sighat2/N+(x-xbar)^2*varb2 #forecast variance
sef <- sqrt(varf) #standard error of forecast
lb <- yhatx-tcr*sef
ub <- yhatx+tcr*sef
```

The result is the confidence interval for the forecast $(104.13, 471.09)$, which is, as expected, larger than the confidence interval of the estimated expected value of y based on Equation (3.9).

Let us calculate confidence intervals of the forecast for all the observations in the sample and draw the upper and lower limits together with the regression line. Figure 4.1 shows the confidence interval band about the regression line.

```
par(cex=1.2,lwd=1.5)
sef <- sqrt(sighat2+sighat2/N+(food$income-xbar)^2*varb2)
yhatv <- fitted.values(m1)
lbv <- yhatv-tcr*sef
ubv <- yhatv+tcr*sef
xincome <- food$income
dplot <- data.frame(xincome, yhatv, lbv, ubv)
dplotord <- dplot[order(xincome), ]
xmax <- max(dplotord$xincome)
xmin <- min(dplotord$xincome)
ymax <- max(dplotord$ubv)
ymin <- min(dplotord$lbv)
plot(dplotord$xincome, dplotord$yhatv,
     xlim=c(xmin, xmax),
     ylim=c(ymin, ymax),
     xlab="Income", ylab="Food Expenditure",
     type="l")
lines(dplotord$ubv~dplotord$xincome, lty=2)
lines(dplotord$lbv~dplotord$xincome, lty=2)
```

A different way of finding point and interval estimates for the *predicted* $E(y|x)$ and *forecasted* y (please see the above mentioned distinction) is to use the predict() function in R. This function requires that the values of the independent variable for which the prediction is being calculated have a data frame structure. The next example shows in parallel point and interval estimates of *predicted* and *forecasted* food expenditures for an income of \$2000. As pointed out before, the point estimate is the same for both prediction and

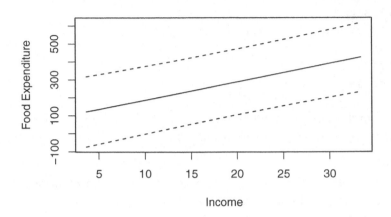

Figure 4.1 Forecast Confidence Intervals for the $food$ Simple Regression

Table 4.1: Predicted and Forecasted Values for b_2

	fit	lwr	upr
Predicted	287.6	258.9	316.3
Forecasted	287.6	104.1	471.1

forecast, but the interval estimates are very different.

```
incomex=data.frame(income=20)
tab1<-predict(m1, newdata=incomex,
          interval="confidence",level=0.95)
tab2<-predict(m1, newdata=incomex,
          interval="prediction",level=0.95)
tab<-data.frame(rbind(tab1,tab2),
          row.names=c("Predicted","Forecasted"))
kable(tab,caption=
      "Predicted and Forecasted Values for $b_{2}$")
```

Let us now use the predict() function to replicate Figure 4.1. The result is Figure 4.2, which shows, besides the interval estimation band, the points in the data set. I create new values for income just for the purpose of plotting.

```
xmin <- min(food$income)
xmax <- max(food$income)
```

```
income <- seq(from=xmin, to=xmax)
ypredict <- predict(m1, newdata=data.frame(income),
                    interval="confidence")
yforecast <- predict(m1, newdata=data.frame(income),
                    interval="predict")
par(cex=1.1,pch=16)
matplot(income, cbind(ypredict[,1], ypredict[,2],
                    ypredict[,3], yforecast[,2],
                    yforecast[,3]),
        type ="l", lty=c(1, 2, 2, 3, 3),
        lwd=c(2,2,2,2,2),
        col=c("black", "red", "red", "blue", "blue"),
        ylab="Food Expenditure", xlab="Income")
points(food$income, food$food_exp,col="grey35")
legend("topleft",
        legend=c("E[y|x]", "lwr_pred", "upr_pred",
                "lwr_forcst","upr_forcst"),
        lty=c(1, 2, 2, 3, 3),
        lwd=c(2,2,2,2,2), bg="white",
        col=c("black", "red", "red", "blue", "blue")
        )
```

Figure 4.2 presents the predicted and forecasted bands on the same graph, to show that they have the same point estimates (the black, solid line) and that the forecasted band is much larger than the predicted one. Put another way, you may think about the distinction between the two types of intervals that we called *prediction* and *forecast* as follows: the prediction interval is not supposed to include, say, 95 percent of the points, but to include the regression line, $E(y|\mathbf{x})$, with a probability of 95 percent; the forecasted interval, on the other hand, should include any true point with a 95 percent probability.

4.2 Goodness-of-Fit

The total variation of y about its sample mean, SST, can be decomposed in variation about the regression line, SSE, and variation of the regression line about the mean of y, SSR, as Equation (4.5) shows.

$$SST = SSR + SSE \qquad (4.5)$$

The **coefficient of determination**, R^2, is defined as the proportion of the variance in y

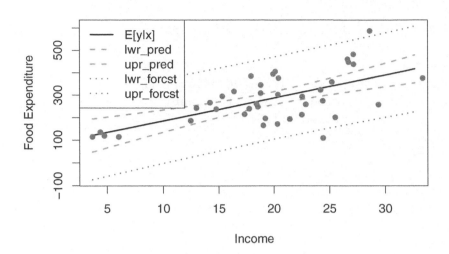

Figure 4.2 Predicted and Forecasted Bands for the *food* Data Set

that is explained by the regression, SSR, in the total variation in y, SST. Dividing both sides of the Equation (4.5) by SST and re-arranging terms gives a formula to calculate R^2, as shown in Equation (4.6).

$$R^2 = \frac{SSR}{SST} = 1 - \frac{SSE}{SST} \qquad (4.6)$$

R^2 takes values between 0 and 1, with higher values showing a closer fit of the regression line to the data. In R, the value of R^2 can be retrieved from the summary of the regression model under the name r.squared; for instance, in our *food* example, $R^2 = 0.385$. R^2 is also printed as part of the summary of a regression model, as the following code sequence shows. (The parentheses around a command tells R to print the result.)

```
(rsq <- sm1$r.squared) #or
```

```
## [1] 0.385
```

```
print(sm1, signif=F) #prints the summary of regression model m1
```

```
##
## Call:
## lm(formula = food_exp ~ income, data = food)
```

Table 4.2: Output Generated by the *anova* Function

	Df	Sum.Sq	Mean.Sq	F.value	Pr..F.
income	1	190627	190627	23.79	0
Residuals	38	304505	8013	NA	NA

```
##
## Residuals:
##     Min      1Q  Median      3Q     Max
## -223.03  -50.82   -6.32   67.88  212.04
##
## Coefficients:
##             Estimate Std. Error t value Pr(>|t|)
## (Intercept)    83.42      43.41    1.92    0.062
## income         10.21       2.09    4.88  1.9e-05
##
## Residual standard error: 89.5 on 38 degrees of freedom
## Multiple R-squared:  0.385,  Adjusted R-squared:  0.369
## F-statistic: 23.8 on 1 and 38 DF,  p-value: 1.95e-05
```

If you need the sum of squared errors, SSE, or the sum of squares due to regression, SSR, use the anova function, which has the structure shown in Table 4.2.

```
anov <- anova(m1)
dfr <- data.frame(anov)
kable(dfr,
  caption="Output Generated by the $anova$ Function")
```

Table 4.2 indicates that $SSE = $ anov[2,2] $= 3.0451 \times 10^5$, $SSR = $ anov[1,2] $= 1.9063 \times 10^5$, and $SST = $ anov[1,2]+anov[2,2] $= 4.9513 \times 10^5$. In our simple regression model, the sum of squares due to regression only includes the variable income. In multiple regression models, which are models with more than one independent variable, the sum of squares due to regression is equal to the sum of squares due to all independent variables. The anova results in Table 4.2 include other useful information: the number of degrees of freedom, anov[2,1], and the estimated variance, $\hat{\sigma}^2 = $ anov[2,3].

4.3 Linear-Log Models

Non-linear functional forms of regression models are useful when the relationship between two variables seems to be more complex than the linear one. One can decide to use a particular functional form based on a mathematical model, reasoning, inspecting a scatter plot of the data, and testing the linear regression model assumptions. In the *food expenditure* model, for example, it is reasonable to believe that the amount spent on food increases faster at lower incomes than at higher incomes. In other words, it increases at a decreasing rate, which makes the regression curve flatten out at higher incomes.

What function could one use to model such a relationship? The logarithmic function fits this profile and, as it turns out, it is relatively easy to interpret, which makes it very popular in econometric models. The general form of a *linear-log* econometric model is provided in Equation (4.7).

$$y_i = \beta_1 + \beta_2 log(x_i) + e_i \tag{4.7}$$

The *marginal effect* of a change in x on y is the slope of the regression curve and is given by Equation (4.8); unlike in the linear form, it depends on x and it is, therefore, only valid for small changes in x.

$$\frac{dy}{dx} = \frac{\beta_2}{x} \tag{4.8}$$

Related to the linear-log model, another measure of interest in economics is the *semi-elasticity* of y with respect to x, which is given by Equation (4.9). Semi-elasticity suggests that a change in x of 1% changes y by $\beta_2/100$ units of y. Since semi-elasticity also changes when x changes, it should only be determined for small changes in x.

$$dy = \frac{\beta_2}{100}(\%\Delta x) \tag{4.9}$$

Another quantity that might be of interest is the *elasticity* of y with respect to x, which is given by Equation (4.10) and indicates that a one percent increase in x produces a (β_2/y) percent change in y.

$$\%\Delta y = \frac{\beta_2}{y}(\%\Delta x) \tag{4.10}$$

Let us estimate a linear-log model for the *food* data set, draw the regression curve, and calculate the marginal effects for some given values of the dependent variable.

```
mod2 <- lm(food_exp~log(income), data=food)
tbl <- data.frame(xtable(mod2))
kable(tbl, digits=5, caption=
    "Linear-Log Model Output for the $food$ Example")
```

Table 4.3: Linear-Log Model Output for the *food* Example

	Estimate	Std..Error	t.value	Pr...t..
(Intercept)	-97.19	84.24	-1.154	0.25582
log(income)	132.17	28.80	4.588	0.00005

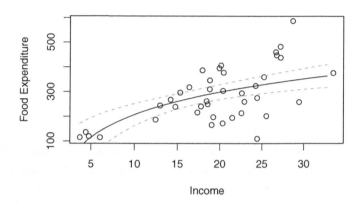

Figure 4.3 Linear-Log Representation for the *food* Data

```
b1 <- coef(mod2)[[1]]
b2 <- coef(mod2)[[2]]
pmod2 <- predict(mod2, newdata=data.frame(income),
            interval="confidence")
par(cex=1.2,lwd=1.5)
plot(food$income, food$food_exp, xlab="Income",
    ylab="Food Expenditure")
lines(pmod2[,1]~income, lty=1, col="black")
lines(pmod2[,2]~income, lty=2, col="red")
lines(pmod2[,3]~income, lty=2, col="red")

x <- 10 #for a household earning #1000 per week
y <- b1+b2*log(x)
DyDx <- b2/x     #marginal effect
DyPDx <- b2/100 #semi-elasticity
PDyPDx <- b2/y  #elasticity
```

The results for an income of $1000 are as follows: $dy/dx = 13.217$, which indicates that

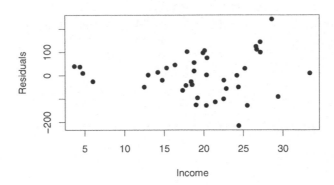

Figure 4.4 Residual Plot for the *food* Linear-Log model

an increase in income of \$100 (i.e., one unit of x) increases expenditure by \$13.217; for a 1% increase in income, that is, an increase of \$10, expenditure increases by \$1.322; and, finally, for a 1% increase in income, expenditure increases by 0.638%.

4.4 Residuals and Diagnostics

Regression results are reliable only to the extent to which the underlying assumptions are met. Plotting the residuals and calculating certain test statistics help deciding whether assumptions such as homoskedasticity, serial correlation, and normality of the errors are not violated. In R, the residuals are stored in the vector `residuals` of the regression output.

```
ehat <- mod2$residuals
par(cex=1.2)
plot(food$income, ehat, pch=16,
     xlab="Income", ylab="Residuals")
```

Figure 4.4 shows the residuals of the of the linear-log equation of the *food expenditure* example. One can notice that the spread of the residuals seems to be higher at higher incomes, which may indicate that the homoskedasticity assumption is violated.

Let us draw a residual plot generated with a simulated model that satisfies the regression assumptions. The data generating process is given by Equation (4.11), where x is a number between 0 and 10, randomly drawn from a uniform distribution, and the error term is randomly drawn from a standard normal distribution. Figure 4.5 illustrates this simulated example.

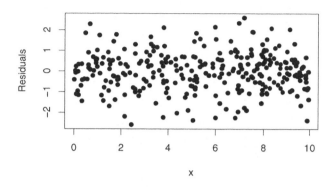

Figure 4.5 Residuals Generated by Simulated Regression

$$y_i = 1 + x_i + e_i, \quad i = 1, ..., N \tag{4.11}$$

```
set.seed(12345)    #sets seed for random number generator
x <- runif(300, 0, 10)
e <- rnorm(300, 0, 1)
y <- 1+x+e
mod3 <- lm(y~x)
ehat <- resid(mod3)
par(cex=1.2,pch=16)
plot(x,ehat, xlab="x", ylab="Residuals")
```

The next example illustrates how the residuals look like when a linear functional form is used, but the true relationship is, in fact, quadratic. The data-generating equation is given in Equation (4.12), where x is uniformly distributed between -2.5 and 2.5), and $e \sim N(0, 4)$. Figure 4.6 shows the residuals from estimating an incorrectly specified, linear econometric model when the correct specification should be quadratic.

$$y_i = 15 - 4x_i^2 + e_i, \quad i = 1, ..., N \tag{4.12}$$

```
set.seed(12345)
x <- runif(150, -2.5, 2.5)
e <- rnorm(150, 0, 4)
y <- 15-4*x^2+e
mod3 <- lm(y~x)
```

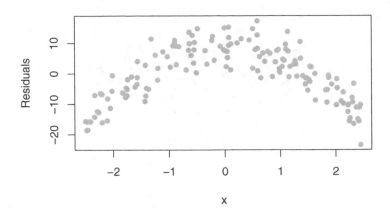

Figure 4.6 Simulated Quadratic Residuals from an Incorrectly Specified Model

```
ehat <- resid(mod3)
ymi <- min(ehat)
yma <- max(ehat)
par(cex=1.2)
plot(x, ehat, ylim=c(ymi, yma),
    xlab="x", ylab="Residuals",col="darkgrey",pch=16)
```

Another assumption that we would like to test is the normality of the residuals, which assures reliable hypothesis testing and confidence intervals even in small samples. This assumption can be assessed by inspecting a histogram of the residuals, as well as performing a Jarque-Bera test, for which the null hypothesis is "Series is normally distributed". Thus, a small p-value rejects the null hypothesis, which means the series fails the normality test. The Jarque-Bera test requires installing and loading the package tseries in R. Figure 4.7 shows a histogram and a superimposed normal distribution for the linear *food expenditure* model.

```
library(tseries)
mod1 <- lm(food_exp~income, data=food)
ehat <- resid(m1)
ebar <- mean(ehat)
sde <- sd(ehat)
par(cex=1.2,lwd=1.5)
hist(ehat, col="grey", freq=FALSE, main="",
    ylab="density", xlab="ehat")
```

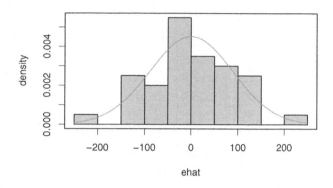

Figure 4.7 Histogram of Residuals from the *food* Linear Model

```
box(bty="o") #builds box around the hystogram
curve(dnorm(x, ebar, sde), col=2, add=TRUE,
      ylab="Density", xlab="ehat")

jarque.bera.test(ehat) #(in package 'tseries')


##
##   Jarque Bera Test
##
## data:   ehat
## X-squared = 0.063, df = 2, p-value = 1
```

While the histogram in Figure 4.7 may not strongly support one conclusion or another about the normlity of ehat, the Jarque-Bera test is unambiguous: there is no evidence against the normality hypothesis.

4.5   Identifying Influential Observations

The set of functions grouped under influence.measures() provide various methods of identifying influential observations. The following code applies some of these to the *food* example and compiles the results in Table 4.4. The methods used are studentized residual (ehatstu), leverage (h), slope dfbeta, and deffits.

Table 4.4: Influential Observations, Various Criteria

	dfbeta	dffits	h	ehatstu	food_exp	income
1	0.029	-0.031	0.163	-0.071	115.2	3.69
2	-0.036	0.039	0.152	0.093	136.0	4.39
3	0.056	-0.062	0.146	-0.150	119.3	4.75
4	0.120	-0.134	0.126	-0.355	115.0	6.03
5	0.046	-0.063	0.053	-0.268	187.1	12.47
31	-0.316	-0.544	0.038	-2.750	109.7	24.42
34	0.204	0.284	0.052	1.215	460.4	26.61
35	0.180	0.248	0.053	1.054	447.8	26.70
36	0.258	0.347	0.056	1.422	482.6	27.14
37	0.162	0.217	0.056	0.890	438.3	27.16
38	0.577	0.722	0.069	2.642	587.7	28.62
39	-0.354	-0.430	0.077	-1.484	257.9	29.40
40	-0.200	-0.222	0.129	-0.578	375.7	33.40

```
data(food)
mod1<-lm(food_exp~income,data=food)
N<-nobs(mod1)
K<-N-df.residual(mod1)
inftab<-data.frame(influence.measures(mod1)$infmat)
inftab$ehatstu <- rstudent(mod1) #studentized residuals
hbar<-K/N #critical value for leverage
dbcr<-2/sqrt(N) #dfbeta criterion
dfcr<-2*sqrt(K/N) #dffits criterion
inftab<-inftab[which(
  inftab$hat > hbar |            #leverage
  abs(inftab$dfb.incm) > dbcr |  #dfbeta
  abs(inftab$dffit) > dfcr |     #dffits
  abs(inftab$ehatstu) > 2        #ehatsu
  ),c(2,3,6,7)]
obs<-as.numeric(rownames(inftab))
tab<-cbind(inftab,food[obs,1:2])
names(tab)<-c("dfbeta","dffits","h",
            "ehatstu","food_exp","income")
kable(tab,caption=
"Influential Observations, Various Criteria",
digits=3, align="c")
```

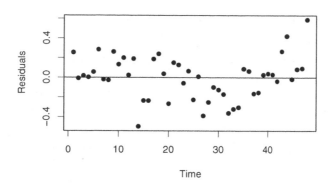

Figure 4.8 Residuals from the Linear *wheat* Model

4.6 Polynomial Models

Regression models may include quadratic or cubic terms to better describe the nature of the data. The following code compares a linear to a cubic model for the `wa_wheat` data set, which gives annual wheat yield in tonnes per hectare in Greenough Shire in Western Australia over a period of 48 years. The linear model is given in Equation (4.13), where the subscript t indicates the observation period.

$$yield_t = \beta_1 + \beta_2 time_t + e_t \tag{4.13}$$

```
data("wa_wheat")
mod1 <- lm(greenough~time, data=wa_wheat)
ehat <- resid(mod1)
par(cex=1.2,pch=16,lwd=1.5)
plot(wa_wheat$time, ehat, xlab="Time", ylab="Residuals")
abline(h=0)
```

Figure 4.8 shows a pattern in the residuals generated by the linear model, which may inspire us to think of a more comples functional form, such as the one in Equation (4.14).

$$yield_t = \beta_1 + \beta_2 time_t^3 + e_t \tag{4.14}$$

Please note in the following code sequence the use of the function `I()`, which is needed in R when an independent variable is transformed by mathematical operators. You do not need

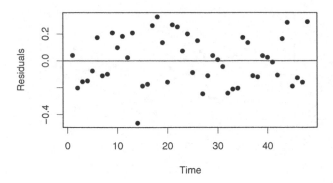

Figure 4.9 Residuals from the Cubic *wheat* Model

the operator I() when an independent variable is transformed through a function such as $log(x)$. In our example, the transformation requiring the use of I() is raising time to the power of 3. Of course, you can create a new variable, x3=x^3 if you wish to avoid the use of I() in a regression equation.

```
mod2 <- lm(wa_wheat$greenough~I(time^3), data=wa_wheat)
ehat <- resid(mod2)
par(cex=1.2,pch=16,lwd=1.5)
plot(wa_wheat$time, ehat, xlab="Time", ylab="Residuals")
abline(h=0)
```

Figure 4.9 displays a much better image of the residuals than Figure 4.8, since the residuals are more evenly spread about the zero line.

4.7   Log-Linear Models

Transforming the dependent variable with the $log()$ function is useful when the variable has a skewed distribution, which is in general the case with amounts that cannot be negative. The $log()$ transformation often makes the distribution closer to normal. The general log-linear model is given in Equation (4.15).

$$log(y_i) = \beta_1 + \beta_2 x_i + e_i \tag{4.15}$$

The following formulas are easily derived from the log-linear Equation (4.15). The semi-

Table 4.5: Log-Linear Model for the *yield* Equation

	Estimate	Std..Error	t.value	Pr...t..
(Intercept)	-0.3434	0.0584	-5.879	0
time	0.0178	0.0021	8.599	0

elasticity has here a different interpretation than the one in the linear-log model: here, an increase in x by one unit (of x) produces a change of $100b_2$ percent in y. For small changes in x, the amount $100b_2$ in the log-linear model can also be interpreted as the growth rate in y (corresponding to a unit increase in x). For instance, if x is time, then $100b_2$ is the growth rate in y per unit of time.

- Prediction: $\hat{y}_n = exp(b_1 + b_2x)$, or $\hat{y}_c = exp(b_1 + b_2x + \hat{\sigma}^2/2)$, with the "natural" predictor $\hat{y}_n$ to be used in small samples and the "corrected" predictor, $\hat{y}_c$, in large samples
- Marginal effect (slope): $dy/dx = b_2y$
- Semi-elasticity: $\%\Delta y = 100b_2\Delta x$

Let us do these calculations first for the *yield* equation using the *wa_wheat* data set.

```
mod4 <- lm(log(greenough)~time, data=wa_wheat)
smod4 <- summary(mod4)
tbl <- data.frame(xtable(smod4))
kable(tbl, caption=
    "Log-Linear Model for the $yield$ Equation")
```

Table 4.5 gives $b_2 = 0.0178$, which indicates that the rate of growth in wheat production has increased at an average rate of approximately 1.78 percent per year.

The *wage* log-linear equation provides another example of calculating a growth rate, but this time the independent variable is not *time*, but *education*. The predictions and the slope are calculated for $educ = 12$ years.

```
data("cps5_small", package="POE5Rdata")
xeduc <- 12
mod5 <- lm(log(wage)~educ, data=cps5_small)
smod5 <- summary(mod5)
tabl <- data.frame(xtable(smod5))
kable(tabl, caption="Log-Linear $wage$ Regression Output")

b1 <- coef(smod5)[[1]]
b2 <- coef(smod5)[[2]]
sighat2 <- smod5$sigma^2
```

Table 4.6: Log-Linear *wage* Regression Output

	Estimate	Std..Error	t.value	Pr...t..
(Intercept)	1.5968	0.0702	22.75	0
educ	0.0988	0.0048	20.39	0

```
g <- 100*b2                     #growth rate
yhatn <- exp(b1+b2*xeduc) #"natural" predictiction
yhatc <- exp(b1+b2*xeduc+sighat2/2) #corrected prediction
DyDx <- b2*yhatn                #marginal effect
```

Here are the results of these calculations: "natural" prediction $\hat{y}_n = 16.149$; corrected prediction, $\hat{y}_c = 18.162$; growth rate $g = 9.875$; and marginal effect $dy/dx = 1.59$. The growth rate indicates that an increase in education by one unit (see the data description using ?cps5_small) increases hourly wage by 9.875 percent.

Figure 4.10 presents the "natural" and the "corrected" regression lines for the *wage* equation, together with the actual data points.

```
education=seq(0,22,2)
yn <- exp(b1+b2*education)
yc <- exp(b1+b2*education+sighat2/2)
par(cex=1.3,pch=16,lwd=1.8)
plot(cps5_small$educ, cps5_small$wage,
     xlab="Education", ylab="Wage", col="grey")
lines(yn~education, lty=2, col="black")
lines(yc~education, lty=1, col="blue")
legend("topleft", legend=c("yc","yn"),
       lty=c(1,2), col=c("blue","black"))
```

The regular R^2 cannot be used to compare two regression models having different dependent variables such as a linear-log and a log-linear models; when such a comparison is needed, one can use the generalized R^2, which is $R_g^2 = [corr(y, \hat{y}]^2$. Let us calculate the generalized R^2 for the quadratic and the log-linear *wage* models.

```
mod4 <- lm(wage~I(educ^2), data=cps5_small)
yhat4 <- predict(mod4)
mod5 <- lm(log(wage)~educ, data=cps5_small)
smod5 <- summary(mod5)
b1 <- coef(smod5)[[1]]
b2 <- coef(smod5)[[2]]
sighat2 <- smod5$sigma^2
```

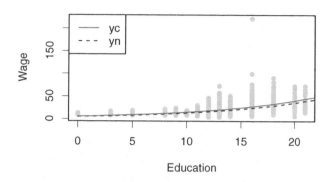

Figure 4.10 Normal and Corrected Lines in the Log-Linear Equation

```
yhat5 <- exp(b1+b2*cps5_small$educ+sighat2/2)
rg4 <- cor(cps5_small$wage, yhat4)^2
rg5 <- cor(cps5_small$wage,yhat5)^2
```

The quadratic model yields $R_g^2 = 0.219$, and the log-linear model yields $R_g^2 = 0.216$; since the former is higher, we conclude that the quadratic model is a better fit to the data than the log-linear one. (However, other tests of how the two models meet the assumptions of linear regression may reach a different conclusion; R^2 is only one of the model selection criteria.)

To determine a forecast interval estimate in the log-linear model, we first construct the interval in logs using the natural predictor $\hat{y}_n$, then take antilogs of the interval limits. The forecasting error is the same as before, given in Equation (4.4). The following calculations use an education level equal to 12 and $\alpha = 0.05$.

```
# The *wage* log-linear model
# Prediction interval for educ = 12
alpha <- 0.05
xeduc <- 12
xedbar <- mean(cps5_small$educ)
mod5 <- lm(log(wage)~educ, data=cps5_small)
b1 <- coef(mod5)[[1]]
b2 <- coef(mod5)[[2]]
df5 <- mod5$df.residual
N <- nobs(mod5)
tcr <- qt(1-alpha/2, df=df5)
```

```
smod5 <- summary(mod5)
varb2 <- vcov(mod5)[2,2]
sighat2 <- smod5$sigma^2
varf <- sighat2+sighat2/N+(xeduc-xedbar)^2*varb2
sef <- sqrt(varf)
lnyhat <- b1+b2*xeduc
lowb <- exp(lnyhat-tcr*sef)
upb <- exp(lnyhat+tcr*sef)
```

The result is the confidence interval (6.24, 41.82). Figure 4.11 shows a 95% confidence band for the log-linear *wage* model. Because of the logarithm, the confidence band is not symmetric with respect to the regression line as it is in the linear model.

```
# Drawing a confidence band for the log-linear
# *wage* equation
xmin <- min(cps5_small$educ)
xmax <- max(cps5_small$educ)+2
education <- seq(xmin, xmax, 2)
lnyhat <- b1+b2*education
yhat <- exp(lnyhat)
varf <- sighat2+sighat2/N+(education-xedbar)^2*varb2
sef <- sqrt(varf)
lowb <- exp(lnyhat-tcr*sef)
upb <- exp(lnyhat+tcr*sef)
par(cex=1.3,pch=16,lwd=1.8)
plot(cps5_small$educ, cps5_small$wage, col="grey35",
     xlab="Education", ylab="Wage", ylim=c(0,100))
lines(yhat~education, lty=1, col="black")
lines(lowb~education, lty=2, col="blue")
lines(upb~education, lty=2, col="blue")
legend("topleft", legend=c("yhat", "lowb", "upb"),
       lty=c(1, 2, 2), col=c("black", "blue", "blue"))
```

4.8 The Log-Log Model

The log-log model has the desirable property that the coefficient of the independent variable is equal to the (constant) elasticity of y with respect to x. Therefore, this model is often used to estimate supply and demand equations. Its standard form is given in Equation (4.16), where y, x, and e are $N \times 1$ vectors.

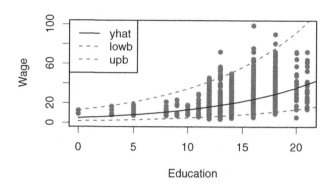

Figure 4.11 Confidence Band for the Log-Linear *wage* Equation

Table 4.7: Log-Log Regression: Demand for Chicken

	Estimate	Std..Error	t.value	Pr...t..
(Intercept)	3.716944	0.0223594	166.23619	0
log(p)	-1.121358	0.0487564	-22.99918	0

$$log(y) = \beta_1 + \beta_2 log(x) + e \tag{4.16}$$

```
# Calculating log-log demand for chicken
data("newbroiler", package="POE5Rdata")
mod6 <- lm(log(q)~log(p), data=newbroiler)
b1 <- coef(mod6)[[1]]
b2 <- coef(mod6)[[2]]
smod6 <- summary(mod6)
tbl <- data.frame(xtable(smod6))
kable(tbl, caption="Log-Log Regression: Demand for Chicken")
```

Table 4.7 gives the log-log regression output. The coefficient on p indicates that an increase in price by 1% changes the quantity demanded by -1.121%.

```
# Drawing the fitted values of the log-log equation
ngrid <- 20 # number of drawing points
xmin <- min(newbroiler$p)
xmax <- max(newbroiler$p)
step <- (xmax-xmin)/ngrid # grid dimension
```

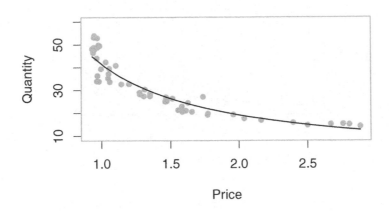

Figure 4.12 Log-Log Demand for Chicken

```
xp <- seq(xmin, xmax, step)
sighat2 <- smod6$sigma^2
yhatc <- exp(b1+b2*log(newbroiler$p)+sighat2/2)
yc <- exp(b1+b2*log(xp)+sighat2/2) #corrected q
par(cex=1.3,lwd=1.8,pch=16, col="darkgrey")
plot(newbroiler$p, newbroiler$q, ylim=c(10,60),
     xlab="Price", ylab="Quantity")
lines(yc~xp, lty=1, col="black")

# The generalized R-squared:
rgsq <- cor(newbroiler$q, yhatc)^2
```

The generalized R^2, wich uses the corrected fitted values, is equal to 0.8818.

Chapter 5

The Multiple Regression Model

```
rm(list=ls())
options(digits=3,scip=TRUE)
library(POE5Rdata)
library(knitr)
library(xtable)
library(effects)
library(car)
library(AER)
library(broom)
library(nlWaldTest)
library(stats)
```

This chapter uses a few new packages: `effects` (Fox et al., 2016), `car` (Fox and Weisberg, 2016), `AER` (Kleiber and Zeileis, 2015), `nlWaldTest` (Komashko, 2016), and `broom` (Robinson, 2016)

5.1 The General Model

A multiple regression model is very similar to the simple regression model, but includes more independent variables. Thus, the interpretation of a slope parameter has to take into account possible changes in other independent variables: a slope parameter, say β_k, gives the change in the (conditional expectation of the) dependent variable, y, when the independent variable x_k increases by one unit, **while all the other factors, including those in the error term, remain constant** (the exogeneity assumption). Equation (5.1) gives

Table 5.1: Summary Statistics for Data Set $andy$

column	n	mean	sd	median	min	max
sales	75	77.375	6.4885	76.50	62.40	91.20
price	75	5.687	0.5184	5.69	4.83	6.49
advert	75	1.844	0.8317	1.80	0.50	3.10

the general form of a multiple regression model, where y, x_k, and e are $N \times 1$ vectors, N is the number of observations in the sample, and $k = 1, ..., K$ indicates the k-th independent variable. The notation used in Equation (5.1) implies that the first independent variable, x_1, is an $N \times 1$ vector of 1s.

$$y = \beta_1 + \beta_2 x_2 + ... + \beta_K x_K + e \tag{5.1}$$

The model assumptions remain the same, with the additional requirement that no independent variable is a linear combination of the others.

5.2   Example: Andy's Hamburger Sales

The *andy* data set includes variables *sales*, which is monthly revenue to the company in \$1000s, *price*, which is a price index of all products sold by Andy's, and *advert*, the advertising expenditure in a given month, in \$1000s. Summary statistics for the *andy* data set are shown in Table 5.1. The basic *andy* model is presented in Equation (5.2).

$$sales = \beta_1 + \beta_2 \, price + \beta_3 \, advert + e \tag{5.2}$$

```
# Summary statistics
data(andy)
s=tidy(andy)[,c(1:5,8,9)]
kable(s,caption="Summary Statistics for Data Set $andy$")

# The basic *andy* model
data("andy",package="POE5Rdata")
mod1 <- lm(sales~price+advert, data=andy)
smod1 <- data.frame(xtable(summary(mod1)))
kable(smod1,
   caption="The Basic Multiple Regression Model",
   col.names=c("Coefficient", "Std. Error", "t-value",
   "p-value"), align="c", digits=3)
```

Table 5.2: The Basic Multiple Regression Model

	Coefficient	Std. Error	t-value	p-value
(Intercept)	118.914	6.352	18.722	0.000
price	-7.908	1.096	-7.215	0.000
advert	1.863	0.683	2.726	0.008

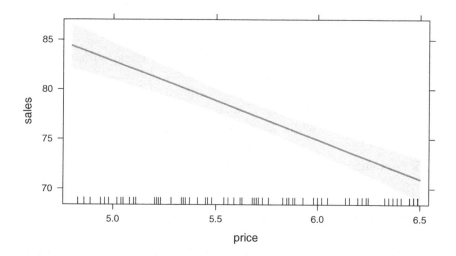

Figure 5.1 The Partial Effect of *price* in the Basic *andy* Regression

Table 5.2 shows that, for any given (but fixed) value of advertising expenditure, an increase in price by \$1 decreases sales by \$7908. On the other hand, for any given price, sales increase by \$1863 when advertising expenditures increase by \$1000.

```
effprice <- Effect("price", mod1)
plot(effprice, main="")

summary(effprice)


##
##  price effect
## price
##     4.8      5.2      5.7      6.1      6.5
## 84.39052 81.22737 77.27345 74.11030 70.94716
##
##  Lower 95 Percent Confidence Limits
## price
```

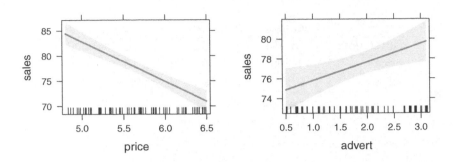

Figure 5.2 Using the Function allEffects in the Basic *andy* Model

```
##      4.8       5.2       5.7       6.1       6.5
## 82.14947 79.67882 76.14838 72.66864 68.84513
##
##  Upper 95 Percent Confidence Limits
## price
##      4.8       5.2       5.7       6.1       6.5
## 86.63156 82.77593 78.39851 75.55197 73.04919
```

Figure 5.1 shows the predicted levels of the dependent variable *sales* and its 95% confidence band for the sample values of the variable *price*. In more complex functional forms, the R function effect() plots the partial effect of a variable for given levels of the other independent variables in the model. The simplest possible call of this function requires, as arguments, the name of the term for which we wish the partial effect (in our example *price*), and the object (model) in question. If not otherwise specified, the confidence intervals (band) are determined for a 95% confidence level and the other variables at their means. A simple use of the effects package is presented in Figure 5.2, which plots the partial effects of all variables in the basic *andy* model. (Function effect() plots only one graph for one variable, while allEffects() plots all variables in the model.)

```
alleffandy <- allEffects(mod1)
plot(alleffandy, main="", cex.axes = .5)

# Another example of using the function effect()
mod2 <- lm(sales~price+advert+I(advert^2), data=andy)
print(summary(mod2),signif=F)
```

```
##
## Call:
## lm(formula = sales ~ price + advert + I(advert^2), data = andy)
```

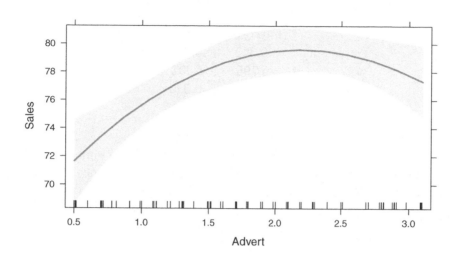

Figure 5.3 Using the Function 'effect' in a Quadratic Model

```
##
## Residuals:
##     Min      1Q   Median      3Q      Max
## -12.255  -3.143   -0.012   2.851   11.805
##
## Coefficients:
##               Estimate Std. Error t value Pr(>|t|)
## (Intercept)   109.719       6.799   16.14  < 2e-16
## price          -7.640       1.046   -7.30  3.2e-10
## advert         12.151       3.556    3.42   0.0011
## I(advert^2)    -2.768       0.941   -2.94   0.0044
##
## Residual standard error: 4.65 on 71 degrees of freedom
## Multiple R-squared:  0.508,  Adjusted R-squared:  0.487
## F-statistic: 24.5 on 3 and 71 DF,  p-value: 5.6e-11
plot(effect("I(advert^2)", mod2), main="",
     xlab="Advert", ylab="Sales")
```

Figure 5.3 is an example of using the effect() function to plot the partial effect of a quadratic independent variable. I chose to insert the I(advert^2) term to indicate that the variable of interest needs to be specified exactly as it appears in the model.

All the methods available in R for simple linear regression models are available for multiple

Table 5.3: Covariance Matrix of the *andy* Model

	(Intercept)	price	advert
(Intercept)	40.343	-6.795	-0.748
price	-6.795	1.201	-0.020
advert	-0.748	-0.020	0.467

models as well. Thus, to extract the information generated by the lm() function, we use the same functions as before. As we have already learned, the command ?mod1 gives a list of all the results stored in the mod1 object. The next code sequence illustrates how to access various regression output items for the basic *andy* equation.

```
mod1 <- lm(sales~price+advert, data=andy)
smod1 <- summary(mod1)
df <- mod1$df.residual
N <- nobs(mod1)
b1 <- coef(mod1)[[1]] #or
b2 <- coef(mod1)[["price"]]
b3 <- coef(mod1)[["advert"]]
sighat2 <- smod1$sigma^2
anov <- anova(mod1)
SSE <- anov[3,2]
SST <- sum(anov[,2]) #sum of column 2 in anova
SSR <- SST-SSE
kable(data.frame(vcov(mod1)), align='c', digits=3,
     caption="Covariance Matrix of the $andy$ Model",
     col.names=c("(Intercept)", "price", "advert"))
```

The *covariance matrix*, or the *variance-covariance* matrix shown in Table 5.3 contains all the estimated variances and covariances of the regression coefficients. These are useful when testing hypotheses about individual coefficients or combinations of those.

The R function predict(), which we have seen before, can also be used in the context of multiple regression, as the following code chunk demonstrates.

```
mod1<- lm(sales~price+advert,data=andy)
x<-data.frame(price=5.5,advert=1.2)
yhat<-predict(mod1,newdata=x,interval="confidence")
yhat[1]
```

```
## [1] 77.66
```

The predicted sales for $price = \$5.5$ and $advert = \$1.2$ is $77.656 with a 95% confidence interval of (76.1781, 79.1329). The next section shows the details of calculating interval estimates for the parameters of a multivariate regression model.

5.3 Interval Estimation in Multiple Regression

Interval estimation is similar to the one we have studied in the simple regression model, except the number of degrees of freedom is now $N - K$, where K is the number of regression coefficients to be estimated. In the *andy* example, $df = 72$ and the variances and covariances of the estimates are given in the following code sequence. Here is the variance-covariance matrix for the *andy* model:

```
vcov(mod1)
```

```
##              (Intercept)    price    advert
## (Intercept)     40.3433 -6.79506 -0.74842
## price           -6.7951  1.20120 -0.01974
## advert          -0.7484 -0.01974  0.46676
```

And here is how we can retrieve various elements from the variance-covariance matrix:

```
varb1 <- vcov(mod1)[1,1]
varb2 <- vcov(mod1)[2,2]
varb3 <- vcov(mod1)[3,3]
covb1b2 <- vcov(mod1)[1,2]
covb1b3 <- vcov(mod1)[1,3]
covb2b3 <- vcov(mod1)[2,3]
seb2 <- sqrt(varb2) #standard error of b2
seb3 <- sqrt(varb3)
```

With the calculated standard error of b_2, $se(b_2) = 1.096$, we can now determine a 95% confidence interval, as shown in the following code lines. The code also shows the use of the R function confint(model, parm, level) to check our results.

```
alpha <- 0.05
tcr <- qt(1-alpha/2, df)
lowb2 <- b2-tcr*seb2
upb2 <- b2+tcr*seb2
lowb3 <- b3-tcr*seb3
upb3 <- b3+tcr*seb3
confints <- confint(mod1,
        parm=c("price", "advert"), level=0.95)
kable(data.frame(confints), caption=
```

Table 5.4: Confidence Intervals for *price* and *advert*

	lowb	upb
price	-10.0927	-5.723
advert	0.5007	3.224

```
"Confidence Intervals for $price$ and $advert$",
  align="c", col.names=c("lowb", "upb"), digits=4)
```

Finding an interval estimate for a **linear combination** of the parameters is often needed. Suppose one is interested in determining an interval estimate for *sales* when the price decreases by 40 cents and the advertising expenditure increases by $800 (see Equation (5.3)) in the *andy* basic equation.

$$\lambda = 0\beta_1 - 0.4\beta_2 + 0.8\beta_3 \tag{5.3}$$

```
alpha <- 0.1
tcr <- qt(1-alpha/2, df)
a1 <- 0
a2 <- -0.4
a3 <- 0.8
L <- a1*b1+a2*b2+a3*b3
varL <- a1^2*varb1+a2^2*varb2+a3^2*varb3+
  2*a1*a2*covb1b2+2*a1*a3*covb1b3+2*a2*a3*covb2b3
seL <- sqrt(varL)
lowbL <- L-tcr*seL
upbL <- L+tcr*seL
```

The calculated confidence interval is $(3.471, 5.836)$.

Let us calculate the variance of a linear combination of regression parameters in a more general way to take advantage of R's excellent capabilities of working with complex data structures such as lists, vectors, and matrices. This code sequence introduces a few new elements, such as matrix transposition and multiplication, as well as turning a list into a vector. The matrix multiplication operator in R is %*% and the transposition operator is t().

```
a <- c(0, -0.4, 0.8) # vector
b <- as.numeric(coef(mod1))# vector of coefficients
L <- sum(a*b) # sum of elementwise products
V <- vcov(mod1) # the variance-covariance matrix
```

```
A <- as.vector(a) # (indeed not necessary)
varL <- as.numeric(t(A) %*% V %*% A)
```

5.4 Hypothesis Testing in Multiple Regression

The process of testing hypotheses about a single parameter is similar to the one we have seen in simple regression, the only difference consisting in the number of degrees of freedom.

A two-tail test. Let us test the significance of the β_2 parameter of the basic *andy* equation. The hypotheses are given in Equation (5.4).

$$H_0 : \beta_2 = 0, \quad H_A : \beta_2 \neq 0 \tag{5.4}$$

```
alpha <- 0.05
df <- mod1$df.residual
tcr <- qt(1-alpha/2, df)
b2 <- coef(mod1)[["price"]]
seb2 <- sqrt(vcov(mod1)[2,2])
t <- b2/seb2
```

The calculated t is equal to -7.215, which is less than $-t_{cr} = -1.993$, indicating that the null hypothesis is rejected and that β_2 is significantly different from zero. As usual, we can perform the same test using the p-value instead of t_{cr}.

```
t <- b2/seb2
pval <- 2*(1-pt(abs(t), df)) #two-tail test
```

The calculated p-value is 4.424×10^{-10}. Since this is less than α we reject, again, the null hypothesis $H_0 : \beta_2 = 0$. Let us do the same for β_3:

```
alpha <- 0.05
df <- mod1$df.residual
tcr <- qt(1-alpha/2, df)
b3 <- coef(mod1)[[3]]
seb3 <- sqrt(vcov(mod1)[3,3])
tval <- b3/seb3
```

Calculated $t = 2.726$, and $t_{cr} = 1.993$. Since $t > t_{cr}$ we reject the null hypothesis and conclude that there is a statistically significant relationship between *advert* and *sales*. The same result can be obtained using the p-value method:

```
pval <- 2*(1-pt(abs(tval), df))
```

Result: p-value $= 0.008 < \alpha$. R shows the two-tail t and p values for coefficients in the regression output (see Table 5.2).

A left-tail test. Let us test the hypothesis described in Equation (5.5) at a 5% significance level. The calculated value of t is the same, but t_{cr} corresponds now not to $\alpha/2$, but to α.

$$H_0 : \beta_2 \geq 0, \quad H_A : \beta_2 < 0 \tag{5.5}$$

```
alpha <- 0.05
tval <- b2/seb2
tcr <- -qt(1-alpha, df) #left-tail test
pval <- pt(tval, df)
```

The results $t = -7.215$, $t_{cr} = -1.666$ show that the calculated t falls in the (left-tail) rejection region. The p-value, which is equal to 2.212×10^{-10}, is less than α, and thus it also rejects the null hypothesis.

Here is how the p-values should be calculated, depending on the type of test:

- Two-tail test ($H_A : \beta_2 \neq 0$), p-value <- 2*(1-pt(abs(t), df))
- Left-tail test ($H_A : \beta_2 < 0$), p-value <- pt(t, df)
- Right-tail test ($H_A : \beta_2 > 0$), p-value <- 1-pt(t, df)

A right-tail test. An example is to test whether an increase of $1000 in advertising expenditure increases revenue by more than $1000. In the hypothesis testing language, we need to test the hypothesis presented in Equation (5.6).

$$H_0 : \beta_3 \leq 1, \quad H_A : \beta_3 > 1 \tag{5.6}$$

```
tval <- (b3-1)/seb3
pval <- 1-pt(tval,df)
```

The calculated p-value is 0.1054, which is greater than α, showing that we cannot reject the null hypothesis $H_0 : \beta_3 \leq 1$ at $\alpha = 0.05$. In other words, increasing advertising expenditure by $1000 may or may not increase sales by more than $1000.

Testing linear combinations of coefficients. Suppose we wish to determine if lowering the price by 20 cents increases sales more than would an increase in advertising expenditure by $500. The hypothesis to test this conjecture is given in Equation (5.7).

$$H_0 : 0\beta_1 - 0.2\beta_2 - 0.5\beta_3 \leq 0, \quad H_A : 0\beta_1 - 0.2\beta_2 - 0.5\beta_3 > 0 \qquad (5.7)$$

Let us practice the matrix form of testing this hypothesis. R functions having names that start with as. coerce a certain structure into another, such as a named list into a vector (names are removed and only numbers remain).

```
A <- as.vector(c(0, -0.2, -0.5))
V <- vcov(mod1)
L <- as.numeric(t(A) %*% coef(mod1))
seL <- as.numeric(sqrt(t(A) %*% V %*% A))
tval <- L/seL
pval <- 1-pt(tval, df) # the result (p-value)
```

The answer is p-value$= 0.0546$, which barely fails to reject the null hypothesis. Thus, the conjecture that a decrease in price by 20 cents is more effective than an increase in advertising by $800 is not supported by the data.

For two-tail linear hypotheses, R has a built-in function, linearHypothesis(model, hypothesis), in the car package. This function tests hypotheses based not on t-statistics as we have done so far, but based on an F-statistic. However, the p-value criterion to reject or not the null hypothesis is the same: reject if the p-value is less than α. Let us use this function to test a two-tail hypothesis similar to the one given in Equation (5.7). (Note that the linearHypothesis() function can test not only one hypothesis, but a set of simultaneous hypotheses.)

```
hypothesis <- "-0.2*price = 0.5*advert"
test <- linearHypothesis (mod1, hypothesis)
Fstat <- test$F[2]
pval <- 1-pf(Fstat, 1, df)
```

The calculated p-value is 0.1092, which shows that the null hypothesis cannot be rejected. There are a few new elements, besides the use of the linearHypothesis function in this code sequence. First, the linearHypothesis() function creates an R object that contains several items, one of which is the F-statistic we are looking for. This object is shown in Table 5.5 and it is named test in our code. The code element test$F[2] extracts the F-statistic from the linearHypothesis() object.

Second, the F-statistic has two 'degrees of freedom' parameters, not only one as the t-statistic does. The first degree of freedom is equal to the number of simultaneous hypotheses to be tested (in our case only one); the second is the number of degrees of freedom in the model, $df = N - K$.

Last, the function that calculates the p-value is pf(Fval, df1, df2), where Fval is

Table 5.5: The 'linearHypothesis()' Object

Res.Df	RSS	Df	Sum of Sq	F	Pr(>F)
73	1782	NA	NA	NA	NA
72	1719	1	62.79	2.63	0.1092

Table 5.6: The Quadratic Version of the *andy* Model

	Estimate	Std. Error	t	p-Value
(Intercept)	109.719	6.799	16.137	0.000
price	-7.640	1.046	-7.304	0.000
advert	12.151	3.556	3.417	0.001
I(advert^2)	-2.768	0.941	-2.943	0.004

the calculated value of the F-statistic, and df1 and df2 are the two degrees of freedom parameters of the F-statistic.

```
kable(test, caption="The `linearHypothesis()` Object")
```

5.5   Polynomial Regression Models

A polynomial multivariate regression model may include several independent variables at various powers. In such models, the partial (or marginal) effect of a regressor x_k on the response y is determined by the partial derivative $\partial y / \partial x_k$. Let us consider again the basic *andy* model with the added *advert* quadratic term as presented in Equation (5.8).

$$sales_i = \beta_1 + \beta_2 \, price_i + \beta_3 \, advert_i + \beta_4 \, advert_i^2 + e_i \qquad (5.8)$$

As we have noticed before, the quadratic term is introduced into the model using the function I() to indicate the presence of a mathematical operator. Table 5.6 presents a summary of the regression output from the model described in Equation (5.8).

```
mod2 <- lm(sales~price+advert+I(advert^2),data=andy)
smod2 <- summary(mod2)
tabl <- data.frame(xtable(smod2))
names(tabl) <- c("Estimate",
            "Std. Error", "t", "p-Value")
kable(tabl, digits=3, align='c',
   caption="The Quadratic Version of the $andy$ Model")
```

Let us calculate the marginal effect of *advert* on *sales* for two levels of *advert*; the relevant partial derivative is the one in Equation (5.9).

$$\frac{\partial sales}{\partial advert} = \beta_3 + 2\beta_4 \, advert \tag{5.9}$$

```
advlevels <- c(0.5, 2)
b3 <- coef(mod2)[[3]]
b4 <- coef(mod2)[[4]]
DsDa <- b3+2*b4*advlevels #Dsales/Dadvert
```

The calculated marginal effects for the two levels of advertising expenditure are, respectively, 9.3833 and 1.0794, which shows, as expected, diminishing returns to advertising at any given price.

Often, marginal effects or other quantities are non-linear functions of the parameters of a regression model. The *delta* method allows calculating the variance of such quantities using a Taylor series approximation. This method is, however, valid only in a vicinity of a point, as any mathematical object involving derivatives.

Suppose we wish to test a hypothesis such as the one in Equation (5.10), where c is a constant.

$$H_0 : g(\beta_1, \beta_2) = c \tag{5.10}$$

The *delta* method consists in estimating the variance of the function $g(\beta_1, \beta_2)$ around some given data point, using the formula in Equation (5.11), where g_i stands for $\partial g / \partial \beta_i$ calculated at the estimated values of the regression coefficients, $b_1, b_2, ..., b_K$.

$$var(g) = g_1^2 var(b_1) + g_2^2 var(b_2) + 2g_1 g_2 cov(b_1, b_2) \tag{5.11}$$

Let us apply this method to find a confidence interval for the optimal level of advertising in the *andy* quadratic equation, g, which is given by Equation (5.12).

$$\hat{g} = \frac{1 - b_3}{2b_4} \tag{5.12}$$

Equation (5.13) shows the derivatives of function g.

$$\hat{g}_3 = -\frac{1}{2b_4}, \quad \hat{g}_4 = -\frac{1 - b_3}{2b_4^2}. \tag{5.13}$$

```
alpha <- 0.05
df <- mod2$df.residual
tcr <- qt(1-alpha/2, df)
g <- (1-b3)/(2*b4)
g3 <- -1/(2*b4)
g4 <- -(1-b3)/(2*b4^2)
varb3 <- vcov(mod2)[3,3]
varb4 <- vcov(mod2)[4,4]
covb3b4 <- vcov(mod2)[3,4]
varg <- g3^2*varb3+g4^2*varb4+2*g3*g4*covb3b4
seg <- sqrt(varg)
lowbg <- g-tcr*seg
upbg <- g+tcr*seg
```

The point estimate of the optimal advertising level is 2.014, with its confidence interval (1.758, 2.271).

5.6   Interaction Terms in Linear Regression

An interaction term is a combination of two or more variables; the variables that make an interaction term may appear in other terms, either by themselves or in combination with other variables. In such models, the slope of one variable may depend on one or several other variables. Partial effects are calculated as partial derivatives, similar to the polynomial equations we have already studied, considering the interaction term as a product of the variables involved.

There are two ways to introduce interaction terms in R; first, with a : (colon) symbol, when only the interaction term is created; second, with the $*$ (star) symbol when all the terms involving the variables in the interaction term should be present in the regression. For instance, the code $x * z$ creates three terms: x, z, and $x : z$ (this last one is x 'interacted' with z, which is a peculiarity of the R system). Consider the following *wage* equation.

$$ln(wage) = \beta_1 + \beta_2\,educ + \beta_3\,exper + \beta_4(educ \times exper) + \beta_5\,exper^2 + e \qquad (5.14)$$

The next code sequence illustrates how to approach such a model; Table 5.7 shows the results.

Table 5.7: The *wage* Problem in a Log-Quadratic Model

term	estimate	std.error	statistic	p.value
(Intercept)	0.6792	0.1561	4.350	0.0000
educ	0.1359	0.0101	13.513	0.0000
exper	0.0489	0.0068	7.145	0.0000
I(exper^2)	-0.0005	0.0001	-6.241	0.0000
educ:exper	-0.0013	0.0003	-3.704	0.0002

```
data("cps5_small",package="POE5Rdata")
mod3 <- lm(log(wage)~educ*exper+I(exper^2),data=cps5_small )
tmod3<-tidy(mod3)
kable(tmod3,caption=
    "The $wage$ Problem in a Log-Quadratic Model")
```

The marginal effect of an extra year of experience is determined, again, by the partial derivative of *wage* with respect to *exper*, as Equation (5.15) shows.

$$\%\Delta wage \cong 100\,(\beta_3 + \beta_4\,educ + 2\,\beta_5\,exper)\Delta exper \qquad (5.15)$$

Here, however, the marginal effect is easier expressed in percentage change, rather than in units of *wage*. Please note that the marginal effect of *exper* depends on both education and experience. Let us calculate this marginal effect for the average values of *educ* and *exper*.

```
data(cps5_small)
meduc <- mean(cps5_small$educ)
mexper <- mean(cps5_small$exper)
mod4 <- lm(log(wage)~educ*exper+I(exper^2), data=cps5_small)
smod4 <- data.frame(xtable(summary(mod4)))
b3 <- coef(mod4)[[3]]
b4 <- coef(mod4)[[4]]
b5 <- coef(mod4)[[5]]
pDwDex <- 100*(b3+b4*meduc+2*b5*mexper)
```

The result of this calculation is $\%\Delta wage = -1.711$, which has, apparently, the wrong sign. What could be the cause? Let us look at a summary of the regression output and identify the terms (see Table 5.8).

```
kable(smod4, caption=
  "The $wage$ Equation with Interaction and Quadratic Terms")
```

Table 5.8: The *wage* Equation with Interaction and Quadratic Terms

	Estimate	Std..Error	t.value	Pr...t..
(Intercept)	0.6792	0.1561	4.350	0.0000
educ	0.1359	0.0101	13.513	0.0000
exper	0.0489	0.0068	7.145	0.0000
I(exper^2)	-0.0005	0.0001	-6.241	0.0000
educ:exper	-0.0013	0.0003	-3.704	0.0002

The output table shows that the order of the terms in the regression equation is not the same as in Equation (5.14), which is the effect of using the compact term $educ * exper$ in the R code. Thee symbol $*$ places the proper interaction term, $educ : exper$ in the last position of all terms containing any of the variables involved in the combined term $educ * exper$. There are a few ways to move the interaction term to a desired location up or down the coefficient list or to retrieve it irrespective of location. One is to write the equation code in full, without the shortcut $educ * exper$; another is to use the names of the terms when retrieving the coefficients, such as b4 <- coef(mod1)[["I(exper^2)"]]; another to change the position of the terms in Equation (5.14) according to Table 5.8 and re-calculate the derivative in Equation (5.15). I am going to use the names of the variables, as they appear in Table 5.8, but I also change the names of the parameters to avoid confusion.

```
bexper <- coef(mod4)[["exper"]]
bint <- coef(mod4)[["educ:exper"]]
bsqr <- coef(mod4)[["I(exper^2)"]]
pDwDex <- 100*(bexper+bint*meduc+2*bsqr*mexper)
```

The new result indicates that the expected wage increases by 0.8725 percent when experience increases by one year, which, at least, has the "right" sign.

An **example** of applying the *Delta* method: The data file *cps5_small* includes 1200 observations on different variables potentially influencing *wage*. Let us consider, again, the *wage* equation, given by Equation (5.16), and seek to estimate the level of education that maximizes *wage*.

$$ln(wage) = \beta_1 + \beta_2\, educ + \beta_3\, exper + \beta_4(educ \times exper) + \beta_5\, exper^2 + e \qquad (5.16)$$

For the model in Equation (5.16), the first-order condition to the maximization problem has the solution

$$exper_0 = \frac{-\beta_3 - \beta_4\, educ}{2\beta_5}$$

The R function `nlConfint` in package `nlWaldTest` calculates confidence intervals for nonlinear functions of the parameters, using the *Delta* method. The expression to be tested must be coded under the form of a string, where the parameters are identified by the symbols `b[k]`, where k is the order of the parameter in the regression output of the model. The following code demonstrates this method.

```
options(digits=4)
foc<-"(-b[3]-16*b[5])/(2*b[4])" #restriction to be tested
nlConfint(mod3,foc) #test function


##                               value 2.5 % 97.5 %
## (-b[3]-16*b[5])/(2*b[4]) 30.17 26.67   33.68
```

5.7 Monte Carlo Simulation for Interval Estimation

Consider an artificially generated data set, with $N/2$ values of x equal to 10 and $N/2$ values equal to 20. Suppose $\beta_1 = 100$, $\beta_2 = 10$, and $\nu_i \sim \chi^2_{(4)}$. Table 5.9 shows the results of a Monte Carlo simulation involving six sample sizes, from 20 to 1000 observations; for each sample size, the results are averages over $10,000$ samples.

```
M<-10000
n<-c(20,40,100,200,500,1000)
b1<-100
b2<-10
sigsq<-2500
stdz<-sqrt(sigsq)
S<-length(n)

  reject<-rep(0,S)
  cover<-rep(0,S)
  b1bar<-numeric(S)
  b2bar<-numeric(S)
  sig2bar<-numeric(S)
  reject<-numeric(S)
  cover<-numeric(S)
  close<-numeric(S)

for(k in 1:S){
  N<-n[k]
  tcr<-qt(0.95,N-2)
  tcr1<-qt(0.975,N-2)
```

```
  rej<-rep(0,M)
  cvr<-rep(0,M)
  x<-c(rep(10,N/2),rep(20,N/2))

  b1hat<-numeric(M)
  b2hat<-numeric(M)
  sig2hat<-numeric(M)
  reje<-numeric(M)
  covr<-numeric(M)
  clos<-numeric(M)

  for(j in 1:M){
    set.seed(j)
    nu<-rchisq(N,df=4)
    z<-(nu-4)/sqrt(8)
    e<-50*z
    y<-b1+b2*x+e
    m1<-lm(y~x)
    sig2hat[j]<-stats::sigma(m1)^2
    b1hat[j]<-tidy(m1)[1,2]
    b2hat[j]<-tidy(m1)[2,2]
    seb2<-tidy(m1)[2,3]
    t2<-(b2hat[j]-b2)/seb2
    if(t2>tcr){rej[j]<-1}
    if(t2 < tcr1 & t2 > -tcr1){cvr[j]<-1}
    if(b2hat[j] > b2-1 & b2hat[j] < b2+1){clos[j]<-1}
  }

  b1bar[k]<-mean(b1hat)
  b2bar[k]<-mean(b2hat)
  sig2bar[k]<-mean(sig2hat)
  reject[k]<-mean(rej)
  cover[k]<-mean(cvr)
  close[k]<-mean(clos)
}

tab<-data.frame(n,b1bar,b2bar,sig2bar,reject,cover,close)
kable(tab,digits=5,caption=
"Simulation of Hypothesis Testing and Interval Estimates")
```

Table 5.9: Simulation of Hypothesis Testing and Interval Estimates

n	b1bar	b2bar	sig2bar	reject	cover	close
20	100.2	9.986	2491	0.0484	0.9507	0.3439
40	100.0	9.998	2497	0.0500	0.9515	0.4814
100	100.1	9.994	2501	0.0482	0.9528	0.6859
200	100.0	10.000	2500	0.0565	0.9468	0.8353
500	100.0	9.999	2499	0.0523	0.9470	0.9729
1000	100.0	9.998	2498	0.0534	0.9489	0.9981

Chapter 6

Further Inference in Multiple Regression

```
rm(list=ls())
options(digits=3,signif=F)
library(POE5Rdata) #for PoE datasets
library(knitr) # for referenced tables with kable()
library(xtable) # makes data frame for kable
library(car)
library(AER)
library(broom) # for tidy lm output glance()
library(ggplot2)
library(nlWaldTest)
library(lrmest) #for function rls(), restricted leasat squares
```

New package: lrmest (Dissanayake and Wijekoon, 2016), used to estimate a least squares model with coefficient restrictions.

6.1 Joint Hypotheses and the F-statistic

A joint hypothesis is a set of relationships among regression parameters, relationships that need to be simultaneously true according to the null hypothesis. Joint hypotheses can be tested using the F-statistic that we have already met. Its formula is given by Equation (6.1). The F-statistic has an F distribution with the degrees of freedom J and $N - K$.

$$F = \frac{(SSE_R - SSE_U)/J}{SSE_U/(N-K)} \sim F_{(J,\,N-K)} \qquad (6.1)$$

In Equation (6.1) the subscript U stands for "unrestricted," that is, the initial regression equation; the "restricted" equation is a new equation, obtained from the initial one, with the relationships in the null hypothesis assumed to hold. For example, if the initial equation is Equation (6.2) and the null hypothesis is Equation (6.3), then the restricted equation is Equation (6.4).

$$y = \beta_1 + \beta_2 x_2 + \beta_3 x_3 + \beta_4 x_4 + e \qquad (6.2)$$

$$H_0 : \beta_2 = 0 \ \ AND \ \ \beta_3 = 0; \quad H_A : \beta_2 \neq 0 \ \ OR \ \ \beta_3 \neq 0 \qquad (6.3)$$

$$y = \beta_1 + \beta_4 x_4 + e \qquad (6.4)$$

The symbol J in the F formula (Equation (6.1)) is the first (*numerator*) degrees of freedom of the F statistic and is equal to the number of simultaneous restrictions in the null hypothesis (Equation (6.3)); the second (the *denominator*) degrees of freedom of the F-statistic is $N-K$, which is the usual degrees of freedom of the unrestricted regression model (Equation (6.2)). The practical procedure to test a joint hypothesis like the one in Equation (6.3) is to estimate the two regressions (unrestricted and restricted) and to calculate the F-statistic.

6.2   Testing Simultaneous Hypotheses

Let us look, again, at the quadratic form of the *andy* equation (Equation (6.5)).

$$sales = \beta_1 + \beta_2 price + \beta_3 advert + \beta_4 advert^2 + e \qquad (6.5)$$

Equation (6.5) has two terms that involve the regressor *advert*, of which at least one needs to be significant for a relationship between *advert* and *sales* to be established. To test if such a relationship exists, we can formulate the following test:

$$H_0 : \beta_3 = 0 \ \ AND \ \ \beta_4 = 0; \quad H_A : \beta_3 \neq 0 \ \ OR \ \ \beta_4 \neq 0 \qquad (6.6)$$

I have already mentioned that R can do an F test quite easily (remember the function linearHypothesis?), but for learning purposes let us calculate the F-statistic in steps. The next code sequence uses information in the anova-type object, which, remember, can be visualized simply by typing the name of the object in the RStudio's Console window.

```
alpha <- 0.05
data(andy)
N <- NROW(andy) #Number of observations in dataset
K <- 4 # four betas in the unrestricted model
J <- 2 # because Ho has two restrictions
fcr <- qf(1-alpha, J, N-K)
mod1 <- lm(sales~price+advert+I(advert^2), data=andy)
anov <- anova(mod1)
anov # prints 'anova' table for the unrestricted model
```

```
## Analysis of Variance Table
##
## Response: sales
##              Df Sum Sq Mean Sq F value  Pr(>F)
## price         1   1219    1219   56.50 1.3e-10
## advert        1    177     177    8.22  0.0054
## I(advert^2)   1    187     187    8.66  0.0044
## Residuals    71   1532      22
```

```
SSEu <- anov[4, 2]
mod2 <- lm(sales~price, data=andy) # restricted
anov <- anova(mod2)
anov # prints the 'anova' table for the restrictred model
```

```
## Analysis of Variance Table
##
## Response: sales
##             Df Sum Sq Mean Sq F value Pr(>F)
## price        1   1219    1219    46.9  2e-09
## Residuals   73   1896      26
```

```
SSEr <- anov[2,2]
fval <- ((SSEr-SSEu)/J) / (SSEu/(N-K))
pval <- 1-pf(fval, J, N-K)
```

The calculated F-statistic is $fval = 8.441$ and the critical value corresponding to a significance level $\alpha = 0.05$ is 3.126, which rejects the null hypothesis that both β_3 and β_4 are zero. The p-value of the test is $p = 5 \times 10^{-4}$.

Using the `linearHypothesis()` function should produce the same result:

```
Hnull <- c("advert=0", "I(advert^2)=0")
linearHypothesis(mod1,Hnull,signif=F)
```

```
## Linear hypothesis test
##
## Hypothesis:
## advert = 0
## I(advert^2) = 0
##
## Model 1: restricted model
## Model 2: sales ~ price + advert + I(advert^2)
##
##   Res.Df  RSS Df Sum of Sq    F  Pr(>F)
## 1     73 1896
## 2     71 1532  2       364 8.44 0.00051
```

The table generated by the `linearHypothesis()` function shows the same values of the F-statistic and p-value that we have calculated before, as well as the residual sum of squares for the restricted and unrestricted models. Please note how I formulate the joint hypothesis as a vector of character values in which the names of the variables perfectly match those in the unrestricted model.

Testing the overall significance of a model amounts to testing the joint hypothesis that all the slope coefficients are zero. R does automatically this test and the resulting F-statistic and p-value are reported in the regression output.

`summary(mod1)`

```
##
## Call:
## lm(formula = sales ~ price + advert + I(advert^2), data = andy)
##
## Residuals:
##     Min      1Q  Median     3Q     Max
## -12.255  -3.143  -0.012  2.851  11.805
##
## Coefficients:
##               Estimate Std. Error t value Pr(>|t|)
## (Intercept)    109.719      6.799   16.14  < 2e-16
## price           -7.640      1.046   -7.30  3.2e-10
## advert          12.151      3.556    3.42   0.0011
```

Table 6.1: Tidy 'summary(mod1)' output

term	estimate	std.error	statistic	p.value
(Intercept)	109.719	6.799	16.137	0.000
price	-7.640	1.046	-7.304	0.000
advert	12.151	3.556	3.417	0.001
I(advert^2)	-2.768	0.941	-2.943	0.004

Table 6.2: 'Tidy(mod1)' output

term	estimate	std.error	statistic	p.value
(Intercept)	109.719	6.799	16.137	0.000
price	-7.640	1.046	-7.304	0.000
advert	12.151	3.556	3.417	0.001
I(advert^2)	-2.768	0.941	-2.943	0.004

```
## I(advert^2)    -2.768        0.941    -2.94    0.0044
##
## Residual standard error: 4.65 on 71 degrees of freedom
## Multiple R-squared:  0.508,  Adjusted R-squared:  0.487
## F-statistic: 24.5 on 3 and 71 DF,  p-value: 5.6e-11
```

The F-statistic can be retrieved from summary(mod1) or by using the function glance(modelname) in package broom, as shown in the following code lines. The function tidy, also from package broom organizes regression output (mainly the coefficients and their statistics) in a neat table. Both glance and tidy create output in the form of data.frame, which makes it suitable for use by other functions such as kable and ggplot2. Please also note that tidy(mod1) and tidy(summary(mod1)) produce the same result, as shown in Tables 6.1 and 6.2. As always, we can use the function names to obtain a list of the quantities available in the output of the glance function.

```
smod1 <- summary(mod1)
kable(tidy(smod1),digits=3,caption=
        "Tidy 'summary(mod1)' output")

fval <- smod1$fstatistic

library(broom)
kable(tidy(mod1),digits=3,caption="'Tidy(mod1)' output")

glance(mod1)$statistic #Retrieves the F-statistic
```

```
## [1] 24.46
```

Table 6.3: Function 'glance(mod1)' output

Rsq	AdjRsq	sig	F	pF	K	logL	AIC	BIC	dev	df.res
0.51	0.49	4.65	24.46	0	4	-219.6	449.1	460.7	1532	71

Table 6.4: Joint hypotheses with 'linearHypothesis'

res.df	rss	df	sumsq	statistic	p.value
73	1780	NA	NA	NA	NA
71	1532	2	247.8	5.741	0.005

```
names(glance(mod1)) #Shows what is available in 'glance'
```

```
## [1] "r.squared"    "adj.r.squared" "sigma"      "statistic"
## [5] "p.value"      "df"            "logLik"     "AIC"
## [9] "BIC"          "deviance"      "df.residual"
```

```
kable(glance(mod1),
  caption="Function 'glance(mod1)' output", digits=2,
  col.names=(c("Rsq","AdjRsq","sig","F",
  "pF","K","logL","AIC","BIC","dev","df.res")))
```

Table 6.3 shows a summary of the quadratic *andy* model (mod1), where I have changed the names of various items so that the table fits the width of the page. When retrieving these variables, make sure you use the original names as indicated by the names(glance(mod1)) command.

When testing a two-tail single (not joint) null hypothesis, the t and F tests are equivalent. However, one-tail tests, single or joint, cannot be easily performed by an F test.

Let us solve one more exercise involving a joint hypothesis with linear combinations of regression coefficients. Suppose we want to test the simultaneous hypotheses that the monthly advertising expenditure $advert_0 = \$1900$ in the quadratic *andy* model (Equation (6.5)) satisfies the profit-maximizing condition $\beta_3 + 2\beta_4 advert_0 = 1$, and that, when $price = \$6$ and $advert = \$1900$ sales revenue is $\$80\,000$.

```
hyp <- c("advert+3.8*I(advert^2)=1",
"(Intercept)+6*price+1.9*advert+3.61*I(advert^2)=80")
lhout <- tidy(linearHypothesis(mod1,hyp))
kable(lhout,digits=3,caption=
  "Joint hypotheses with 'linearHypothesis' ")
```

Table 6.4 includes the F-statistic of the test, $F = 5.7412$ and its p-value $p = 0.0049$. Please be aware that the function tidy changes the names in the output of linearHypothesis. A useful exercise is to compare the raw output of linearHypothesis with the output generated by tidy(linearHypothesis(mod1)).

There are several other possibilities to compare two regression models, such as a restricted and unrestricted ones in R, such as the anova() function or Wald tests. These are going to be mentioned in later chapters.

6.2.1   Building the t_test function

The function t_test, created in the next code chunk, tests a single one- or two-tail hypothesis about a linear combination of coefficients; as a by-product, it also calculates a confidence interval for the same linear combination. More precisely, let L be a linear combination of regression coefficients,

$$L = \sum_{k=1}^{K} a_k \beta_k,$$

where a_k are real numbers; the types of hypothesis that form the object of the t_test function are the following:

$$H_0 : L \geq c, \;\; H_A : L < c \;\; (\text{"less"})$$

$$H_0 : L = c, \;\; H_A : L \neq c \;\; (\text{"notequal"})$$

$$H_0 : L \leq c, \;\; H_A : L > c \;\; (\text{"greater"})$$

where c is a real number. The t_test function requires the following arguments:

- modelName, the name of the model to be tested; such a model is of any type that is recognized by the R functions coef() and vcov()
- lhs, the vector of coefficients in the left-hand side of the linear combination to be tested. The size of the lhs vector must be equal to the number of the β coefficients in the model
- rhs, the number that appears to the right-hand side of the hypothesis
- altHyp, the nature of the alternative hypothesis; it can be one of "greater", "notequal", or "less"
- level, the desired confidence level for the construction of the interval estimate

The results of the function t_test consist in three numbers, in the following order: the p-value, the lower bound of a confidence interval for the linear combination, and the upper bound.

```
t_test<-function(modelName,lhs,rhs,altHyp,level=0.95){
  V<-vcov(modelName)
  L<-as.numeric(t(lhs) %*% coef(modelName))
  varL<-as.numeric(t(lhs) %*% V %*% lhs)
  tratio<-(L-rhs)/sqrt(varL)
  df<-df.residual(modelName)
  if(altHyp=="greater"){pval<-1-pt(tratio,df)}
  if(altHyp=="notequal"){pval<-2*(1-pt(abs(tratio),df))}
  if(altHyp=="less"){pval<-pt(tratio,df)}
  tcr<-qt(1-(1-level)/2,df)
  lwbL<-L-tcr*sqrt(varL)
  upbL<-L+tcr*sqrt(varL)
  list<-c(pval,lwbL,upbL)
  return(list)
}
```

Let us use the newly-created function, t-test, on Example 6.6, which requires to test the hypothesis:

$$H_0 : \beta_3 + 3.8\beta_4 \leq 1, \quad H_A : \beta_3 + 3.8\beta_4 > 1$$

```
a<-c(0,0,1,3.8)
c<-1
p1<-t_test(mod1,a,c,"greater")
p2<-t_test(mod1,a,c,"notequal")
p3<-t_test(mod1,a,c,"less")
cat(" p-value= ",p1[[1]],"\n",
    "Confidence interval= (",p1[[2]],",",p1[[3]],")")
## p-value= 0.1683
## Confidence interval= ( 0.3286 , 2.937 )
```

The result is a p-value equal to 0.168, which does not reject the null hypothesis that the optimal advertising expenditure is less than \$1000. The other two lines in the above code chunk test the other two possible alternative hypotheses.

Here is another application of the t_test function, this time involving a negative t-ratio:

$$H_0 : \beta_3 + 3.8\beta_4 \leq 3, \quad H_A : \beta_3 + 3.8\beta_4 > 3$$

```
a<-c(0,0,1,3.8)
c<-3
p<-t_test(mod1,a,c,"greater")
cat(" p-value = ",p[1],"\n",
```

```
    "Confidence interval = (",p[2],",",p1[3],")")
## p-value =  0.9799
## Confidence interval = ( 0.3286 , 2.937 )
```

Since the p-value is, in this last example equal to 0.98, we cannot reject the null hypothesis that $L \leq 3$.

Example 6.8

The goal of this example is to show how the F-test and the χ^2 tests yield different p-values in the *andy* quadratic equation.

```
chisqtest<-nlWaldtest(mod1,"(1-b[3])/(2*b[4])=1.9")
pvalchisq<-chisqtest[[4]]
ftest<-linearHypothesis(mod1,c(0,0,1,3.8),1)
pvalf<-ftest[2,6]
cat(" p-value from the F test = ",pvalf,"\n",
    "p-value from the Chi-square test = ",pvalchisq)
```

```
## p-value from the F test =  0.3365
## p-value from the Chi-square test =  0.3744
```

Example 6.9

The R function rls() in the package lrmest performs restricted least square estimation; the restrictions are given as a system of linear equations such as those in the following example with two restrictions and P parameters.

$$r_1 = R_{11}\beta_1 + R_{12}\beta_2 + ... + R_{1P}\beta_P + \delta_1$$

$$r_2 = R_{21}\beta_1 + R_{22}\beta_2 + ... + R_{2P}\beta_P + \delta_2$$

In general, the number of restrictions is J. Thus, r is a vector of J constants, *delta* is also a vector of J constants, and R is a $J \times P$ matrix. Let us apply this function to the *beer* dataset.

```
data(beer)
rls(log(q)~log(pb)+log(pl)+log(pr)+log(i),
        r=0,R=c(0,1,1,1,1),delt=0, data=beer)
```

```
## $`*****Restricted Least Square Estimator*****`
##              Estimate Standard_error t_statistic pvalue
## (Intercept)  -4.7978         3.6114            0      1
## log(pb)      -1.2994         0.1612           NA     NA
## log(pl)       0.1868         0.2765           NA     NA
```

```
## log(pr)        0.1667         0.0749        NA      NA
## log(i)         0.9458         0.4153        NA      NA
##
## $`*****Mean square error value******`
##    MSE
## 13.32
```

The regression coefficients can be interpreted as various demand elasticities.

6.3   Omitted Variable Bias

Consider the general model with two regressors in Equation (6.7), a model that I will call the *true* model.

$$y = \beta_1 + \beta_2 x_2 + \beta_3 x_3 + e \tag{6.7}$$

Suppose we are only interested in estimating β_2, but there is no data available for x_3, or for other reasons x_3 is omitted from the model in Equation (6.7). What is the error in the estimate of β_2 introduced by omitting x_3?

Equation (6.8) shows what is left of the *true* model after omitting x_3.

$$y = \beta_1 + \beta_2 x_2 + u \tag{6.8}$$

Let b_2^* be the estimate of β_2 when x_3 is omitted. Equation (6.9) gives the bias in this simple, two-regressor case. The formula shows that bias depends on the direct relationship between the omitted regressor and the response variable through β_3, as well as the correlation between the omitted and the included regressors. When β_3 and $cov(x_2, x_3)$ are both positive or both negative the bias is positive (the incorrect model overestimates the true β_2), and when they are of opposite signs the bias is negative (β_2 is underestimated)

$$bias(b_2^*) = E(b_2^*) - \beta_2 = \beta_3 \frac{\widehat{cov(x_2, x_3)}}{var(x_2)} \tag{6.9}$$

The example in this section uses the dataset *edu_inc*, and two models: one where the response variable *family income* (*faminc*) in *logs* is explained by the regressors *husband's education* (he) and *wife's education* (we), and another model, where the we regressor is omitted. The purpose is to compare the estimates coming from the two models and see if there is a significant difference between them.

Table 6.5: The Correct Model

term	estimate	std.error	statistic	p.value
(Intercept)	10.2647262	0.1219950	84.140540	0.0000000
he	0.0438546	0.0087226	5.027698	0.0000007
we	0.0390327	0.0115843	3.369445	0.0008219

Table 6.6: The Incorrect Model (*we* omitted)

term	estimate	std.error	statistic	p.value
(Intercept)	10.5385285	0.0920910	114.436010	0
he	0.0613226	0.0070995	8.637531	0

```
data(edu_inc)
mod1 <- lm(log(faminc)~he+we, data=edu_inc)
mod2 <- lm(log(faminc)~he, data=edu_inc)
kable(tidy(mod1), caption="The Correct Model")

kable(tidy(mod2),
  caption="The Incorrect Model ($we$ omitted)")
```

The marginal effect of husband's education is higher in the incorrect model. Let us apply the logic of Equation (6.9) to the *edu_inc* model. The direct effect of the omitted regressor (*we*) on response (*faminc*) is likely to be positive in theory (higher education generates higher income); the correlation between husband's and wife's education is also likely to be positive if we believe that people generally marry persons within their entourage. Thus, we should expect that omitting the regressor *we* should produce an overestimated marginal effect of *he*. Our data happen to confirm this supposition, though there is some chance that they might not.

Understanding the problem of omitted variable can justify the choice of a model. If one is not interested in the effect of variable x_3 on y and can convince that x_3 is uncorrelated with x_2, one can argue against criticism about omitting the important regressor x_3.

The following code calculates the correlation matrix for the *income_edu* dataset with the variable *faminc* in *log*; the results are displayed in Table 6.7

```
attach(edu_inc)# Attaches a data file
log_faminc<-log(faminc)
kable(cor(cbind(log_faminc,he,we,kl6,xtra_x5,xtra_x6)),
    digits=3, caption=
    "Correlation Matrix for the $income-edu$ Data")
```

Table 6.7: Correlation Matrix for the $income - edu$ Data

	log_faminc	he	we	kl6	xtra_x5	xtra_x6
log_faminc	1.000	0.386	0.349	-0.085	0.315	0.364
he	0.386	1.000	0.594	0.105	0.836	0.821
we	0.349	0.594	1.000	0.129	0.518	0.799
kl6	-0.085	0.105	0.129	1.000	0.149	0.160
xtra_x5	0.315	0.836	0.518	0.149	1.000	0.900
xtra_x6	0.364	0.821	0.799	0.160	0.900	1.000

Table 6.8: Correct $faminc$ Model

term	estimate	std.error	statistic	p.value
(Intercept)	10.2378	0.1210	84.619	0.0000
he	0.0448	0.0086	5.191	0.0000
we	0.0421	0.0115	3.662	0.0003
kl6	-0.1733	0.0542	-3.196	0.0015

```
detach(edu_inc)# Detaches a data file
```

6.4　Irrelevant Variables

We have seen the effect of omitting a relevant regressor (the effect is biased estimates and lower variances of the included regressors). But what happens if irrelevant variables are incorrectly included? Not surprisingly, this increases the variances (lowers the precision) of the other estimates in the model. The next example uses the same (edu_inc) data set as above, but includes two artificially generated variables, $xtra\_x5$ and $xtra\_x6$ that are correlated with he and we but, obviously, have no role in determining y. Let us compare two models, of which one includes these irrelevant variables.

```
mod3 <- lm(log(faminc)~he+we+kl6, data=edu_inc)
mod4 <- lm(log(faminc)~he+we+kl6+xtra_x5+xtra_x6,
           data=edu_inc)
kable(tidy(mod3), digits=4,
      caption="Correct $faminc$ Model")

kable(tidy(mod4), digits=4,
  caption="Incorrect $faminc$ with Irrelevant Variables")
```

Table 6.9: Incorrect $faminc$ with Irrelevant Variables

term	estimate	std.error	statistic	p.value
(Intercept)	10.2393	0.1214	84.3659	0.0000
he	0.0460	0.0136	3.3956	0.0007
we	0.0492	0.0247	1.9932	0.0469
kl6	-0.1724	0.0547	-3.1531	0.0017
xtra_x5	0.0054	0.0243	0.2216	0.8247
xtra_x6	-0.0069	0.0215	-0.3229	0.7469

Table 6.10: The $wage$ Equation without $score$

	Estimate	Std. Error	t value	Pr($>$|t|)
(Intercept)	0.8872	0.2929	3.030	0.0025
educ	0.0728	0.0091	8.013	0.0000
exper	0.1268	0.0403	3.150	0.0017
I(exper^2)	-0.0057	0.0017	-3.453	0.0006

A comparison of the two models shown in Tables 6.8 and 6.9 indicates that the inclusion of the two irrelevant variables has increased the marginal effects, standard errors, and the p-values of he and we. Thus, including irrelevant variables may incorrectly diminish the significance of the "true" regressors.

Example 6.13: A Control Variable for Ability

This example uses the dataset $koop\_tobias\_87$. Tables 6.10 and 6.11 display the results of a wage equation, with and without $score$, a variable that measures ability. Comparing the two models shows that omitting $score$ inflates the effect of education on wage.

```
data(koop_tobias_87)
mod5<-lm(log(wage)~educ+exper+I(exper^2),
    data=koop_tobias_87)
mod6<-lm(log(wage)~educ+exper+I(exper^2)+score,
    data=koop_tobias_87)
kable(coefficients(summary(mod5)), digits=4,
    caption="The $wage$ Equation without $score$")

mod6<-lm(log(wage)~educ+exper+I(exper^2)+score,
    data=koop_tobias_87)
kable(coefficients(summary(mod6)), digits=4,
    caption="The $wage$ Equation with $score$")
```

Table 6.11: The *wage* Equation with *score*

	Estimate	Std. Error	t value	Pr(>|t|)
(Intercept)	1.0547	0.2967	3.555	0.0004
educ	0.0592	0.0101	5.881	0.0000
exper	0.1231	0.0401	3.067	0.0022
I(exper^2)	-0.0054	0.0016	-3.262	0.0011
score	0.0604	0.0195	3.089	0.0021

6.5   Model Selection Criteria

The main tools of building a model should be economic theory, sound reasoning based on economic principles, and making sure that the model satisfies the Gauss-Markov assumptions. One should also consider the possibility of omitted variable bias, as well as the exclusion of irrelevant variables that may increase variability in the estimates. After all these aspects have been considered and a model established, there are a few quantities that help comparing different models. These are R^2, adjusted R^2 ($\bar{R}^2$), the Akaike information criterion (AIC), and the Schwarz (or Bayesian information) criterion (SC or BIC).

We have already seen how to calculate the coefficient of determination, R^2 and how it measures the distance between the regression line and the observation points. A major disadvantage of R^2 is that it increases every time a new regressor is included in the model, whether the regressor is relevant or not. The idea of counterbalancing this property of R^2 has lead to a new measure, adjusted R^2, denoted by $\bar{R}^2$, given by Equation (6.10).

$$\bar{R}^2 = 1 - \frac{SSE / (N - K)}{SST / (N - 1)} \tag{6.10}$$

Adjusted R^2, while addressing the problem with R^2, introduces other problems. In general, no single goodness of fit measure is perfect. The Akaike information criterion (AIC) and the Schwarz criterion use the same idea of penalizing the introduction of extra regressors. Their formulas are given in Equations (6.11) and (6.12).

$$AIC = ln\left(\frac{SSE}{N}\right) + \frac{2K}{N} \tag{6.11}$$

$$SC = ln\left(\frac{SSE}{N}\right) + \frac{K\,ln(N)}{N} \tag{6.12}$$

Among several models, the best fit is the one that maximizes R^2 or $\bar{R}^2$. On the contrary, the best model must **minimize** AIC or BIC. Some computer packages, R included, calculate

AIC and BIC differently than Equations (6.11) and (6.12) indicate. However, the ranking of the various models is the same.

The following code sequence needs some explanation. Function as.numeric extracts only the numbers from an object such as glance(mod1), which also contains row and column names. The purpose is to put together a table with information coming from several models. Function rbind gathers several rows in a matrix, which then is made into a data.frame and given the name tab. The part of code [,c(1,2,8,9)] at the end of rbind instructs R to pick all rows, but only columns 1, 2, and 9 from the glance table. Function row.names assigns or changes the row names in a data frame; finally, kable, which we have already encountered several times, prints the table, assigns column names, and gives a caption to the table. While there are many ways to create a table in R, I use kable from package knitr because it allows me to cross-reference tables within this book. kable only works with data frames. The function resettest() in package lmtest performs a Ramsey specification test; the input to this function is a regression object.

```
data(edu_inc)
mod2 <- lm(log(faminc)~he, data=edu_inc)
mod1 <- lm(log(faminc)~he+we, data=edu_inc)
mod3 <- lm(log(faminc)~he+we+kl6, data=edu_inc)
mod4 <- lm(log(faminc)~he+we+kl6+xtra_x5+xtra_x6, data=edu_inc)
r1 <- as.numeric(glance(mod1))
r2 <- as.numeric(glance(mod2))
r3 <- as.numeric(glance(mod3))
r4 <- as.numeric(glance(mod4))
c5<-c(resettest(mod1)$p.value,resettest(mod2)$p.value,
       resettest(mod3)$p.value,resettest(mod4)$p.value)
tab <- data.frame(rbind(r1, r2, r3, r4))[,c(1,2,8,9)]
tab<-cbind(tab,c5)
row.names(tab) <- c("he,we","he","he, we, kl6",
                    "he, we, kl6, xtra_x5, xtra_x6")
kable(tab,
 caption="Model comparison, 'faminc' ", digits=4,align="c",
 col.names=c("Rsq","AdjRsq","AIC","BIC","RESET"))
```

Table 6.12 shows the four model selection criteria for four different models based on the *edu_inc* data set, with the first column showing the variables included in each model. It is noticeable that three of the criteria indicate the third model as the best fit, while one, namely R^2 prefers the model that includes the irrelevant variables $xtra\_x5$ and $xtra\_x6$. The $RESET$ criterion does not seem to be very useful in this case, since it only rejects the simplest of the models, but it does not discriminate among the others.

Table 6.12: Model comparison, 'faminc'

	Rsq	AdjRsq	AIC	BIC	RESET
he,we	0.1712	0.1673	516.7622	532.9987	0.1491
he	0.1490	0.1470	526.0454	538.2228	0.0431
he, we, kl6	0.1907	0.1849	508.5742	528.8698	0.2796
he, we, kl6, xtra_x5, xtra_x6	0.1909	0.1813	512.4492	540.8630	0.2711

A few words about the Ramsey specification test are in order. This method automatically adds higher-order polynomial terms to your model and tests the joint hypothesis that their coefficients are all zero. Thus, the null hypothesis of the test is H_0: "No higher-order polynomial terms are necessary"; if we reject the null hypothesis we need to consider including such terms.

The R function that performs a RESET test is resettest in package lmtest. This function requires the following arguments: formula, the formula of the model to be tested or the name of an already calculated lm object; alternatively, resettest accepts the name of an lm object; power, a set of integers indicating the powers of the polynomial terms to be included; type, which could be one of "fitted", "regressor", or "princomp", indicating whether the additional terms should be powers of the regressors, fitted values, or the first principal component of the regressor matrix; and, finally, data, which specifies the data set to be used if a formula has been provided and not a model object. The following code applies the test to the third *faminc* model, first using only quadratic terms of the fitted values, then using both quadratic and cubic terms.

```
mod3 <- lm(log(faminc)~he+we+kl6, data=edu_inc)
resettest(mod3, power=2, type="fitted")


##
##   RESET test
##
## data:  mod3
## RESET = 1.7, df1 = 1, df2 = 420, p-value = 0.2

resettest(mod3, power=2:3, type="fitted")


##
##   RESET test
##
## data:  mod3
## RESET = 1.3, df1 = 2, df2 = 420, p-value = 0.3
```

The number labeled as RESET in the output is the F-statistic of the test under the null hypothesis, followed by the two types of degrees of freedom of the F distribution and the p-value. In our case, both p-values are greater than 0.05, indicating that the model specification is correct.

As a side note, a quick way of extracting the information criteria from an `lm()` object is illustrated in the following code fragment.

```
library(stats)
smod1 <- summary(mod1)
Rsq <- smod1$r.squared
AdjRsq <- smod1$adj.r.squared
aic <- AIC(mod1)
bic <- BIC(mod1)
c(Rsq, AdjRsq, aic, bic)
```

```
## [1]   0.1712   0.1673 516.7622 532.9987
```

6.6   Prediction in Multivariate Linear Models

This section uses the R function `predict`, which we have already encountered.

```
data(andy)
m6<-lm(sales~price+advert+I(advert^2),data=andy)
x0<-data.frame(price=6,advert=1.9)
predict(m6,newdata=x0, interval="predict")
```

```
##     fit   lwr   upr
## 1 76.97 67.53 86.42
```

Given a set of regressors, how can we build a model that is best suited for prediction?

Example 6.16

We are going to compare a number of models, all using the *house price* data in the $br5$ data set, with the dependent variable in logs, all using only $sqft$ and age as independent variables; the difference among models is their functional form. The criteria of choosing the best model are the same as in a previous example, plus the **root mean square error**.

```
data(br5)
#Make a random sample of 800 observations from br5
set.seed(246789)
nr<-sample(nrow(br5))
br5<-br5[nr,]
```

```r
train<-br5[1:800,] #the "train" set
test<-br5[801:900,] #the remaining 100 observations
m1<-lm(log(price)~age+sqft,data=train)
m2<-lm(log(price)~age+sqft+I(age^2),data=train)
m3<-lm(log(price)~age+sqft+I(sqft^2),data=train)
m4<-lm(log(price)~age*sqft,data=train)
m5<-lm(log(price)~age+sqft+I(age^2)+I(sqft^2),data=train)
m6<-lm(log(price)~age*sqft+I(age^2),data=train)
m7<-lm(log(price)~age*sqft+I(sqft^2),data=train)
m8<-lm(log(price)~age*sqft+I(sqft^2)+I(age^2),data=train)
r1 <- as.numeric(glance(m1))
r2 <- as.numeric(glance(m2))
r3 <- as.numeric(glance(m3))
r4 <- as.numeric(glance(m4))
r5 <- as.numeric(glance(m5))
r6 <- as.numeric(glance(m6))
r7 <- as.numeric(glance(m7))
r8 <- as.numeric(glance(m8))
tab <- data.frame(rbind(r1,r2,r3,r4,r5,r6,r7,r8))[,c(1,2,8,9)]

# Function to calculate RMSE
# Arguments: x = model_name, newx = new_data, yi = true_y
rmsef<-function(x,newx,yi){
    yh <- predict(x,newx)
    rmse<-sqrt(sum((yi-yh)^2)/nrow(newx))
    return(rmse)
  } #End of function

lsm<-paste0("m",1:8)
tab$RMSE<-numeric(8)
for(i in 1:8){
  m<-get(lsm[[i]])
  tab$RMSE[i]<-rmsef(m,test,log(test$price))
}
row.names(tab)<-c(
  "None","age^2","sqft^2","age*sqft",
  "age^2, sqft^2","age^2, age*sqft","sqft^2, age*sqft",
  "sqft^2, age^2, age*sqft")
kable(tab, caption="Model Comparison, $br5$ ",
  digits=4,align="c", col.names=
```

Table 6.13: Model Comparison, $br5$

	Rsq	AdjRsq	AIC	BIC	RMSE
None	0.7096	0.7089	234.5662	253.3046	0.2957
age^2	0.7295	0.7285	179.7970	203.2201	0.2793
sqft^2	0.7104	0.7093	234.4199	257.8430	0.2958
age*sqft	0.7106	0.7095	233.9514	257.3745	0.2947
age^2, sqft^2	0.7297	0.7284	181.1183	209.2259	0.2795
age^2, age*sqft	0.7298	0.7284	181.0855	209.1931	0.2789
sqft^2, age*sqft	0.7116	0.7102	232.9921	261.0998	0.2946
sqft^2, age^2, age*sqft	0.7301	0.7284	182.1485	214.9408	0.2792

```
c("Rsq","AdjRsq","AIC","BIC","RMSE"))
```

Table 6.13 gives the results of our measures of prediction. It shows that most measures seem to prefer model 2 over the others (RMSE, however, slightly favors model 6). One should keep in mind, though, that these numbers only reflect one choice of the "training" and "testing" sub-samples.

6.7 Collinearity

There is collinearity among regressors when two or more regressors move closely with each other or display little variability. A consequence of collinearity is large variance in the estimated parameters, which increases the chances of not finding them significantly different from zero. The estimates are, however, unbiased since (imperfect) collinearity does not technically violate the Gauss-Markov assumptions. Collinearity tends to show insignificant coefficients even when measures of goodness-of-fit such as R^2 or overall significance (the F-statistic) may be quite large.

A test that may be useful in detecting collinearity is to calculate the *variance inflation factor*, VIF, for each regressor. The rule of thumb is that a regressor produces collinearity if its VIF is greater than 10. Equation (6.13) shows the formula for the variance inflation factor, where R_k^2 is the R^2 from regressing the regressor x_k on all the remaining regressors.

$$VIF_k = \frac{1}{1 - R_k^2} \qquad (6.13)$$

Let us consider the example of the data set *rice5*, where *prod* is in tonnes, *area* is in hectares, *labor* is in person-days, and *fert* is in kilograms. For the moment, let us restrict the data

Table 6.14: Unrestricted Model with Data from 1994

term	estimate	std.error	statistic	p.value	VIF
(Intercept)	-1.9473	0.7385	-2.6369	0.0119	N/A
log(area)	0.2106	0.1821	1.1567	0.2543	9.15
log(labor)	0.3776	0.2551	1.4804	0.1466	17.73
log(fert)	0.3433	0.1280	2.6823	0.0106	7.68

to year 1994 only .

```
data("rice5",package="POE5Rdata")
rice5<-rice5[rice5$year==1994,]
mod1 <- lm(log(prod)~log(area)+log(labor)+log(fert),
          data=rice5)
vf1<-vif(mod1)
VIF<-c("N/A",round(as.numeric(vf1),2))
tbl<-cbind(tidy(mod1),VIF)
kable(tbl, caption="Unrestricted Model with Data from 1994",
      digits=4,align="c")

smod1<-summary(mod1)
Rsq<-smod1$r.squared
```

This model has $R^2 = 0.8745$, which is unexpectedly high given that two of the independent variables are not statistically significant. This situation could be a sign of collinearity in the model. Let us impose the constant returns constraint on the model, which amounts to imposing the constraint $\beta_2 + \beta_3 + \beta_4 = 1$. The R function rls(), which we've already met, estimates a restricted model. The data are, still, restricted to 1994.

```
mod1r<-rls(log(prod)~log(area)+log(labor)+log(fert),
      r=1,R=c(0,1,1,1),delt=0,data=rice5)
df<-nrow(rice5)-nrow(
  mod1r$`*****Restricted Least Square Estimator*****`)
estimates<-as.numeric(
  mod1r$`*****Restricted Least Square Estimator*****`[,1])
stderr<-as.numeric(
  mod1r$`*****Restricted Least Square Estimator*****`[,2])
statistic<-estimates/stderr
pvalues<-2*(1-pt(abs(statistic),df))
tab<-data.frame(estimates,stderr,statistic,pvalues)
row.names(tab)=
  c("constant","ln(area)","ln(labor)","ln(fert)")
```

Table 6.15: Restricted Model with Data from 1994

	estimates	stderr	statistic	pvalues
constant	-2.1683	0.7061	-3.0708	0.0038
ln(area)	0.2262	0.1814	1.2470	0.2197
ln(labor)	0.4834	0.2331	2.0738	0.0446
ln(fert)	0.2904	0.1170	2.4821	0.0174

Table 6.16: Unrestricted Model with Full Dataset

term	estimate	std.error	statistic	p.value	VIF
(Intercept)	-1.8694	0.4565	-4.0947	0.0001	N/A
log(area)	0.2108	0.1083	1.9466	0.0549	7.7047
log(labor)	0.3997	0.1306	3.0591	0.0030	10.0512
log(fert)	0.3195	0.0635	5.0303	0.0000	4.455

```
kable(tab,digits=4,
  caption="Restricted Model with Data from 1994")
```

Table 6.15 shows the results of the model with constant-returns restriction.

An alternative solution for dealing with collinearity is increasing the sample size. Let us run again the unrestricted model, but this time using the full data set; the results are shown in Table 6.16.

```
data(rice5) #restores the dataset
mod1 <- lm(log(prod)~log(area)+log(labor)+log(fert),
        data=rice5)
vf1<-vif(mod1)
VIF<-c("N/A",round(as.numeric(vf1),4))
tbl<-cbind(tidy(mod1),VIF)
kable(tbl, caption=
  "Unrestricted Model with Full Dataset", digits=4)

smod1<-summary(mod1)
Rsq<-smod1$r.squared
cat("R squared = ",round(Rsq,4))
```

```
## R squared =  0.8791
```

Table 6.17: Influential Observations in the *house* Dataset

	h	ehatstu	dffits	dfb.sqrt	dfb.age	dfb.age^2
411	0.032	-4.980	-0.904	-0.658	0.106	-0.327
524	0.017	-4.314	-0.560	0.174	0.230	-0.381
150	0.064	1.961	0.511	-0.085	-0.332	0.448

6.7.1   Influential Observations

In a previous chapter, we have met the R set of functions collectively named
`influence.measures()`, which are in the base R, so that no external package is
necessary. Let us follow the same steps as those in Chapter 4 to identify the influential
observations in the br5 data set.

```
data(br5)
mod1<-lm(log(price)~sqft+age+I(age^2),data=br5)
N<-nobs(mod1)
K<-N-df.residual(mod1)
inftab<-data.frame(influence.measures(mod1)$infmat)
inftab$ehatstu <- rstudent(mod1)#studentized residuals
hbar<-K/N
dbcr<-2/sqrt(N) #dfbeta criterion
dfcr<-2*sqrt(K/N)#dffits criterion
inftab<-inftab[which(
  inftab$hat > hbar |  #leverage
  abs(inftab$dfb.sqft)> dbcr |    #dfbeta
  abs(inftab$dfb.age) > dbcr |
  abs(inftab$dfb.I..2)> dbcr |
  abs(inftab$dffit) > dfcr |      #dffits
  abs(inftab$ehatstu) > 2         #ehatsu
  ),c(8,9,5,2,3,4)]
obs<-as.numeric(rownames(inftab))
tab<-inftab[c("411","524","150"),]
names(tab)<-c("h","ehatstu","dffits","dfb.sqrt",
   "dfb.age","dfb.age^2")
kable(tab, digits=3, caption=
"Influential Observations in the $house$ Dataset")
```

A small sample of the influential observations identified (chosen to match those in the
textbook) are shown in Table 6.17.

Table 6.18: NLS Applied to Example 6.19

term	estimate	std.error	statistic	p.value
b	1.161	0.1307	8.887	0

Table 6.19: NLS Applied to the *steel* Dataset

term	estimate	std.error	statistic	p.value
alpha	0.8143748	0.0510500	15.95250	0
beta	-1.3776710	0.0563556	-24.44603	0
delta	0.0572226	0.0043039	13.29555	0

6.8 Nonlinear Least Squares

Consider the following non-linear model and the data set *nls*.

$$y_i = \beta x_{i1} + \beta^2 x_{i2} + e_i$$

Let us apply the function nls (base R) to determine an estimate for the parameter β, using the *nlls* data set. I choose the starting value for the nls algorithm (argument start= in the following code) completely arbitrarily, but this may not always work. You may need to try a more educated guess when a first attempt does not work. Table 6.18 shows the results.

```
data(nlls)
nl1<-nls(y~b*x1+b^2*x2, start=list(b=0.5), data=nlls)
kable(tidy(nl1), caption="NLS Applied to Example 6.19")
```

In Example 6.20, it is required to fit a logistic curve to U.S. steel production data. The regression equation for this model is

$$eaf_i = \frac{\alpha}{e^{-\beta - \delta t}},$$

where eaf_i is electric arc furnace share of U.S. steel production from 1070 to 2015.

```
data("steel",package="POE5Rdata")
g1<-nls(eaf~alpha/(1+exp(-beta-delta*t)),
    start=list(alpha=1,beta=-.5,delta=0.1),data=steel)
kable(tidy(g1), caption="NLS Applied to the $steel$ Dataset")
```

Table 6.19 shows the results from applying the function nls to the *steel* data, while Figure 6.1 shows the observation points and the fitted curve, which, not surprisingly, is not a straight line.

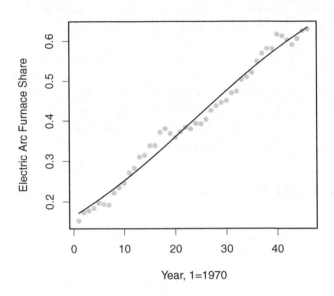

Figure 6.1 NLS Estimate of the *steel* Model

```
par(cex=1.3,lwd=2,pch=16)
plot(steel$t,steel$eaf, col="grey",
    ylab="Electric Arc Furnace Share", xlab="Year, 1=1970")
lines(steel$t,fitted(g1),col="black")
```

Chapter 7

Using Indicator Variables

```
rm(list=ls())
options(digits=3)
library(bookdown)
library(POE5Rdata)#for PoE datasets
library(knitr)   #for referenced tables with kable()
library(effects)
library(car)# for linearHypothesis, among othe things
library(AER)
library(broom) #for tidy lm output and function glance()
library(lmtest)#for coeftest() and other test functions
library(stargazer) #nice and informative tables
```

This chapter introduces the package `lmtest` (Hothorn et al., 2015).

7.1 Factor Variables

Indicator variables show the presence of a certain non-quantifiable attribute, such as whether an individual is male or female, or whether a house has a swimming pool. In R, an indicator variable is called *factor*, *category*, or *ennumerated type* and there is no distinction between binary (such as yes-no, or male-female) or multiple-category factors.

Factors can be either numerical or character variables, ordered or not. R automatically creates dummy variables for each category within a factor variable and excludes a (baseline) category from a model. The choice of the baseline category, as well as which categories should be included can be changed using the function `contrasts()`.

Table 7.1: Summary for the *utown* Data Set

price	sqft	age	utown	pool	fplace
Min. :134	Min. :20.0	Min. : 0.00	0:481	0:796	0:482
1st Qu.:216	1st Qu.:22.8	1st Qu.: 3.00	1:519	1:204	1:518
Median :246	Median :25.4	Median : 6.00	NA	NA	NA
Mean :248	Mean :25.2	Mean : 9.39	NA	NA	NA
3rd Qu.:278	3rd Qu.:27.8	3rd Qu.:13.00	NA	NA	NA
Max. :345	Max. :30.0	Max. :60.00	NA	NA	NA

Table 7.2: The *house* Model

term	estimate	std.error	statistic	p.value
(Intercept)	24.5000	6.1917	3.957	0.0001
utown1	27.4530	8.4226	3.259	0.0012
sqft	7.6122	0.2452	31.048	0.0000
age	-0.1901	0.0512	-3.712	0.0002
pool1	4.3772	1.1967	3.658	0.0003
fplace1	1.6492	0.9720	1.697	0.0901
utown1:sqft	1.2994	0.3320	3.913	0.0001

The following code fragment loads the `utown` data, declares the indicator variables `utown`, `pool`, and `fplace` as factors, and displays a summary statistics table (Table 7.1). The factor variables are represented in the summary table as count data, i.e., how many observations are in each category.

```
library(stargazer); library(ggplot2)
data("utown", package="POE5Rdata")
utown$utown <- as.factor(utown$utown)
utown$pool <- as.factor(utown$pool)
utown$fplace <- as.factor(utown$fplace)
kable(summary.data.frame(utown),
        caption="Summary for  the $utown$ Data Set")
```

Example 7.1 House Prices

This example uses the `utown` data set, where prices are in thousands, `sqft` is the living area in hundreds of square feet, and `utown` marks houses located near university.

```
mod4<-lm(price~utown*sqft+age+pool+fplace, data=utown)
kable(tidy(mod4), caption="The $house$ Model")
```

```
bsqft<-1000*coef(mod4)[["sqft"]]
bsqft1<-1000*(coef(mod4)[["sqft"]]+coef(mod4)[["utown1:sqft"]])
```

Notice how the model in the above code lines has been specified: the term `utown*sqft` created three terms: `utown`, `sqft`, and the interaction term `utown:sqft`. Table 7.2 shows the estimated coefficients and their statistics; please notice how the factor variables have been market at the end of their names with 1 to show which category they represent. For instance, `utown1` is the equivalent of a dummy variable equal to 1 when `utown` is equal to 1. When a factor has n categories the regression output will show $n - 1$ dummies marked to identify each category.

According to the results in Table 7.2, an extra hundred square feet increases the price by `bsqft`=$7612.18 if the house is not near university and by `bsqft1` = $8911.58 if the house is near university. This example shows how interaction terms allow distinguishing the marginal effect of a continuous variable (`sqft`) for one category (`utown=1`) from the marginal effect of the same continuous variable within another category (`utown=0`).

In general, the marginal effect of a regressor on the response is, as we have seen before, the partial derivative of the response with respect to that regressor. For example, the marginal effect of `sqft` in the *house prices* model is as shown in Equation (7.1).

$$\frac{\partial \widehat{price}}{\partial sqft} = b[sqft] + utown \times b[utown : sqft] \tag{7.1}$$

Example 7.2 Indicator Interaction

Let us look at another example, the *wage* equation using the data set *cps5_small*.

```
data("cps5_small", package="POE5Rdata")
names(cps5_small)
```

```
## [1] "black"   "educ"    "exper"   "faminc"  "female"  "metro"   "midwest"
## [8] "south"   "wage"    "west"
```

This data set already includes dummy variables for gender, race, and region, so that we do not need R's capability of building these dummies for us. Although usually it is useful to declare the categorical variables as factors, I will not do so this time. Let us consider the model in Equation (7.2).

$$wage = \beta_1 + \beta_2 educ + \delta_1 black + \delta_2 female + \gamma(black \times female) + e \tag{7.2}$$

Table 7.3: A Wage-Discrimination Model

term	estimate	std.error	statistic	p.value
(Intercept)	-9.4821	1.9580	-4.8428	0.0000
educ	2.4737	0.1351	18.3096	0.0000
black	-2.0653	2.1616	-0.9554	0.3396
female	-4.2235	0.8249	-5.1198	0.0000
black:female	0.5329	2.8020	0.1902	0.8492

```
mod5 <- lm(wage~educ+black*female, data=cps5_small)
delta1 <- coef(mod5)[["black"]]
delta2 <- coef(mod5)[["female"]]
gamma <- coef(mod5)[["black:female"]]
blfm <- delta1+delta2+gamma
kable(tidy(mod5), caption="A Wage-Discrimination Model")
```

What are the expected wages for different categories, according to Equation (7.2) and Table 7.3?

- white male: $\beta_1 + \beta_2 educ$ (the baseline category)
- black male: $\beta_1 + \beta_2 educ + \delta_1$
- white female: $\beta_1 + \beta_2 educ + \delta_2$
- black female: $\beta_1 + \beta_2 educ + \delta_1 + \delta_2 + \gamma$

These formulas help evaluating the differences in wage expectations between different categories. For instance, given the same education, the difference between black female and white male is $\delta_1 + \delta_2 + \gamma = -5.76$, which means that the average black female is paid less by \$5.76 than the average white male.

To test the hypothesis that neither race nor gender affects wage is to test the joint hypothesis $H_0 : \delta_1 = 0, \quad \delta_2 = 0, \quad \gamma = 0$ against the alternative that at least one of these coefficients is different from zero. We have learned already how to perform an F-test the hard way and how to retrieve the quantities needed for the F-statistic (SSE_R, SSE_U, J, and $N - K$). Let us this time use R's linearHypothesis function.

```
hyp <- c("black=0", "female=0", "black:female=0")
tab <- tidy(linearHypothesis(mod5, hyp))
kable(tab,
caption="Testing a Joint Hypothesis for the $wage$ Equation")
```

The results in Table 7.4 indicate that the null hypothesis of no discrimination can be rejected.

Table 7.4: Testing a Joint Hypothesis for the *wage* Equation

res.df	rss	df	sumsq	statistic	p.value
1198	220062	NA	NA	NA	NA
1195	214401	3	5661	10.52	0

Table 7.5: A Wage-Discrimination Model

term	estimate	std.error	statistic	p.value
(Intercept)	-8.3708	2.1540	-3.8862	0.0001
educ	2.4670	0.1351	18.2603	0.0000
black	-1.8777	2.1799	-0.8614	0.3892
female	-4.1861	0.8246	-5.0768	0.0000
south	-1.6523	1.1557	-1.4297	0.1531
midwest	-1.9392	1.2083	-1.6049	0.1088
west	-0.1452	1.2027	-0.1207	0.9039
black:female	0.6190	2.8008	0.2210	0.8251

Example 7.3 A *Wage* Equation with Regional Indicators

Equation (7.3) show the same *wage* model as before, but with three region indicator variables.

$$wage = \beta_1 + \beta_2 educ + \delta_1 black + \delta_2 female + \gamma(black \times female) +$$

$$\delta_3 south + \delta_4 midwest + \delta_5 west + e \tag{7.3}$$

Table 7.5 displays the results, which suggest that none of the regional indicators is significant at the 10 percent level.

```
mod5a <- lm(wage~educ+black*female+south+midwest+west,
            data=cps5_small)
kable(tidy(mod5a),digits=4,
      caption="A Wage-Discrimination Model")
```

Let us use, again, the `linearHypothesis` function in package `lmtest` to test the hypothesis that all three regional coefficients are zero,

$$H_0 : \delta_3 = 0, \ \delta_4 = 0, \ \delta_5 = 0, \ H_A : \text{At least one is} \neq 0$$

```
hyp73<-c("south=0","midwest=0","west=0")
lh73<-linearHypothesis(mod5a,hyp73)
lh73$F[2]
```

```
## [1] 1.579
```

The F-statistic of this test is stored in the lh73 object, under the name lh73$F[2], and is equal to 1.5792; the p-value can be retrieved under the name of lh73$"Pr(>F)", and is equal to 0.1926, which fails to reject the null hypothesis that all three regional coefficients are zero. How would you know what information is stored after running a certain function such as linearHypothesis? You may remember that we have used the function str(), which shows the "structure," or the content of a certain object. We have also used the function names() for the same purpose.

7.2   Comparing Two Regressions: the Chow Test

By interacting a binary indicator variable with all the terms in a regression and testing that the new terms are insignificant we can determine if a certain category is significantly different than the other categories. Starting with the *wage* regression in Equation (7.2), let us include the indicator variable "south". To see how this works, let us separate the *south* data from the rest and run the same regression on each data set (dsouth stands for "data south" and dnosouth stands for "data no-south."); then, we try to get the same result, but, instead of manually separating the data, we interact the dummy with all the regressors.

```
dnosouth <- cps5_small[which(cps5_small$south==0),]#no south
dsouth <- cps5_small[which(cps5_small$south==1),] #south
mod5ns <- lm(wage~educ+black*female, data=dnosouth)
mod5s <- lm(wage~educ+black*female, data=dsouth)
mod6 <- lm(wage~educ+black*female+south/(educ+black*female),
                  data=cps5_small)
stargazer(mod6, mod5ns, mod5s, header=FALSE,
  type=.stargazertype,
  title="Model Comparison for the $wage$ Equation",
  keep.stat="n",digits=2, single.row=TRUE,
  intercept.bottom=FALSE)
```

The table titled "Model Comparison for the $Wage$ Equation" presents the results of three equations: equation (1) is the full *wage* model with all terms interacted with variable *south*; equation (2) is the basic 'wage' model shown in Equation (7.2) with the sample restricted to non-south regions, and, finally, equation (3) is the same as (2) but with the sample

Table 7.6: Model Comparison for the *wage* Equation

	Dependent variable:		
	wage		
	(1)	(2)	(3)
Constant	−10.00*** (2.39)	−10.00*** (2.23)	−8.42** (3.87)
educ	2.53*** (0.16)	2.53*** (0.15)	2.36*** (0.27)
black	1.13 (3.52)	1.13 (3.29)	−3.49 (3.17)
female	−4.15*** (0.98)	−4.15*** (0.92)	−4.34** (1.71)
south	1.58 (4.18)		
black:female	−4.45 (4.49)	−4.45 (4.19)	3.67 (4.18)
educ:south	−0.17 (0.29)		
black:south	−4.62 (4.51)		
female:south	−0.19 (1.81)		
black:female:south	8.12 (5.82)		
Observations	1,200	810	390

Note: $^{*}p<0.1$; $^{**}p<0.05$; $^{***}p<0.01$

Table 7.7: Chow Test for the *wage* Equation

Res.Df	RSS	Df	Sum of Sq	F	Pr(>F)
1195	214401	NA	NA	NA	NA
1190	213774	5	626.9	0.698	0.625

restricted only to the south region. (This table is constructed with the function `stargazer` from the package by the same name (Hlavac, 2015).)

In R, however, it is not necessary to split the data manually as I did in the above code sequence; instead, we can just write two equations like mod5 and mod6 and ask R to do a Chow test to see if the two equations are statistically identical. The Chow test is performed in R by the function anova, with the results presented in Table 7.7, where the F statistic is equal to 0.698 and the corresponding p-value of 0.625.

```
kable(anova(mod5, mod6),
    caption="Chow Test for the $wage$ Equation")
```

Table 7.7 indicates that the null hypothesis that the equations are equivalent cannot be rejected. In other words, our test provides no evidence that wages in the south region are statistically different from the rest of the regions.

7.3 Indicator Variables in Log-Linear Models

An indicator regressor is essentially no different from a continuous one and its interpretation is very similar to the one we have studied in the context of log-linear models. In a model like $log(y) = \beta_1 + \beta_2 x + \delta D$, where D is an indicator variable, the percentage difference between the two categories represented by D can be calculated in two ways, both using the coefficient δ:

- approximate: $\%\Delta y \cong 100\delta$
- exact: $\%\Delta y = 100(e^\delta - 1)$

Let us calculate these two effects in a log-linear wage equation based on the data set *cps4_small*.

```
data("cps5_small", package="POE5Rdata")
mod1 <- lm(log(wage)~educ+female, data=cps5_small)
approx <- 100*coef(mod1)[["female"]]
exact <- 100*(exp(coef(mod1)[["female"]])-1)
```

The results indicate a percentage difference in expected wage between females and males as follows: $\%\Delta wage = -17.78\%$ (approximate), or $\%\Delta wage = -16.29\%$ (exact).

7.4 The Linear Probability Model

Linear probability models are regression models in which the response, rather than a regressor, is a binary indicator variable. However, since the regressors can be either continuous or factor variables, the fitted values will be continuous. Equation (7.4), where $y \in \{0, 1\}$ shows a general linear probability model.

$$y = \beta_1 + \beta_2 x_2 + ... + \beta_k x_k + e \qquad (7.4)$$

How can a continuous fitted variable be interpreted when the actual response is binary? As it turns out, the fitted value represents the *probability* that the response takes the value 1, $\hat{y} = Pr(y = 1)$. There are two major problems with this model. First, the model is heteroskedastic, with the variance being larger in the middle range of the fitted values; second, the fitted variable being continuous, it can take values, unlike a probability function, outside the interval $[0, 1]$.

The next example, based on the data set *coke*, estimates the probability that a customer chooses *coke* when *coke* or *pepsi* are displayed. Besides the two indicator variables *disp_coke* and *disp_pepsi*, the model includes the price ratio between *coke* and *pepsi*.

Table 7.8: Linear Probability Model, the *coke* Example

term	estimate	std.error	statistic	p.value
(Intercept)	0.8902	0.0655	13.594	0.000
pratio	-0.4009	0.0613	-6.534	0.000
disp_coke	0.0772	0.0344	2.244	0.025
disp_pepsi	-0.1657	0.0356	-4.654	0.000

```
# Linear probability example
data("coke", package="POE5Rdata")
mod2 <- lm(coke~pratio+disp_coke+disp_pepsi, data=coke)
kable(tidy(mod2),
 caption="Linear Probability Model, the $coke$ Example")

# Graph for the linear probability model
b00 <- coef(mod2)[[1]]
b10 <- b00+coef(mod2)[["disp_coke"]]
b11 <- b10+coef(mod2)[["disp_pepsi"]]
b01 <-b11-coef(mod2)[["disp_coke"]]
b2 <- coef(mod2)[["pratio"]]
par(cex=1.2,lwd=2.5,pch=16)
plot(coke$pratio, coke$coke, col="darkgrey",ylab=
   "Probability of Choosing Coke", xlab="Price Ratio")
abline(b00, b2, lty=2, col=2)
abline(b10,b2, lty=6, col=6)
abline(b11,b2, lty=4, col=4)
abline(b01,b2, lty=5, col=5)
legend("topright", c("00","10","11","01"),bg="white",
      lty=c(2,6,4,5), col=c(2,6,4,5))
```

Figure 7.1 plots the probability of choosing *coke* with respect to the price ratio for the four possible combinations of the indicator variables *disp_coke* and *disp_pepsi*. In addition, the graph shows the observation points, all located at a height of either 0 or 1. In the legend, the first digit is 0 if *coke* is not displayed and 1 otherwise; the second digit does the same for *pepsi*. Thus, the highest probability of choosing *coke* for any given *pratio* happens when *coke* is displayed and *pepsi* is not (the line marked 10).

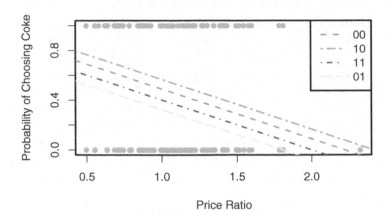

Figure 7.1 Linear probability: the *coke* Example

7.5   Treatment Effects

Treatment effects models aim at measuring the differences between a *treatment* group and a *control* group. The **difference estimator** is the simplest such a model and consists in constructing an indicator variable to distinguish between the two groups. Consider Equation (7.5), where $d_i = 1$ if observation i belongs to the treatment group and $d_i = 0$ otherwise.

$$y_i = \beta_1 + \beta_2 d_i + e_i \qquad (7.5)$$

Thus, the expected value of the response is β_1 for the control group and $\beta_1 + \beta_2$ for the treatment group. Put otherwise, the coefficient on the dummy variable represents the difference between the treatment and the control group. Moreover, it turns out that b_2, the estimator of β_2, is equal to the difference between the sample averages of the two groups:

$$b_2 = \bar{y}_1 - \bar{y}_0 \qquad (7.6)$$

The data set *star* contains information on students from kindergarten to the third grade and was built to identify the determinants of student performance. Let us use this data set for an example of a difference estimator, as well as an example of selecting just part of the variables and observations in a data set.

The next piece of code presents a few new elements, which are used to select only a set of all the variables in the data set, then to split the data set in two parts: one for small classes, and one for regular classes. Lets look at these elements in the order in which they appear in the code. The function `attach(dataset_name)` allows subsequent use of variable names without specifying from which database they come. While in general doing this is not advisable, I used it to simplify the next lines of code, which lists the variables I want to extract and assigns them to variable `vars`. As soon as I am done with splitting my data set, I `detach()` the data set to avoid subsequent confusion.

The line `starregular` is the one that actually retrieves the wanted variables and observations from the data set. In essence, it picks from the data set `star` the observations (rows) for which `small==0` (see, no need for `star$small` as long as `star` is still attached). The same about the variable `starsmall`. Another novelty in the following code fragment is the use of the R function `stargazer()` to visualize a summary table instead of the usual function `summary`; `stargazer` shows a more familiar version of the summary statistics table.

```
# An application of the simple difference estimator
# Cases of regular class sizes with aid removed
data("star", package="POE5Rdata")
star<-star[(star$small==1 | star$regular==1),] #restrict
attach(star)
vars <- c("totalscore","small","tchexper","boy",
          "freelunch","white_asian","tchwhite",
          "tchmasters", "schurban","schrural")
starregular <- star[which(regular==1),vars]
starsmall <- star[which(small==1),vars]
detach(star)
stargazer(starregular, type=.stargazertype, header=FALSE,
title="Data Set $star$ for Regular Classes")

stargazer(starsmall, type=.stargazertype, header=FALSE,
title="Dataset $star$ for Small Classes")
```

The two tables titled "Data set *star*..." display summary statistics for a number of variables in data set *star*. The difference in the means of `totalscore` is equal to 13.899, which should also be equal to β_2 in Equation (7.7).

$$totalscore = \beta_1 + \beta_2\,small + e \qquad (7.7)$$

```
mod3 <- lm(totalscore~small, data=star)
b2 <- coef(mod3)[["small"]]
```

Table 7.9: Data Set *star* for Regular Classes

Statistic	N	Mean	St. Dev.	Min	Max
totalscore	2,005	918.000	73.140	635	1,229
small	2,005	0.000	0.000	0	0
tchexper	2,005	9.068	5.724	0	24
boy	2,005	0.513	0.500	0	1
freelunch	2,005	0.474	0.499	0	1
white_asian	2,005	0.681	0.466	0	1
tchwhite	2,005	0.798	0.402	0	1
tchmasters	2,005	0.365	0.482	0	1
schurban	2,005	0.301	0.459	0	1
schrural	2,005	0.500	0.500	0	1

Table 7.10: Dataset *star* for Small Classes

Statistic	N	Mean	St. Dev.	Min	Max
totalscore	1,738	931.900	76.360	747	1,253
small	1,738	1.000	0.000	1	1
tchexper	1,738	8.995	5.732	0	27
boy	1,738	0.515	0.500	0	1
freelunch	1,738	0.472	0.499	0	1
white_asian	1,738	0.685	0.465	0	1
tchwhite	1,738	0.862	0.344	0	1
tchmasters	1,738	0.318	0.466	0	1
schurban	1,738	0.306	0.461	0	1
schrural	1,738	0.463	0.499	0	1

Table 7.11: Class Sizes in the *star* Data Set

term	estimate	std.error	statistic	p.value
(Intercept)	918.0	1.667	550.664	0
small	13.9	2.447	5.681	0

```
kable(tidy(mod3),caption=
    "Class Sizes in the $star$ Data Set")
```

The difference estimated based on Equation (7.7) is $b_2 = 13.899$, which coincides with the difference in means we calculated above.

If the students were randomly assigned to small or regular classes and the number of observations is large, there would be no need for additional regressors (there is no omitted variable bias if other regressors are not correlated with the variable small). In some instances, however, including other regressors may improve the difference estimator. Here is a model that includes a 'teacher experience' variable and some school characteristics that sometimes are called 'fixed effects' (the students were randomized within schools, but schools were not randomized).

```
school <- as.factor(star$schid)#dummies for schools
mod4 <- lm(totalscore~small+tchexper, data=star)
mod5 <- lm(totalscore~small+tchexper+school,data=star)
b2n <- coef(mod4)[["small"]]
b2s <- coef(mod5)[["small"]]
tidy(anova(mod4, mod5))
```

```
##    res.df      rss df   sumsq statistic    p.value
## 1    3740 20683680 NA      NA       NA         NA
## 2    3662 15957534 78 4726146      13.9 6.651e-152
```

By the introduction of school *fixed effects*, the difference estimate has increased from 13.9833 to 16.0656. The anova() function, which tests the equivalence of the two regressions, yields a very low p-value, indicating that the difference between the two models is significant.

I have mentioned already, in the context of collinearity, that a way to check if there is a relationship between an independent variable and the others is to regress that variable on the others and check the overall significance of the regression. The same method allows checking if the assignments to the treated and control groups are random. If we regress small on the other regressors and the assignment was random we should find no significant relationship.

Table 7.12: Checking Random Assignment in the *star* Data Set

term	estimate	std.error	statistic	p.value
(Intercept)	0.4664623	0.0251564	18.5424954	0.0000000
boy	0.0014108	0.0163385	0.0863456	0.9311963
white_asian	0.0044057	0.0195970	0.2248133	0.8221368
tchexper	-0.0006025	0.0014389	-0.4187685	0.6754094
freelunch	-0.0008859	0.0181931	-0.0486930	0.9611666

```
mod6<-lm(small~boy+white_asian+tchexper+freelunch, data=star)
kable(tidy(mod6), caption=
    "Checking Random Assignment in the $star$ Data Set")

fstat <- glance(mod6)$statistic
pf <- glance(mod6)$p.value
```

The F-statistic of the model in Table 7.12 is $F = 0.059$ and its corresponding p-value 0.994, which shows that the model is overall insignificant at the 5% level or lower. The coefficients of the independent variables are insignificant or extremely small (the coefficient on *tchexper* is statistically significant, but its marginal effect is a change in the probability that $small = 1$ of about 0.3 percent). Again, these results provide fair evidence that the students' assignment to small or regular classes was random.

7.6 The Difference-in-Differences Estimator

In many economic problems, which do not benefit from the luxury of random samples, the selection into one of the two groups is by choice, thus introducing a selection bias. When this is the case, the difference estimator is biased and, therefore, inadequate. The more complex **difference-in-differences** estimator is more appropriate in such cases. While the simple *difference* estimator assumes that before the treatment all units are identical or, at least, that the assignment to the treatment and control group is random, the *difference-in-differences* estimator takes into account any initial heterogeneity between the two groups.

The two 'differences' in the *diference-in-differences* estimator are: (i) the difference in the means of the *treatment* and *control* groups in the response variable **after** the treatment, and (ii) the difference in the means of the *treatment* and *control* groups in the response variable **before** the treatment. The 'difference' is between *after* and *before*.

Let us denote four averages of the response, as follows:

- $\bar{y}_{T,A}$ Treatment, After
- $\bar{y}_{C,A}$ Control, After
- $\bar{y}_{T,B}$ Treatment, Before
- $\bar{y}_{C,B}$ Control, Before

The *difference-in-differences* estimator, $\hat{\delta}$, is defined as in Equation (7.8).

$$\hat{\delta} = (\bar{y}_{T,A} - \bar{y}_{C,A}) - (\bar{y}_{T,B} - \bar{y}_{C,B}) \tag{7.8}$$

Instead of manually calculating the four means and their difference-in-differences, it is possible to estimate the *difference-in-differences* estimator and its statistical properties by running a regression that includes indicator variables for *treatment* and *after* and their interaction term. The advantage of a regression over simply using Equation (7.8) is that the regression allows taking into account other factors that might influence the treatment effect. The simplest *difference-in-differences* regression model is presented in Equation (7.9), where y_{it} is the response for unit i in period t. In the typical *difference-in-differences* model there are only two periods, *before* and *after*.

$$y_{it} = \beta_1 + \beta_2 T + \beta_3 A + \delta T \times A + e_{it} \tag{7.9}$$

With a little algebra, it can be seen that the coefficient δ on the interaction term in Equation (7.9) is exactly the *difference-in-differences* estimator defined in Equation (7.8). The following example calculates this estimator for the data set $njmin3$, where the response is *fte*, the full-time equivalent employment, d is the *after* dummy, with $d = 1$ for the *after* period and $d = 0$ for the *before* period, and nj is the dummy that marks the treatment group ($nj_i = 1$ if unit i is in New Jersey, where the minimum wage law has been changed, and $nj_i = 0$ if unit i in Pennsylvania, where the minimum wage law has not changed). In other words, units (fast-food restaurants) located in New Jersey form the treatment group, and units located in Pennsylvania form the control group.

```
data("njmin3", package="POE5Rdata")
mod1 <- lm(fte~nj*d, data=njmin3)
mod2 <- lm(fte~nj*d+
              kfc+roys+wendys+co_owned, data=njmin3)
mod3 <- lm(fte~nj*d+
              kfc+roys+wendys+co_owned+
              southj+centralj+pa1, data=njmin3)
stargazer(mod1,mod2,mod3,
          type=.stargazertype,
          title="Difference in Differences Example",
```

```
header=FALSE, keep.stat="n",digits=2,
single.row=TRUE, intercept.bottom=FALSE)
```

Table 7.13: Difference in Differences Example

	(1)	(2)	(3)
		Dependent variable:	
		fte	
Constant	23.33*** (1.07)	25.95*** (1.04)	25.32*** (1.21)
nj	−2.89** (1.19)	−2.38** (1.08)	−0.91 (1.27)
d	−2.17 (1.52)	−2.22 (1.37)	−2.21 (1.35)
kfc		−10.45*** (0.85)	−10.06*** (0.84)
roys		−1.62* (0.86)	−1.69** (0.86)
wendys		−1.06 (0.93)	−1.06 (0.92)
co_owned		−1.17 (0.72)	−0.72 (0.72)
southj			−3.70*** (0.78)
centralj			0.01 (0.90)
pa1			0.92 (1.38)
nj:d	2.75 (1.69)	2.85* (1.52)	2.81* (1.50)
Observations	794	794	794

Note: *p<0.1; **p<0.05; ***p<0.01

```
# t-ratio for delta, the D-in-D estimator:
tdelta <- summary(mod1)$coefficients[4,3]
```

The coefficient on the term $nj : d$ in the table titled "Difference-in-Differences Example" is δ, our difference-in-differences estimator. If we want to test the null hypothesis $H_0 : \delta \geq 0$, the rejection region is at the left tail; since the calculated t, which is equal to 1.6309 is positive, we cannot reject the null hypothesis. In other words, there is no evidence that an increased minimum wage reduces employment at fast-food restaurants.

Figure 7.2 displays the change of fte from the period before ($d = 0$) to the period after the change in minimum wage ($d = 1$) for both the treatment and the control groups. The line labeled "counterfactual" shows how the treatment group would have changed in the absence of the treatment, assuming its change would mirror the change in the control group. The graph is plotted using Equation (7.9).

```
b1 <- coef(mod1)[[1]]
b2 <- coef(mod1)[["nj"]]
```

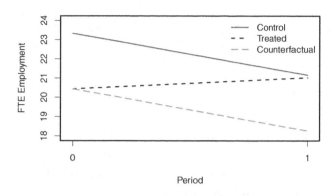

Figure 7.2 Difference-in-Differences for $njmin3$

```
b3 <- coef(mod1)[["d"]]
delta <- coef(mod1)[["nj:d"]]
C <- b1+b2+b3+delta
E <- b1+b3
B <- b1+b2
A <- b1
D <- E+(B-A)
# This creates an empty plot:
par(cex=1.1,lwd=2)
plot(1, type="n", xlab="Period",
     ylab="FTE Employment",xaxt="n",
     xlim=c(-0.01, 1.01), ylim=c(18, 24))
segments(x0=0,y0=A,x1=1,y1=E,lty=1,col="blue")#control
segments(x0=0,y0=B,x1=1,y1=C,lty=2,col="black")#treated
segments(x0=0, y0=B, x1=1, y1=D,          #counterfactual
         lty=5, col="red")
legend("topright", legend=c("Control", "Treated",
    "Counterfactual"), lty=c(1,2,5), bty="n",
    col=c("blue","black","red"))
axis(side=1, at=c(0,1), labels=NULL)
```

Table 7.14: Difference in Differences with Panel Data

term	estimate	std.error	statistic	p.value
(Intercept)	-2.283	0.7313	-3.123	0.0019
nj	2.750	0.8152	3.373	0.0008

7.7 Using Panel Data

The *difference-in-differences* method does not require that the same units be observed both periods, since it works with averages–before and after. If we observe a number of units within the same time period, we construct a *cross-section*; if we construct different cross-sections in different periods we obtain a data structure named *repeated cross-sections*. Sometimes, however, we have information about *the same* units over several periods. A data structure in which the same (cross-sectional) units are observed over two or more periods is called a **panel data** and contains more information than a repeated cross-section. Let us re-consider the simplest $njmin3$ equation (Equation (7.10)), with the unit and time subscripts reflecting the panel data structure of the data set. The time-invariant term c_i has been added to reflect unobserved, individual-specific attributes.

$$fte_{it} = \beta_1 + \beta_2 nj_i + \beta_3 d_t + \delta(nj_i \times d_t) + c_i + e_{it} \tag{7.10}$$

In the data set $njmin3$, some restaurants, belonging to either group have been observed in both periods. If we restrict the data set to only those restaurants we obtain a short (two period) panel data. Let us re-calculate the difference-in-differences estimator using this panel data. To do so, we notice that, if we write Equation (7.10) twice, once for each period and subtract the *before* from the *after* equation we obtain Equation (7.11), where the response, $dfte$, is the after-minus-before difference in employment and the only regressor that remains is the *treatment* dummy, nj, whose coefficient is δ, the very *difference-in-differences* estimator we are trying to estimate.

$$dfte_i = \alpha + \delta nj_i + u_i \tag{7.11}$$

```
mod3 <- lm(demp~nj, data=njmin3)
kable(tidy(summary(mod3)),
   caption="Difference in Differences with Panel Data")

(smod3 <- summary(mod3))

##
## Call:
```

```
## lm(formula = demp ~ nj, data = njmin3)
##
## Residuals:
##    Min      1Q Median      3Q     Max
## -39.22   -3.97    0.53    4.53   33.53
##
## Coefficients:
##                 Estimate Std. Error t value Pr(>|t|)
## (Intercept)       -2.283      0.731   -3.12  0.00186 **
## nj                 2.750      0.815    3.37  0.00078 ***
## ---
## Signif. codes:  0 '***' 0.001 '**' 0.01 '*' 0.05 '.' 0.1 ' ' 1
##
## Residual standard error: 8.96 on 766 degrees of freedom
##   (52 observations deleted due to missingness)
## Multiple R-squared:  0.0146, Adjusted R-squared:  0.0134
## F-statistic: 11.4 on 1 and 766 DF,  p-value: 0.00078
```

$$R^2 = 0.0146, \quad F = 11.3802, \quad p = 7.796 \times 10^{-4}$$

Table 7.14 shows a value of the estimated *difference-in-differences* coefficient very close to the one we estimated before. Its t-statistic is still positive, indicating that the null hypothesis H_0 : "An increase in minimum wage increases employment" cannot be rejected.

7.8   R Practicum

7.8.1   Extracting Various Information

Here is a reminder on how to extract various results after fitting a linear model. The function names(lm.object) returns a list of the names of different items contained in the object. Suppose we run an lm() model and name it mod5. Then, mod5$name returns the item identified by the name. Like about everything in R, there are many ways to extract values from an lm() object. I will present three objects that contain about everything we will need. These are the lm() object itself, summary(lm()), and the function glance(lm()) in package broom. The next code shows the name lists for all three objects and a few examples of extracting various statistics.

```
library(broom)
mod5 <- lm(wage~educ+black*female, data=cps5_small)
smod5 <- summary(mod5)
```

```
gmod5 <- glance(mod5) #from package 'broom'
names(mod5)
```

```
## [1] "coefficients"  "residuals"     "effects"       "rank"
## [5] "fitted.values" "assign"        "qr"            "df.residual"
## [9] "xlevels"       "call"          "terms"         "model"
```

```
names(smod5)
```

```
## [1] "call"           "terms"         "residuals"     "coefficients"
## [5] "aliased"        "sigma"         "df"            "r.squared"
## [9] "adj.r.squared"  "fstatistic"    "cov.unscaled"
```

```
names(gmod5)
```

```
## [1] "r.squared"      "adj.r.squared" "sigma"         "statistic"
## [5] "p.value"        "df"            "logLik"        "AIC"
## [9] "BIC"            "deviance"      "df.residual"
```

```
# Examples:
head(mod5$fitted.values)
```

```
##         1        2        3        4        5        6
## 18.45257 20.92627 30.82106 22.67603 18.45257 25.87366
```

```
head(mod5$residuals)#head of residual vector
```

```
##          1         2          3          4         5         6
##  25.987434 -4.926265 -15.441061 -9.136031  6.547434 -1.823663
```

```
smod5$r.squared
```

```
## [1] 0.22772
```

```
smod5$fstatistic # F-stat. and its degrees of freedom
```

```
##      value       numdf       dendf
##   88.09155     4.00000  1195.00000
```

```
gmod5$statistic #the F-statistic of the model
```

```
## [1] 88.09155
```

```
mod5$df.residual
```

```
## [1] 1195
```

Table 7.15: Example of Using the Function 'tidy'

term	estimate	std.error	statistic	p.value
(Intercept)	-9.4821	1.9580	-4.8428	0.0000
educ	2.4737	0.1351	18.3096	0.0000
black	-2.0653	2.1616	-0.9554	0.3396
female	-4.2235	0.8249	-5.1198	0.0000
black:female	0.5329	2.8020	0.1902	0.8492

For some oftenly used statistics, such as coefficients and their statistics, fitted values, or residuals, there are specialized functions to extract them from regression results. Here are a few:

```
N <- nobs(mod5)
yhat <- fitted(mod5) # fitted values
ehat <- resid(mod5)   # estimated residuals
allcoeffs <- coef(mod5) # only coefficients, no statistics
coef(mod5)[[2]] #or:
```

```
## [1] 2.474
```

```
coef(mod5)[["educ"]]
```

```
## [1] 2.474
```

```
coeftest(mod5)# all coefficients and their statistics
```

```
##
## t test of coefficients:
##
##              Estimate Std. Error t value Pr(>|t|)
## (Intercept)   -9.482      1.958   -4.84  1.4e-06 ***
## educ           2.474      0.135   18.31  < 2e-16 ***
## black         -2.065      2.162   -0.96     0.34
## female        -4.223      0.825   -5.12  3.6e-07 ***
## black:female   0.533      2.802    0.19     0.85
## ---
## Signif. codes:  0 '***' 0.001 '**' 0.01 '*' 0.05 '.' 0.1 ' ' 1
```

```
# The 'tidy()' function is from the package 'broom':
tabl <- tidy(mod5) #this gives the same result as coeftest()
kable(tabl, caption=" Example of Using the Function 'tidy'")
```

Chapter 8

Heteroskedasticity

```
rm(list=ls()) #Removes all items in Environment!
options(digits=3)
library(lmtest) #for coeftest() and bptest().
library(broom) #for glance() and tidy()
library(POE5Rdata) #for POE5 datasets
library(car) #for hccm() robust standard errors
library(sandwich)
library(knitr)
library(stargazer) # draws tables to compare models
library(dplyr) # for data manipulation
library(ggplot2)
library(gridExtra) # for arranging plots
```

New packages: `sandwich` (Lumley and Zeileis, 2015) and `dplyr` (Wickham et al., 2017).

One of the assumptions of the Gauss–Markov theorem is **homoskedasticity**, which requires that all observations of the response (dependent) variable come from distributions with the same variance, σ^2. In many economic applications, however, the spread of y tends to depend on one or more of the regressors x. For example, in the *food* simple regression model (Equation (8.1)) expenditure on food stays closer to its mean (regression line) at lower incomes but spreads about its mean at higher incomes; people with higher income have more choices whether to spend their income on more expensive food or on something else.

$$food\_exp_i = \beta_1 + \beta_2\,income_i + e_i \tag{8.1}$$

141

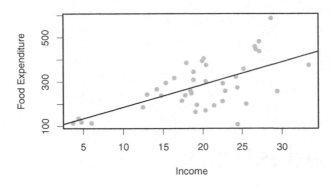

Figure 8.1 Heteroskedasticity in the *food* Data

In the presence of heteroskedasticity, the coefficient estimators are still unbiased, but their variance is incorrectly calculated by the usual OLS method, which makes confidence intervals and hypothesis testing incorrect as well. Thus, new methods need to be applied to correct the variances.

8.1   Spotting Heteroskedasticity in Scatter Plots

When the conditional variance of y, or e, is not constant, we say that the response or the residuals are **heteroskedastic**. Figure 8.1 shows, again, a scatter diagram of the *food* data set with the regression line to show how the observations tend to be more spread at higher income.

```
data(food)
mod1 <- lm(food_exp~income, data=food)
par(cex=1.2,pch=16,lwd=2)
plot(food$income,food$food_exp, type="p",col="darkgrey",
     xlab="Income", ylab="Food Expenditure")
abline(mod1)
```

Another useful method to visualize possible heteroskedasticity is to plot the residuals against the regressors suspected of creating heteroskedasticity, or, more generally, against the fitted values of the regression. Figure 8.2 shows both these options for the simple *food_exp* model.

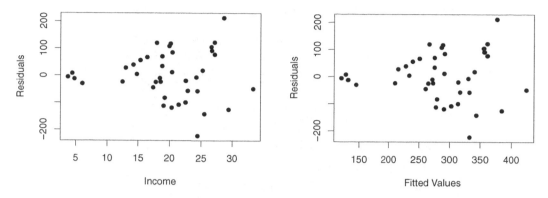

Figure 8.2 Residual plots in the 'food' model

```
par(cex=1.4,mar=c(4,4,1,2))
res <- residuals(mod1)
yhat <- fitted(mod1)
plot(food$income,res, xlab="Income", ylab="Residuals",pch=16)
plot(yhat,res, xlab="Fitted Values", ylab="Residuals",pch=16)
```

8.2 Heteroskedasticity-Robust Variance Estimator

Since the presence of heteroskedasticity makes the least-squares standard errors incorrect, we need another method to calculate them. *White* robust standard errors is such a method.

The R function that does this job is hccm(), which is part of the car package and yields a heteroskedasticity-robust coefficient covariance matrix. This matrix can then be used with other functions, such as coeftest() (instead of summary), waldtest() (instead of anova), or linearHypothesis() to perform hypothesis testing. The function hccm() takes several arguments, among which is the model for which we want the robust standard errors and the type of standard errors we wish to calculate. type can be "constant" (the regular homoskedastic errors), "hc0", "hc1", "hc2", "hc3", or "hc4"; "hc1" is the default type in some statistical software packages. Let us compute robust standard errors for the basic *food* equation and compare them with the regular (incorrect) ones.

```
foodeq <- lm(food_exp~income,data=food)
kable(tidy(foodeq),caption=
  "Regular Standard Errors in the $food$ Equation")
```

Table 8.1: Regular Standard Errors in the *food* Equation

term	estimate	std.error	statistic	p.value
(Intercept)	83.42	43.410	1.922	0.0622
income	10.21	2.093	4.877	0.0000

Table 8.2: Robust (HC1) Standard Errors in the *food* Equation

term	estimate	std.error	statistic	p.value
(Intercept)	83.42	27.464	3.037	0.0043
income	10.21	1.809	5.644	0.0000

```
cov1 <- hccm(foodeq, type="hc1") #needs package 'car'
food.HC1 <- coeftest(foodeq, vcov.=cov1)
kable(tidy(food.HC1),caption=
  "Robust (HC1) Standard Errors in the $food$ Equation")
```

When comparing Tables 8.1 and 8.2, it can be observed that the robust standard errors are smaller and, since the coefficients are the same, the t-statistics are higher and the p-values are smaller than in the regular standard errors case. Lower p-values with robust standard errors is, however, the exception rather than the rule.

Next is an example of using robust standard errors when performing a fictitious linear hypothesis test on the basic *andy* model, to test the hypothesis $H_0 : \beta_2 + \beta_3 = 0$

```
data("andy", package="POE5Rdata")
andy.eq <- lm(sales~price+advert, data=andy)
bp <- bptest(andy.eq) #Heteroskedasticity test
b2 <- coef(andy.eq)[["price"]]
b3 <- coef(andy.eq)[["advert"]]
H0 <- "price+advert=0"
kable(tidy(linearHypothesis(andy.eq, H0,
  vcov=hccm(andy.eq, type="hc1"))),
  caption="Linear Hypothesis with Robust Standard Errors")
```

Table 8.3: Linear Hypothesis with Robust Standard Errors

res.df	df	statistic	p.value
73	NA	NA	NA
72	1	23.38698	7.3e-06

Table 8.4: Linear Hypothesis with Regular Standard Errors

res.df	rss	df	sumsq	statistic	p.value
73	2254.715	NA	NA	NA	NA
72	1718.943	1	535.7719	22.44145	1.06e-05

```
kable(tidy(linearHypothesis(andy.eq, H0)),
  caption="Linear Hypothesis with Regular Standard Errors")
```

This example demonstrates how to introduce robust standards errors in a linearHypothesis function. It also shows that, when heteroskedasticity is not significant (bptest does not reject the homoskedasticity hypothesis) the robust and regular standard errors (and therefore the F statistics of the tests) are very similar.

Just for completeness, I should mention that a similar function, with similar uses is the function vcov, which can be found in the package sandwich.

Example 8.3 GLS/WLS with *food* Data

Consider the regression model described by Equation (8.2), where the errors are assumed heteroskedastic.

$$y_i = \beta_1 + \beta_2 x_i + e_i, \quad var(e_i) = \sigma_i \qquad (8.2)$$

Heteroskedasticity implies different variances of the error term for each observation. Ideally, one should be able to estimate the N variances in order to obtain reliable standard errors, but this is not possible. The second best in the absence of such estimates is an assumption of how variance depends on one or several of the regressors. The estimator obtained when using such an assumption is called a **generalized least squares** estimator, **gls**, involving a linear relationship between variance and the regressor x_i with the unknown parameter σ^2 as a proportionality factor. Equation (8.3) shows such a structure of the error term.

$$var(e_i) = \sigma_i^2 = \sigma^2 x_i \qquad (8.3)$$

One way to circumvent guessing a proportionality factor σ^2 is to transform the initial model in Equation (8.2) such that the error variance in the new model has the structure proposed in Equation (8.3). This can be achieved if the initial model is divided through by $\sqrt{x_i}$ and the new model, shown in Equation (8.4), is estimated. If Equation (8.4) is correct, then the resulting estimator is BLUE.

$$y_i^* = \beta_1 x_{i1}^* + \beta_2 x_{i2}^* + e_i^* \qquad (8.4)$$

Table 8.5: OLS Estimates for the *food* Equation

term	estimate	std.error	statistic	p.value
(Intercept)	83.42	43.410	1.922	0.0622
income	10.21	2.093	4.877	0.0000

Table 8.6: WLS Estimates for the *food* Equation

term	estimate	std.error	statistic	p.value
(Intercept)	78.68	23.789	3.308	0.0021
income	10.45	1.386	7.541	0.0000

In general, if the initial variables are multiplied by quantities that are specific to each observation, the resulting estimator is called a **weighted least squares** estimator, **wls**. Unlike the robust standard errors method for heteroskedasticity correction, **gls** or **wls** methods change the estimates of the regression coefficients.

The function `lm()` can do **wls** estimation if the argument `weights` is provided under the form of a vector of the same size as the other variables in the model. R multiplies the variables in the regression by the square root of the weights that you provide. Thus, if you wish to multiply the model by $1/\sqrt{x_i}$, you should provide the weights $w_i = 1/x_i$.

Let us apply these ideas to re-estimate the *food* equation, which we have determined to be affected by heteroskedasticity.

```
w <- 1/food$income
food.wls <- lm(food_exp~income, weights=w, data=food)
vcvfoodeq <- coeftest(foodeq, vcov.=cov1)
kable(tidy(foodeq),
  caption="OLS Estimates for the $food$ Equation")

kable(tidy(food.wls),
  caption="WLS Estimates for the $food$ Equation" )

kable(tidy(vcvfoodeq),caption=
"OLS Estimates with Robust Standard Errors" )
```

Table 8.7: OLS Estimates with Robust Standard Errors

term	estimate	std.error	statistic	p.value
(Intercept)	83.42	27.464	3.037	0.0043
income	10.21	1.809	5.644	0.0000

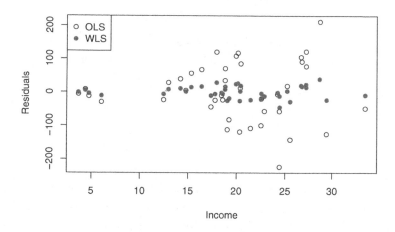

Figure 8.3 OLS and WLS Residuals

Tables 8.5, 8.6, and 8.7 compare the ordinary least squares model to a weighted least squares model and to OLS with robust standard errors. The WLS model multiplies the variables by $1 / \sqrt{income}$; therefore, the weights provided have to be $w = 1/income$. The effect of introducing the weights is a slightly lower intercept and, more importantly, different standard errors. Please note that the WLS standard errors are closer to the robust (HC1) standard errors than to the OLS ones. Figure 8.3 shows, for comparison, the residuals from the OLS and WLS models side by side.

```
plot(food$income,foodeq$residuals,
    xlab="Income",ylab="Residuals")
points(food$income,food.wls$residuals/sqrt(food$income),
      pch=16,col="blue")
legend("topleft",c("OLS","WLS"),pch=c(1,16),
      col=c("black","blue"))
```

8.3 Generalized Least Squares: Unknown Form of Variance

Suppose we wish to estimate the model in Equation (8.5), where the errors are known to be heteroskedastic but their variance is an unknown function of S variables, z_s that might or might not be among the regressors in our model.

$$y_i = \beta_1 + \beta_2 x_{i2} + ...\beta_k x_{iK} + e_i \tag{8.5}$$

Equation (8.6) uses the residuals from Equation (8.5) as estimates of the variances of the error terms and serves at estimating the functional form of the variance. If the assumed functional form of the variance is the exponential function $var(e_i) = \sigma_i^2 = \sigma^2 x_i^\gamma$, then the regressors z_{is} in Equation (8.6) are the logs of the initial regressors x_{is}, $z_{is} = log(x_{is})$.

$$ln(\hat{e}_i^2) = \alpha_1 + \alpha_2 z_{i2} + ... + \alpha_S z_{iS} + \nu_i \tag{8.6}$$

The variance estimates for each error term in Equation (8.5) are the fitted values, $\hat{\sigma}_i^2$ of Equation (8.6), which can then be used to construct a vector of weights for the regression model in Equation (8.5). Let us follow these steps on the *food* basic equation where we assume that the variance of error term i is an unknown exponential function of income. So, the purpose of the following code fragment is to determine the weights and to supply them to the `lm()` function. Remember, `lm()` **multiplies** each observation by the **square root** of the weight you supply. For instance, if you want to multiply the observations by $1/\sigma_i$, you should supply the weight $w_i = 1/\sigma_i^2$.

```
data("food", package="POE5Rdata")
food.ols <- lm(food_exp~income, data=food)
ehatsq <- resid(food.ols)^2
sighatsq.ols  <- lm(log(ehatsq)~log(income), data=food)
vari <- exp(fitted(sighatsq.ols))
food.fgls <- lm(food_exp~income, weights=1/vari^2, data=food)

stargazer(food.ols, food.HC1, food.wls, food.fgls,
   header=FALSE,
   title="Comparing Various $food$ Models",
   type=.stargazertype, # "html" or "latex" (in index.Rmd)
   keep.stat="n",  # what statistics to print
   omit.table.layout="n",
   star.cutoffs=NA,
   digits=3,
#  single.row=TRUE,
   intercept.bottom=FALSE, #moves the intercept coef to top
   column.labels=c("OLS","HC1","WLS","FGLS"),
   dep.var.labels.include = FALSE,
   model.numbers = FALSE,
   dep.var.caption="Dependent variable: $food-exp$",
```

```
model.names=FALSE,
star.char=NULL) #supresses the stars
```

Table 8.8: Comparing Various *food* Models

	Dependent variable: $food - exp$			
	OLS	HC1	WLS	FGLS
Constant	83.416	83.416	78.684	79.913
	(43.410)	(27.464)	(23.789)	(5.551)
income	10.210	10.210	10.451	9.889
	(2.093)	(1.809)	(1.386)	(1.219)
Observations	40		40	40

The table titled "Comparing Various 'food' Models" shows that the FGLS with unknown variances model substantially lowers the standard errors of the coefficients, which in turn increases the t-ratios (since the point estimates of the coefficients remain about the same), making an important difference for hypothesis testing.

For a few classes of variance functions, the weights in a GLS model can be calculated in R using the `varFunc()` and `varWeights()` functions in the package `nlme`.

8.4 Heteroskedastic partition

We have seen already (Equation (8.12)) how a dichotomous indicator variable splits the data in two groups that may have different variances. The generalized least squares method can account for group heteroskedasticity, by choosing appropriate weights for each group; if the variables are transformed by multiplying them by $1/\sigma_j$ for group j, the resulting model is homoskedastic. Since σ_j is unknown, we replace it with its estimate $\hat{\sigma}_j$. This method is named **feasible generalized least squares**. Before illustrating this method, let us synthesize some descriptive statistics for a subset of the `cps5_small` package, namely the observations for which `midwest=1`.

```
t1<-cps5_small%>% # I use the "pipe" here
  filter(metro==1,midwest==1)%>%
  dplyr::select(wage,educ,exper)%>%
  tidy%>%
```

Table 8.9: metro=1

Variable	N	Mean	StDev
wage	213	24.25	14.00
educ	213	14.25	2.77
exper	213	23.15	13.17

Table 8.10: metro=0

Variable	N	Mean	StDev
wage	84	18.86	8.52
educ	84	13.99	2.26
exper	84	24.30	14.32

```
  dplyr::select(1:4)
kable(t1,caption="metro=1",digits=2,
     col.names=c("Variable","N","Mean","StDev"))

t2<-cps5_small%>%
  filter(metro==0,midwest==1)%>%
  dplyr::select(wage,educ,exper)%>%
  tidy%>%
  dplyr::select(1:4)
kable(t2,caption="metro=0",digits=2,
     col.names=c("Variable","N","Mean","StDev"))
```

The above code fragment shows a few novel elements, which come from the package dplyr (Wickham et al., 2017), a relatively new data manipulation system. This is just an example of using the package dplyr; the remaining of this manual uses mostly base R functions, with only sparse references to dplyr. One of the novelties in the deplyr system is the use of the "pipe", symbolized by %>%, which allows constructing a chain of command lines having the same object (usually a data set name) at its root. Other new elements are the functions filter, which selects the observations that satisfy a certain logical condition, and select, which selects a number of columns (variables) in the data set. As an exercise, you may wish to write the base R instructions that would accomplish the same task as the above code lines.

For the same subset, let us build and compare a few heteroskedasticity-consistent models. The table titled "OLS vs. FGLS Estimates for the *wage* Equation" helps comparing the coefficients and standard errors of four models: OLS for rural area, OLS for metro area, feasible GLS with the whole data set but with two types of weights, one for each area, and, finally, OLS with heteroskedasticity-consistent (HC1) standard errors. Please keep in mind that the regular OLS standard errors are not to be trusted in the presence of heteroskedasticity.

```r
data("cps5_small", package="POE5Rdata")
cps5_small<-cps5_small[cps5_small$midwest==1,]
rural.lm <- lm(wage~educ+exper,
               data=cps5_small, subset=(metro==0))
sigR <- summary(rural.lm)$sigma
metro.lm <- lm(wage~educ+exper,
               data=cps5_small, subset=(metro==1))
sigM <- summary(metro.lm)$sigma
cps5_small$wght <- rep(0, nrow(cps5_small))
# Create a vector of weights
n<-nrow(cps5_small)
for (i in 1:n)
{
  if (cps5_small$metro[i]==0){cps5_small$wght[i]<-1/sigR^2}
  else{cps5_small$wght[i]<-1/sigM^2}
}
wge.fgls <- lm(wage~educ+exper+metro, weights=wght,
               data=cps5_small)
wge.lm <- lm(wage~educ+exper+metro, data=cps5_small)
wge.hce <- coeftest(wge.lm, vcov.=hccm(wge.lm, data=cps5_small))
stargazer(rural.lm, metro.lm, wge.fgls,wge.hce,
  header=FALSE,
  title="OLS vs. FGLS Estimates for the $wage$ Equation",
  type=.stargazertype, # "html" or "latex" (in index.Rmd)
  keep.stat="n",   # what statistics to print
  omit.table.layout="n",
  star.cutoffs=NA,
  digits=3,
# single.row=TRUE,
  intercept.bottom=FALSE, #moves the intercept coef to top
  column.labels=c("Rural","Metro","FGLS", "HC1"),
  dep.var.labels.include = FALSE,
  model.numbers = FALSE,
  dep.var.caption="Dependent variable: $wage$",
  model.names=FALSE,
  star.char=NULL) #supresses the stars
```

Table 8.11: OLS vs. FGLS Estimates for the *wage* Equation

| | Dependent variable: *wage* | | | |
	Rural	Metro	FGLS	HC1
Constant	−9.965	−15.728	−16.326	−18.450
	(5.801)	(4.800)	(3.717)	(4.087)
educ	1.848	2.457	2.222	2.339
	(0.375)	(0.303)	(0.236)	(0.265)
exper	0.123	0.214	0.169	0.189
	(0.059)	(0.064)	(0.043)	(0.048)
metro			4.999	4.991
			(1.173)	(1.169)
Observations	84	213	297	

The previous code sequence needs some explanation. It runs two regression models, `rural.lm` and `metro.lm` just to estimate $\hat{\sigma}_R$ and $\hat{\sigma}_M$ needed to calculate the weights for each group. The subsets, this time, were selected directly in the `lm()` function through the argument `subset=`, which takes as argument some logical expression that may involve one or more variables in the data set. Then, it creates a new vector of a size equal to the number of observations in the data set, a vector that will be populated over the next few code lines with weights. This vector is created as a new column of the data set `cps5_small`, a column named `wght`. With this, the hard part is done. One just needs to run an `lm()` model with the option `weights=wght`, and that gives the FGLS coefficients and standard errors.

The next lines make a `for` loop running through each observation. If observation i is a rural area observation, it receives a weight equal to $1/\sigma_R^2$; otherwise, it receives the weight $1/\sigma_M^2$. Why did I square those *sigmas*? Because, remember, the argument `weights` in the `lm()` function requires the square of the factor multiplying the regression model in the WLS method.

The remaining part of the code repeats models we ran before and places them in one table for making comparison easier.

8.5   Detecting Heteroskedasticity

Suppose the regression model we want to test for heteroskedasticity is the one in Equation (8.7).

$$y_i = \beta_1 + \beta_2 x_{i2} + \ldots + \beta_K x_{iK} + e_i \qquad (8.7)$$

The test we are constructing assumes that the variance of the errors is a function h of a number of variables z_s, which may or may not be present in the initial regression model that we want to test. Equation (8.8) shows the general form of the variance function.

$$var(y_i) = E(e_i^2) = h(\alpha_1 + \alpha_2 z_{i2} + \ldots + \alpha_S z_{iS}) \qquad (8.8)$$

The variance $var(y_i)$ is constant only if all the coefficients of the regressors z in Equation (8.8) are zero, which provides the null hypothesis of our heteroskedasticity test shown in Equation (8.9).

$$H_0 : \alpha_2 = \alpha_3 = \ldots \alpha_S = 0 \qquad (8.9)$$

Since we do not know the true variances of the response variable y_i, all we can do is to estimate the residuals from the initial model in Equation (8.7) and replace e_i^2 in Equation (8.8) with the estimated residuals. For a linear function $h()$, the test equation is, finally, Equation (8.10).

$$\hat{e}_i^2 = \alpha_1 + \alpha_2 z_{i2} + \ldots + \alpha_S z_{iS} + \nu_i \qquad (8.10)$$

Te relevant test statistic is χ^2, given by Equation (8.11), where R^2 is the one resulted from Equation (8.10).

$$\chi^2 = N \times R^2 \sim \chi^2_{(S-1)} \qquad (8.11)$$

The **Breusch-Pagan** heteroskedasticity test uses the method we have just described, where the regressors z_s are the variables x_k in the initial model. Let us apply this test to the *food* model. The function to determine a critical value of the χ^2 distribution for a significance level α and $S - 1$ degrees of freedom is qchisq(1-alpha, S-1).

```
alpha <- 0.05
mod1 <- lm(food_exp~income, data=food)
ressq <- resid(mod1)^2
#The test equation:
modres <- lm(ressq~income, data=food)
N <- nobs(modres)
gmodres <- glance(modres)
S <- gmodres$df #Number of Betas in model
#Chi-square is always a right-tail test
chisqcr <- qchisq(1-alpha, S-1)
Rsqres <- gmodres$r.squared
chisq <- N*Rsqres
pval <- 1-pchisq(chisq,S-1)
```

Our test yields a value of the test statistic χ^2 of 7.38, which is to be compared to the critical χ^2_{cr} having $S - 1 = 1$ degrees of freedom and $\alpha = 0.05$. This critical value is $\chi^2_{cr} = 3.84$. Since the calculated χ^2 exceeds the critical value, we reject the null hypothesis of homoskedasticity, which means there is heteroskedasticity in our data and model. Alternatively, we can find the p-value corresponding to the calculated χ^2, $p = 0.007$.

Let us now do the same test, but using a **White** version of the residuals equation, in its quadratic form.

```
modres <- lm(ressq~income+I(income^2), data=food)
gmodres <- glance(modres)
Rsq <- gmodres$r.squared
S <- gmodres$df #Number of Betas in model
chisq <- N*Rsq
pval <- 1-pchisq(chisq, S-1)
```

The calculated p-value in this version is $p = 0.023$, which also implies rejection of the null hypothesis of homoskedasticity.

The function bptest() in package lmtest does (the robust version of) the Breusch-Pagan test in R. The following code applies this function to the basic *food* equation, showing the results in Table 8.12, where 'statistic' is the calculated χ^2.

```
mod1 <- lm(food_exp~income, data=food)
kable(tidy(bptest(mod1)),
caption="Breusch-Pagan Heteroskedasticity Test")
```

The **Goldfeld-Quandt** heteroskedasticity test is useful when the regression model to be tested includes an indicator variable among its regressors. The test compares the variance

Table 8.12: Breusch-Pagan Heteroskedasticity Test

statistic	p.value	parameter	method
7.384	0.0066	1	studentized Breusch-Pagan test

of one group of the indicator variable (say group 1) to the variance of the benchmark group (say group 0), as the null hypothesis in Equation(8.12) shows.

$$H_0 : \hat{\sigma}_1^2 = \hat{\sigma}_0^2, \quad H_A : \hat{\sigma}_1^2 \neq \hat{\sigma}_0^2 \tag{8.12}$$

The test statistic when the null hypothesis is true, given in Equation (8.13), has an F distribution with its two degrees of freedom equal to the degrees of freedom of the two subsamples, respectively $N_1 - K$ and $N_0 - K$.

$$F = \frac{\hat{\sigma}_1^2}{\hat{\sigma}_0^2} \tag{8.13}$$

Let us apply this test to a *wage* equation based on the data set *cps5_small*, where $metro$ is an indicator variable equal to 1 if the individual lives in a metropolitan area and 0 for rural area. I will split the data set in two based on the indicator variable $metro$ and apply the regression model (Equation (8.14)) separately to each group.

$$wage = \beta_1 + \beta_2 educ + \beta_3 exper + \beta_4 metro + e \tag{8.14}$$

```
alpha <- 0.05 #two tail, will take alpha/2
data("cps5_small", package="POE5Rdata")
#Create the two groups, m (metro) and r (rural)
m <- cps5_small[which(cps5_small$metro==1),]
r <- cps5_small[which(cps5_small$metro==0),]
wg1 <- lm(wage~educ+exper, data=m)
wg0 <- lm(wage~educ+exper, data=r)
df1 <- wg1$df.residual #Numerator degrees of freedom
df0 <- wg0$df.residual #Denominatot df
sig1squared <- glance(wg1)$sigma^2
sig0squared <- glance(wg0)$sigma^2
fstat <- sig1squared/sig0squared
Flc <- qf(alpha/2, df1, df0)#Left (lower) critical F
Fuc <- qf(1-alpha/2, df1, df0) #Right (upper) critical F
```

The results of these calculations are as follows: calculated F statistic $F = 2.32$, the lower tail critical value $F_{lc} = 0.82$, and the upper tail critical value $F_{uc} = 1.24$. Since the calculated amount is greater than the upper critical value, we reject the hypothesis that the two variances are equal, facing, thus, a heteroskedasticity problem. If one expects the variance in the metropolitan area to be higher and wants to test the (alternative) hypothesis $H_0 : \sigma_1^2 \leq \sigma_0^2, \quad H_A : \sigma_1^2 > \sigma_0^2$, one needs to re-calculate the critical value for $\alpha = 0.05$ as follows:

```
Fc <- qf(1-alpha, df1, df0) #Right-tail test
```

The critical value for the right tail test is $F_c = 1.2$, which still implies rejecting the null hypothesis.

Example 8.7 The GQ Test in the *food* Model

The Goldfeld-Quant test can be used even when there is no indicator variable in the model or in the data set. One can split the data set in two using an arbitrary rule. Let us apply the method to the basic *food* equation, with the data split in low-income (li) and high-income (hi) halves. The cutoff point is, in this case, the median income, and the hypothesis to be tested

$$H_0 : \sigma_{hi}^2 \leq \sigma_{li}^2, \quad H_A : \sigma_{hi}^2 > \sigma_{li}^2$$

```
alpha <- 0.05
data("food", package="POE5Rdata")
medianincome <- median(food$income)
li <- food[which(food$income<=medianincome),]
hi <- food[which(food$income>=medianincome),]
eqli <- lm(food_exp~income, data=li)
eqhi <- lm(food_exp~income, data=hi)
dfli <- eqli$df.residual
dfhi <- eqhi$df.residual
sigsqli <- glance(eqli)$sigma^2
sigsqhi <- glance(eqhi)$sigma^2
fstat <- sigsqhi/sigsqli #The larger var in numerator
Fc <- qf(1-alpha, dfhi, dfli)
pval <- 1-pf(fstat, dfhi, dfli)
```

The resulting F statistic in the *food* example is $F = 3.61$, which is greater than the critical value $F_{cr} = 2.22$, rejecting the null hypothesis in favor of the alternative hypothesis that variance is higher at higher incomes. The p-value of the test is $p = 0.0046$.

In the package lmtest, R has a specialized function to perform Goldfeld-Quandt tests, the function gqtest which takes, among other arguments, the formula describing the model to be tested, a break point specifying how the data should be split (percentage of the number of observations), what is the alternative hypothesis ("greater", "two.sided", or "less"), how the data should be ordered (order.by=), and data=. Let us apply gqtest() to the *food* example with the same partition as we have just done.

```
foodeq <- lm(food_exp~income, data=food)
tst <- gqtest(foodeq, point=0.5, alternative="greater",
        order.by=food$income)
tst
```

```
##
##  Goldfeld-Quandt test
##
## data:  foodeq
## GQ = 3.6, df1 = 18, df2 = 18, p-value = 0.005
## alternative hypothesis: variance increases from segment 1 to 2
```

Please note that the results from applying the gqtest function are the same as those we have already calculated.

8.5.1 Model Specification and Heteroskedasticity

Log–linear models are useful when the conditional distribution of the dependent variable is skewed but the relationship between $log(y)$ and x is linear and homoskedastic.

Example 8.8 Variance-Stabilizing Log Transformation

This example looks at the relationship between entertainment expenditure and income, based on the *cex5_small* data set. First, let us draw the distribution of entertainment expenditure, in levels and in logs. Let us practice, this time, using the ggplot function to plot the two histograms. As the next code lines show, we can calculate the histogram in percentages within the geom_histogram function. Another novelty of this code is the function grid.arrange from the package gridExtra, which arranges the two graphs next to each other; the labs function allows customizing the axis labels. The histograms are shown in Figure 8.4, where one can observe how taking logs makes the distribution more balanced.

```
data(cex5_small)
cex5_small<-cex5_small[cex5_small$entert>0,]
h1<-ggplot(cex5_small)+
  geom_histogram(aes(x=entert,
              y=..count../sum(..count..)*100))+
  labs(x="Entertainment Expenditure", y="Percent")
```

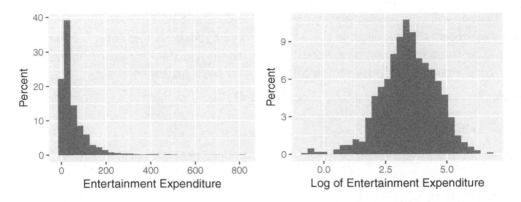

Figure 8.4 Histograms of Entertainment Expenditures in Levels and Logs

```
h2<-ggplot(cex5_small)+
  geom_histogram(aes(log(entert),
               y=..count../sum(..count..)*100))+
  labs(x="Log of Entertainment Expenditure",
       y="Percent")
grid.arrange(h1,h2, nrow=1, ncol=2)
```

Figure 8.5 shows a scatter plot and regression line for entertainment expenditure in the left panel; the right-hand side panel shows the same variables, but with entertainment expenditure in logs. One can observe how the observation points are more evenly distributed around the regression line along the income dimension in the log model.

```
data(cex5_small)
cex5_small<-cex5_small[cex5_small$entert>0,]
s1<-ggplot(cex5_small, aes(x=income, y=entert))+
  geom_point(alpha=0.2)+
  geom_smooth(aes(x=income, y=entert), method="lm",
      formula=y~x)+
  labs(x="Income", y="Entertainment Expenditure")
s2<-ggplot(cex5_small,aes(x=income,y=log(entert)))+
  geom_point(alpha=0.2)+
  geom_smooth(method="lm",formula=y~x)+
  labs(x="Income",y="Log of Entertainment Expenditure")
grid.arrange(s1,s2,nrow=1,ncol=2)
```

A heteroskedasticity test confirms the idea that the log-linear model reduces heteroskedasticity in the entertainment expenditure model, as the following code lines show:

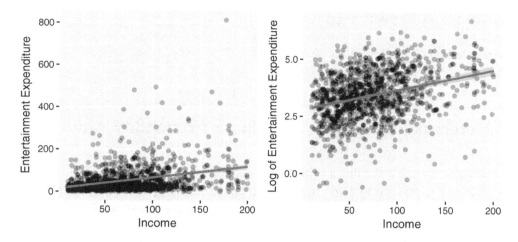

Figure 8.5 Entertainment Expenditure: Linear and Log–Linear Models

```
data(cex5_small)
nrow(cex5_small) # the length of the initial data set
```

```
## [1] 1200
```

```
cex5_small<-cex5_small%>% # you need dplyr package
            filter(entert>0)
nrow(cex5_small) # to check that the filter worked
```

```
## [1] 1100
```

```
m1<-lm(entert~income+college+advanced, data=cex5_small)
res2<-resid(m1)^2
mr2<-lm(res2~income,data=cex5_small)
n<-nobs(mr2)
R.sq<-summary(mr2)$r.squared
Chisq<-n*R.sq
Chisq.cr<-qchisq(0.99,1)#df= #of slope parameters in mr2
```

The results of the calculations in the previous code lines are: $\chi^2_{calculated} = 31.337$, and $\chi^2_{critical} = 6.6349$. Thus, we reject the homoskedasticity hypothesis. The same result can be obtained using the R function bptest, as follows:

```
m1<-lm(entert~income+college+advanced,data=cex5_small)
bptest(m1, ~income, data=cex5_small)
```

```
##
```

```
##  studentized Breusch-Pagan test
##
## data:  m1
## BP = 31, df = 1, p-value = 2e-08
```

8.6   Heteroskedasticity in the Linear Probability Model

As we have already seen, the linear probability model is, by definition, heteroskedastic, with the variance of the error term given by its binomial distribution parameter p, the probability that y is equal to 1, $var(y) = p(1 - p)$, where p is defined in Equation (8.15).

$$\hat{p}_i = \beta_1 + \beta_2 x_{i2} + ... + \beta_K x_{iK} \tag{8.15}$$

Thus, the linear probability model provides a known variance to be used with GLS, taking care that none of the estimated variances is negative. One way to avoid negative or greater than one probabilities is to artificially limit them to the interval $(0, 1)$.

Example 8.9 *Coke* vs. *Pepsi*

Let us revise the *coke* model in data set *coke* using the linear probability model. The table titled "Comparing Various *coke* Models" shows the results of various heteroskedasticity models.

```
data("coke", package="POE5Rdata")
coke.ols <- lm(coke~pratio+disp_coke+disp_pepsi,
               data=coke)
coke.hc1 <- coeftest(coke.ols,
               vcov.=hccm(coke.ols, type="hc1"))
p <- fitted(coke.ols)
# Truncate negative or >1 values of p
pt<-p
pt[pt<0.01] <- 0.01
pt[pt>0.99] <- 0.99
sigsq <- pt*(1-pt)
wght <- 1/sigsq
coke.gls.trunc <- lm(coke~pratio+disp_coke+disp_pepsi,
                  data=coke, weights=wght)
# Eliminate negative or >1 values of p
p1 <- p
p1[p1<0.01 | p1>0.99] <- NA
```

```r
sigsq <- p1*(1-p1)
wght <- 1/sigsq
coke.gls.omit <- lm(coke~pratio+disp_coke+disp_pepsi,
                    data=coke, weights=wght)

stargazer(coke.ols, coke.hc1, coke.gls.trunc, coke.gls.omit,
  header=FALSE,
  title="Comparing Various 'Coke' Models",
  type=.stargazertype, # "html" or "latex" (in index.Rmd)
  keep.stat="n",   # what statistics to print
  omit.table.layout="n",
  star.cutoffs=NA,
  digits=4,
# single.row=TRUE,
  intercept.bottom=FALSE, #moves the intercept coef to top
  column.labels=c("OLS","HC1","GLS-trunc","GLS-omit"),
  dep.var.labels.include = FALSE,
  model.numbers = FALSE,
  dep.var.caption="Dependent variable: 'choice of coke'",
  model.names=FALSE,
  star.char=NULL) #supresses the stars
```

Table 8.13: Comparing Various 'Coke' Models

| | Dependent variable: 'choice of coke' | | | |
	OLS	HC1	GLS-trunc	GLS-omit
Constant	0.8902	0.8902	0.6505	0.8795
	(0.0655)	(0.0653)	(0.0568)	(0.0594)
pratio	−0.4009	−0.4009	−0.1652	−0.3859
	(0.0613)	(0.0604)	(0.0444)	(0.0527)
disp_coke	0.0772	0.0772	0.0940	0.0760
	(0.0344)	(0.0339)	(0.0399)	(0.0353)
disp_pepsi	−0.1657	−0.1657	−0.1314	−0.1587
	(0.0356)	(0.0344)	(0.0354)	(0.0360)
Observations	1,140		1,140	1,124

Chapter 9

Time-Series: Stationary Variables

```
rm(list=ls()) #Removes all items in Environment!
library(dynlm) #for the `dynlm()` function
library(orcutt) # for the `cochrane.orcutt()` function
library(nlWaldTest) # for the `nlWaldtest()` function
library(zoo) # for time series functions (not much used here)
library(pdfetch) # for retrieving data (just mentioned here)
library(lmtest) #for `coeftest()` and `bptest()`.
library(broom) #for `glance(`) and `tidy()`
library(car) #for `hccm()` robust standard errors
library(sandwich)
library(knitr) #for kable()
library(forecast)
library(dplyr)
library(POE5Rdata)
library(stats)
```

New packages: dynlm (Zeileis, 2014); orcutt (Spada et al., 2012); nlWaldTest (Komashko, 2016); zoo [R-zoo]; pdfetch (Reinhart, 2015); and forecast (Hyndman, 2016).

Time series are data on several variables on an observational unit (such as an individual, country, or firm) when observations span several periods. Correlation among subsequent observations, the importance of the natural order in the data, and dynamics (past values of data influence present and future values) are features of time series that do not occur in cross-sectional data.

Time series models assume, in addition to the usual linear regression assumptions, that the series are **stationary**, that is, the distribution of the variable, as well as the correlation

163

between the current value of a variable and its past values are constant over time. Constant distribution requires, in particular, that the variable does not display a trend in its mean or variance; constant correlation implies no clustering of observations in certain periods.

9.1   An Overview of Time Series Tools in R

R creates a time series variable or data set using the function ts(), with the following main arguments: your data file in matrix or data frame form, the start period, the end period, the frequency of the data (1 is annual, 4 is quarterly, and 12 is monthly), and the names of your column variables. Another class of time series objects is created by the function zoo() in the package zoo, which, unlike ts(), can handle irregular or high-frequency time series. Both ts and zoo classes of objects can be used by the function dynlm() in the package with the same name to solve models that include lags and other time series specific operators.

In standard R, two functions are very useful when working with time series: the *difference* function, $diff(y_t) = y_t - y_{t-1}$, and the *lag* function, $lag(y_t) = y_{t-1}$.

The package pdfetch is a very useful tool for getting R-compatible time series data from different online sources such as the World Bank, Eurostat, European Central Bank, and Yahoo Finance. The package WDI retrieves data from the very rich World Development Indicators database, maintained by the World Bank.

Example 9.1 U.S. Unemployment Plot

Figure 9.1 is an example of a time series plot; it shows the fluctuations in U.S. unemployment rate over a period of more than six decades. One may note that the unemployment rate in the financial crisis period (2008-2009) has reached the maximum of the previous three decades.

```
data("usmacro", package="POE5Rdata")
u.ts<-ts(usmacro$u,start=c(1948,1),end=c(2016,1),frequency=4)
par(cex=1.2,lwd=1.8)
ts.plot(u.ts, ylab="Unemployment Rate",xlab=NULL)
```

The evolution of U.S. growth rate is another example of time series, which is illustrated in Figure 9.2.

```
g.ts<-ts(usmacro$g,start=c(1948,1),end=c(2016,1),frequency=4)
par(cex=1.2,lwd=1.5)
ts.plot(g.ts,ylab="Growth Rate",xlab=NULL)
```

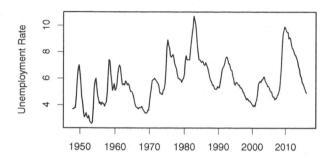

Figure 9.1 U.S. Unemployment Rate, 1948-2016

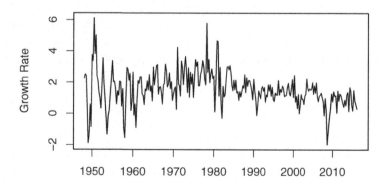

Figure 9.2 U.S. Growth Rate, 1948-2016

9.2   Modeling Dynamic Relations

Finite Distributed Lags

A *finite distributed lag* model (FDL) assumes a linear relationship between a dependent variable y and several lags of an independent variable x. Equation (9.1) shows a finite distributed lag model **of order q.**

$$y_t = \alpha + \beta_0 x_t + \beta_1 x_{t-1} + ... + \beta_q x_{t-q} + e_t \qquad (9.1)$$

The coefficient β_s is an s-**period delay multiplier**, and the coefficient β_0, the immediate (contemporaneous) impact of a change in x on y, is an **impact multiplier**. If x increases by one unit today, the change in y will be $\beta_0 + \beta_1 + ... + \beta_s$ after s periods; this quantity is called the s-period **interim multiplier**. The **total multiplier** is equal to the sum of all βs in the model.

Let us look at Okun's law as an example of an FDL model and an opportunity to introduce a few of R's time series elements. Okun's law relates contemporaneous (time t) change in unemployment rate, DU_t, to present and past levels of economic growth rate, G_{t-s}.

One should be careful when using the lag function, because there are two such functions, which work slightly differently. One is in base R, and requires a negative integer for denoting a period in the past; the other is in the deplyr package and uses a positive integer for denoting the same past period. The deplyr::lag function does not accept negative number of lags at all; for that purpose, one should use the deplyr::lead function. When loading the deplyr package, the base R lag is "masked", so that any further reference to lag will silently refer to the deplyr one. Perhaps the best strategy to avoid errors is to specify which lag function you mean to use by placing either stats:: or dplyr:: in front of lag.

```
library(dynlm)
data("okun5_aus")
okun<-okun5_aus[,c(2,3)]
is.okun.ts<-is.ts(okun) # "is 'okun' structured as time series?"
okun.ts <- ts(okun, start=c(1978,2), end=c(2016,2),frequency=4)
okun.tab <- cbind(okun.ts,
                  stats::lag(okun.ts[,2], -1),
                  diff(okun.ts[,2], lag=1),
                  stats::lag(okun.ts[,1], -1),
                  stats::lag(okun.ts[,1], -2),
                  stats::lag(okun.ts[,1], -3))
```

Table 9.1: The *okun* Data Set with Differences and Lags

g	u	uL1	du	gL1	gL2	gL3
0.9	6.3	NA	NA	NA	NA	NA
1.4	6.3	6.3	0.0	0.9	NA	NA
0.8	6.3	6.3	0.0	1.4	0.9	NA
2.8	6.3	6.3	0.0	0.8	1.4	0.9
-1.6	6.3	6.3	0.0	2.8	0.8	1.4
1.0	6.2	6.3	-0.1	-1.6	2.8	0.8

```
kable(head(okun.tab),
      caption="The $okun$ Data Set with Differences and Lags",
      col.names=c("g","u","uL1","du","gL1","gL2","gL3"))
```

Table 9.1 shows how lags and differences work. Please note how each lag uses up an observation period.

Example 9.2 Sample Autocorrelation for Unemployment

We have already created the unemployment time series u.ts using the data set *usmacro*. Let us calculate the first four autocorrelations for this series; an autocorrelation of order s is given by

$$r_s = \frac{\sum_{t=s+1}^{T} (x_t - \bar{x})(x_{t-s} - \bar{x})}{\sum_{t=1}^{T} (x_t - \bar{x})^2}$$

```
u.ts1<-stats::lag(u.ts,-1)
u.ts2<-stats::lag(u.ts,-2)
u.ts3<-stats::lag(u.ts,-3)
u.ts4<-stats::lag(u.ts,-4)
ubar<-mean(u.ts)
# In the following lines, we remove the observations with NAs
r1<-sum((u.ts-ubar)*(u.ts1-ubar))/sum((u.ts-ubar)^2)
r2<-sum((u.ts-ubar)*(u.ts2-ubar))/sum((u.ts-ubar)^2)
r3<-sum((u.ts-ubar)*(u.ts3-ubar))/sum((u.ts-ubar)^2)
r4<-sum((u.ts-ubar)*(u.ts4-ubar))/sum((u.ts-ubar)^2)
r1;r2;r3;r4
```

```
## [1] 0.9674
```

```
## [1] 0.8978
```

```
## [1] 0.8107
```

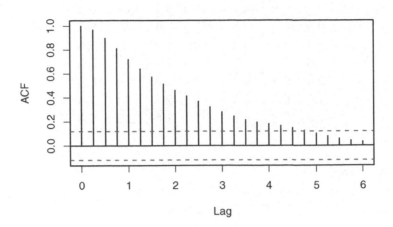

Figure 9.3 Correlogram for U.S. Unemployment

```
## [1] 0.7209
```

Autocorrelations in a time series can also be determined using R's function acf(). The next code lines demonstrate its use. First, autocorrelations for four lags are calculated and printed; then, a correlogram showing more lags is drawn in Figure 9.3.

```
acf(u.ts,lag.max=4,type="correlation",plot=FALSE)
```

```
##
## Autocorrelations of series 'u.ts', by lag
##
##   0.00   0.25   0.50   0.75   1.00
## 1.000 0.967 0.898 0.811 0.721
```

```
par(cex=1.1,lwd=1.8)
acf(u.ts, main="")
```

Example 9.3 Correlogram for U.S. Growth Rate

The correlogram is displayed in Figure 9.4; this autocorrelation structure involves shorter spans, but somehow cyclical.

```
par(cex=1.1,lwd=1.8)
data(usmacro)
g.ts<-ts(usmacro$g,start=c(1948,1),end=c(2016,1),frequency=4)
acf(g.ts,lag.max=45,main="")
```

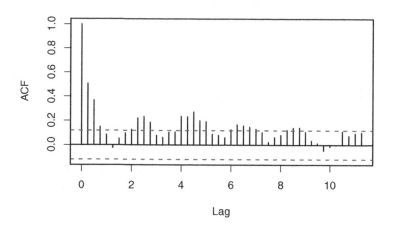

Figure 9.4 Correlogram for U.S. GDP Growth Rate

9.3 Forecasting

Example 9.5 Forecasting Unemployment with an AR(2) Model

Let us consider first an autoregressive (AR) model, exemplified by the U.S. unemployment problem with two lags specified in Equation (9.2).

$$u_t = \delta + \theta_1 u_{t-1} + \theta_2 u_{t-2} + e_t \tag{9.2}$$

Once the coefficients of this model are estimated, they can be used to predict (forecast) out-of-sample, future values of the response variable. Let us do this for periods $T+1$, $T+2$, and $T+3$, where T is the last period in the sample. Equation (9.3) gives the forecast for period s into the future.

$$u_{T+s} = \delta + \theta_1 u_{T+s-1} + \theta_2 u_{T+s-2} + e_{T+s} \tag{9.3}$$

```
data("usmacro", package="POE5Rdata")
u.ts<-ts(usmacro$u,start=c(1948,1),end=c(2016,1),frequency=4)
u.ar2 <- dynlm(u.ts~L(u.ts, 1:2))
kable(tidy(u.ar2), caption=
      "The AR(2) Unemployment Model", digits=3)
```

Table 9.2: The AR(2) Unemployment Model

term	estimate	std.error	statistic	p.value
(Intercept)	0.289	0.067	4.332	0
L(u.ts, 1:2)1	1.613	0.046	35.295	0
L(u.ts, 1:2)2	-0.662	0.046	-14.528	0

Table 9.3: Unemployment forcasts with AR(2)

	Point.Forecast	Lo.80	Hi.80	Lo.95	Hi.95
2016 Q2	4.881	4.505	5.256	4.306	5.455
2016 Q3	4.916	4.204	5.629	3.826	6.006
2016 Q4	4.986	3.967	6.005	3.428	6.544

Table 9.2 shows the results of the AR(2) model. R uses the function forecast() in package forecast to automatically calculate forecasts based on autoregressive or other time series models. One such model is ar(), which fits an autoregressive model to a univariate time series. The arguments of ar() include: x= the name of the time series, aic=TRUE, if we want automatic selection of the number of lags based on the AIC information criterion; otherwise, aic=FALSE; order.max= the maximum lag order in the autoregressive model.

```
ar2u <- ar(u.ts, aic=FALSE, order.max=2, method="ols")
fcst <- data.frame(forecast(ar2u, 3))
kable(fcst, digits=3,
caption="Unemployment forcasts with AR(2)", align="c")
```

Table 9.3 shows the forecasted values of unemployment rate for three future periods, using the AR(2) growth model.

```
par(cex=1.2,lwd=1.8)
plot(forecast(ar2u,3), main="",
     xlab="Year",ylab="Unemployment Rate")
```

Figure 9.5 illustrates the forecasts produced by the AR(2) model of US GDP and their interval estimates.

Example 9.7 An ARDL(2,1) Unemployment Model

Using more information under the form of additional regressors can improve the accuracy of forecasting. We are already familiar with ARDL models; let us use an ARDL(2,1) model to forecast the rate of unemployment based on past unemployment and GDP growth data. The data set is still *usmacro*, and the model is an ARDL(2,1) as the one in Equation (9.4).

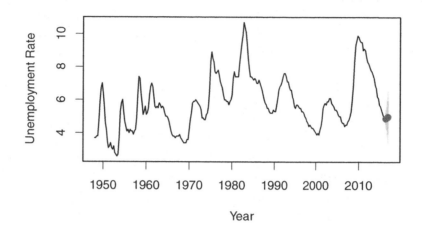

Figure 9.5 Forcasts and Confidence Intervals for Three Future Periods

$$u_t = \delta + \theta_1 u_{t-1} + \theta_2 u_{t-2} + \delta_1 g_{t-1} + e_t \tag{9.4}$$

The variances of the forecasts for the next three periods can be calculated using the following formulas, where $\hat{\sigma}$ is the regression standard error from Equation (9.4):

$$\hat{\sigma}_{f1}^2 = \hat{\sigma}^2$$

$$\hat{\sigma}_{f2}^2 = \hat{\sigma}^2(1 + \theta_1)$$

$$\hat{\sigma}_{f2}^2 = \hat{\sigma}^2[(\theta_1^2 + \theta_2)^2 + \theta_1^2 + 1]$$

The following code fragment reproduces the results in the textbook, using the above equations.

```
data(usmacro)
u<-ts(usmacro$u,start=c(1948,1),end=c(2016,1),frequency=4)
g<-ts(usmacro$g,start=c(1948,1),end=c(2016,1),frequency=4)
u1<-stats::lag(u,-1)
u2<-stats::lag(u,-2)
g1<-stats::lag(g,-1)
df<-ts.union(u,u1,u2,g1)
```

Table 9.4: Forecasts for Unemployment from ARDL(2,1)

Quarter	Forecast	Std. Err. of Forecast	Lower Bound	Upper Bound
2016Q2	4.950	0.292	4.375	5.525
2016Q3	5.058	0.534	4.005	6.110
2016Q4	5.184	0.743	3.721	6.647

```
us.lm<-lm(u~u1+u2+g1, data=df)
T<-length(u)

# Forecast, forecast eror, and forecast interval for T+1
 df1<-data.frame(u1=u[T], u2=u[T-1],g1=g[T])
 uT1<-predict(us.lm,newdata=df1)
 sigT1<-stats::sigma(us.lm)
 lwbT1<-uT1-1.9689*sigT1
 upbT1<-uT1+1.9689*sigT1

# Forecast, forecast eror, and forecast interval for T+2
 df2<-data.frame(u1=uT1,u2=df[T,1],g1=0.869)
 uT2<-predict(us.lm,newdata=df2)
 sigT2<-sigT1*sqrt(1+coef(us.lm)[["u1"]]^2)
 lwbT2<-uT2-1.9689*sigT2
 upbT2<-uT2+1.9689*sigT2

# Forecast, forecast eror, and forecast interval for T+3
 df3<-data.frame(u1=uT2,u2=uT1,g1=1.069)
 uT3<-predict(us.lm,newdata=df3)
 sigT3<-sigT1*sqrt((coef(us.lm)[["u1"]]^2+
        coef(us.lm)[["u2"]])^2+coef(us.lm)[["u1"]]^2+1))
 lwbT3<-uT3-1.9689*sigT3
 upbT3<-uT3+1.9689*sigT3

kable(tibble(
  Quarter=c("2016Q2","2016Q3","2016Q4"),
  Forecast = c(uT1, uT2,uT3),
  "Std. Err. of Forecast"=c(sigT1,sigT2,sigT3),
  "Lower Bound"=c(lwbT1,lwbT2,lwbT3),
  "Upper Bound"=c(upbT1,upbT2,upbT3)),
  digits=3,align='c',caption=
  "Forecasts for Unemployment from ARDL(2,1)")
```

Table 9.5: Unemployment Forecasts with Arima

	Point.Forecast	Lo.95	Hi.95
2016 Q2	4.869	4.302	5.436
2016 Q3	4.871	3.790	5.952
2016 Q4	4.923	3.371	6.476

Table 9.4 collects the forecasts and their 95% confidence intervals for the unemployment ARDL(2,1)model.

Forecasts and their standard confidence intervals can be calculated in R directly using the Arima function. An ARDL(2,1) model requires the argument order=c(2,0,0) in the Arima function; the additional regressors are given by the argument xreg. Table 9.5 shows the point and interval estimates of the three-period forecasts for given values of the growth rates; Figure 9.6 shows a plot of the forecast estimates. This forecast is based on Equation (9.4). The results, however, seem to be slightly different from those found by the previous method.

```
data(usmacro)
u<-ts(usmacro$u,start=c(1948,1),end=c(2016,1),frequency=4)
g<-ts(usmacro$g,start=c(1948,1),end=c(2016,1),frequency=4)
uArima<-Arima(u,order=c(2,0,0),xreg=stats::lag(g,-1))
uf<-forecast(uArima,
          xreg= c(g[length(g)],0.869,1.069),level=95)
tbl<-data.frame(uf)
kable(tbl, digits=3, caption=
        "Unemployment Forecasts with Arima")

par(cex=1.1,lwd=1.8)
plot(uf, main="", xlab="Year",ylab="Unemployment Rate")
```

Choosing the Lag Lengths in an ARDL(p,q) Model

Consider the ARDL(p,q) model in the following equation, with p lags of the dependent variable and q lags of an independent variable:

$$u_t = \delta + \theta_1 u_{t-1} + \dots + \theta_p u_{t-p} + \delta_1 g_{t-1} + \dots + \delta_q g_{t-q} + e_t$$

We can choose the number of lags, p and q, by calculating one of the AIC or BIC (SC) criteria for different combinations of lag numbers and choosing the model having the lowest of these measures.

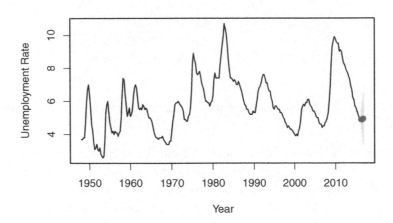

Figure 9.6 Forecasts from Regression with ARDL(2,1)

Example 9.8 Choosing an ARDL Model

This example determines the optimal ARDL(p,q) model for unemployment rate, using the *usmacro* data. The formula to calculate the *SC* value is

$$SC = ln\left(\frac{SSE}{N}\right) + \frac{K\,ln(N)}{N}$$

```
data(usmacro)
us.ts<-ts(usmacro,start=c(1948,1),end=c(2016,1),frequency=4)
bics <- matrix(0,nrow=9,ncol=8)#initializing the SC matrix
for(p in 1:8){  # First, a loop for q=0
    ari <- dynlm(u~L(u,1:p),data=us.ts)
    SSE<-sum(residuals(ari)^2)
    N<-nobs(ari)
    K<-N-ari$df.residual
    bics[1,p] <- log(SSE/N)+K*log(N)/N
}
for (p in 1:8){
  for (q in 1:8){
    ari <- dynlm(u~L(u,1:p)+L(g,1:q), data=us.ts)
    SSE<-sum(residuals(ari)^2)
    N<-nobs(ari)
    K<-N-ari$df.residual
```

Table 9.6: Lag Order Selection for an AR Model

q/p	1	2	3	4	5	6	7	8
0	-1.836	-2.393	-2.378	-2.363	-2.374	-2.372	-2.352	-2.331
1	-2.076	-2.395	-2.379	-2.361	-2.367	-2.365	-2.345	-2.323
2	-2.056	-2.379	-2.359	-2.341	-2.347	-2.344	-2.324	-2.302
3	-2.073	-2.398	-2.378	-2.354	-2.356	-2.349	-2.328	-2.306
4	-2.097	-2.390	-2.370	-2.352	-2.349	-2.340	-2.319	-2.297
5	-2.136	-2.398	-2.378	-2.360	-2.340	-2.353	-2.333	-2.312
6	-2.119	-2.393	-2.372	-2.355	-2.334	-2.336	-2.313	-2.292
7	-2.096	-2.368	-2.347	-2.329	-2.309	-2.312	-2.293	-2.271
8	-2.109	-2.368	-2.347	-2.327	-2.306	-2.307	-2.289	-2.269

```
    bics[q+1,p] <- log(SSE/N)+K*log(N)/N
  }
}
tbl <- data.frame(cbind(0:8,bics))
names(tbl) <- c("q/p",1:8)
kable(tbl, digits=3, align='c',
      caption="Lag Order Selection for an AR Model")
```

The previous code fragment needs some explanation. The third line initializes the matrix that is going to hold the SC results. The problem of automatically changing the number of regressors is addressed by using the convenient function L() inside of two loops over all possible combinations of lags.

Table 9.6 displays the SC (or BIC) values for 64 autoregressive models on the U.S. unemployment rate in data set *usmacro* with a number of lags $p = 1, ..., 8$ and $q = 0, ..., 8$.

Here is how we can determine the coordinates of the minimum element in the matrix of SC values, thus identifying the structure of the SC-best model.

```
mOpt <- which(bics==min(bics), arr.ind=TRUE)
cat("Optimal model: p = ",mOpt[[2]], ", q = ",mOpt[[1]]-1)
```

```
## Optimal model: p =  2 , q =  3
```

The lowest SC value indicates the model with only two lags of the dependent variable as the winner. Other criteria may be taken into account in such a situation, for instance the correlogram, which agrees with the BIC's choice of model.

Example 9.9 Granger Causality

Table 9.7: Granger Causality Test for the Unemployment Equation

res.df	rss	df	sumsq	statistic	p.value
268	23.28	NA	NA	NA	NA
267	22.75	1	0.5221	6.126	0.0139

In general, a variable x does not "Granger" cause another variable, y, if the lags of x are not significant in a y–x ARDL model.

Consider the following model of unemployment rate determination:

$$u_t = \delta + \theta_1 u_{t-1} + \theta_2 u_{t-2} + \delta_1 g_{t-1} + e_t,$$

where the unemployment rate, u, and the growth rate, g, come from the data set *usmacro*. Testing for Granger causality is equivalent to test the hypothesis that all the lags of an independent variable are insignificant. In our case, the Granger causality hypothesis is

$$H_0 : \delta_1 = 0, \quad H_A : \delta_1 \neq 0$$

```
u21<-dynlm(u~L(u,1:2)+L(g,1))
hnull<-"L(g, 1)=0"
lH<-linearHypothesis(u21,hnull)
kable(tidy(lH), digits=4, align='c', caption=
  "Granger Causality Test for the Unemployment Equation")
```

With a p-value of 0.0139 (see Table 9.7), the test rejects the null hypothesis at the 5% level, implying that g Granger causes u.

Let us examine the same problem, but with four lags of the independent variable g, as in the following equation

$$u_t = \delta + \theta_1 u_{t-1} + \theta_2 u_{t-2} + \delta_1 g_{t-1} + \delta_2 g_{t-2} + \delta_3 u_{t-3} + \delta_4 u_{t-4} + e_t,$$

and the hypothesis to be tested

$$H_0 : \delta_1 = 0, \; \delta_2 = 0, \; \delta_3 = 0, \; \delta_4 = 0$$

$$H_1 : \text{At least one } \delta_i \neq 0$$

```
u24<-dynlm(u~L(u,1:2)+L(g,1:4))
h0<-c("L(g, 1:4)1=0","L(g, 1:4)2=0",
    "L(g, 1:4)3=0", "L(g, 1:4)4=0")
lH<-linearHypothesis(u24,h0)
kable(tidy(lH),digits=4,align='c',caption=
  "Granger Test with Four Lags of the Growth Variable")
```

Table 9.8: Granger Test with Four Lags of the Growth Variable

res.df	rss	df	sumsq	statistic	p.value
266	23.25	NA	NA	NA	NA
262	21.30	4	1.945	5.981	0.0001

Again, the test rejects the null hypothesis, as shown in Table 9.8.

9.4 Testing for Serially Correlated Errors

Time series regressions are only valid when there is no serial correlation in the errors.

Example 9.10 Residual Correlogram

Consider, again, the ARDL(2,1) unemployment model,

$$u_t = \delta + \theta_1 u_{t-1} + \theta_2 u_{t-2} + \delta_1 g_{t-1} + e_t$$

As we have already seen, a good tool for identifying serial correlation in a time series is the correlogram. Let us calculate the errors from the above model and draw their correlogram.

```
par(cex=1.1,lwd=1.8)
u21<-dynlm(u~L(u,1:2)+L(g,1))
resd<-residuals(u21)
acf(resd,main="")
```

Figure 9.7 shows no evidence of serial correlation in the errors for this model.

While visualizing the data and plotting the correlogram are powerful methods of spotting autocorrelation, in many applications we need a precise criterion, a test statistic to decide whether autocorrelation is a problem. One such a method is the **Lagrange Multiplier** test. Suppose we want to test for autocorrelation in the residuals of the model given in Equation (9.5), where we assume that the errors have the autocorrelation structure described in Equation (9.6).

$$y_t = \beta_1 + \beta_2 x_t + e_t \tag{9.5}$$

$$e_t = \rho e_{t-1} + \nu_t \tag{9.6}$$

A test for autocorrelation would be based on the hypothesis in Equation (9.7).

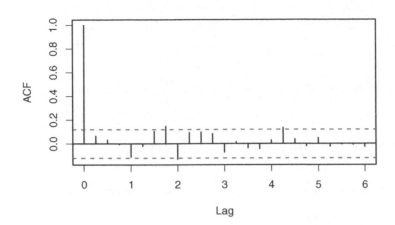

Figure 9.7 Correlogram for an ARDL(2,1) Model Errors

$$H_0 : \rho = 0, \quad H_A : \rho \neq 0 \qquad (9.7)$$

After little algebraic manipulation, the auxiliary regression that the LM test actually uses is the one in Equation (9.8).

$$\hat{e}_t = \gamma_1 + \gamma_2 x_t + \rho \hat{e}_{t-1} + \nu_t \qquad (9.8)$$

The test statistic is $T \times R^2$, where R^2 is the coefficient of determination resulted from estimating the auxiliary equation (9.8). In R, all these calculations can be done in one command, `bgtest`, which is the **Breusch-Godfrey** autocorrelation test. The `bgtest` function can test for autocorrelation of higher orders, which requires including higher lags for $\hat{e}$ in the auxiliary equation.

Example 9.12 Testing Serial Correlation in the Unemployment Equation

Let us do this test for two functional forms of the unemployment example, ARDL(1,1) and ARDL(2,1).

```
u11<-dynlm(u~L(u,1)+L(g,1))
u21<-dynlm(u~L(u,1:2)+L(g,1))
a1 <- bgtest(u11, order=1, type="Chisq")
b1 <- bgtest(u11, order=2, type="Chisq")
c1 <- bgtest(u11, order=3, type="Chisq")
```

Table 9.9: Breusch-Godfrey Test for the Unemployment Example

k	(1,1) Chisq	(1,1) p-Value	(2,1) Chisq	(2,1) p-Value
1	66.90	0	2.489	0.1146
2	73.38	0	6.088	0.0476
3	73.38	0	9.253	0.0261
4	73.55	0	9.390	0.0521

```
d1 <- bgtest(u11, order=4, type="Chisq")

a2 <- bgtest(u21, order=1, type="Chisq")
b2 <- bgtest(u21, order=2, type="Chisq")
c2 <- bgtest(u21, order=3, type="Chisq")
d2 <- bgtest(u21, order=4, type="Chisq")

dfr <- data.frame(rbind(
  c(a1$statistic,a1$p.value,a2$statistic,a2$p.value),
  c(b1$statistic,b1$p.value,b2$statistic,b2$p.value),
  c(c1$statistic,c1$p.value,c2$statistic,c2$p.value),
  c(d1$statistic,d1$p.value,d2$statistic,d2$p.value)
            ))
dfrm <- cbind(1:4, dfr)
names(dfrm)<-c("k", "(1,1) Chisq", "(1,1) p-Value",
                "(2,1) Chisq", "(2,1) p-Value" )
kable(dfrm, digits=4, align="c", caption=
  "Breusch-Godfrey Test for the Unemployment Example")
```

Table 9.9 shows the results of the test, where all the four tests reject the hypothesis of no serial correlation in the errors for the ARDL(1,1) model. For the second model, the first and the fourth-order tests do not reject H_0 at 5% level, but the second and the third order tests do reject H_0, indicating that serial correlation in the errors exists.

How many lags should be considered when performing the autocorrelation test? One suggestion would be to limit the test to the number of lags that the correlogram shows to exceed the confidence band.

R can perform another autocorrelation test, **Durbin-Watson**, which is being used less and less today because of its limitations. However, it may be considered when the sample is small. The following code line can be used to perform this test, showing that its results are consistent with our previous assessments.

```
dwtest(u11);dwtest(u21)
```

```
##
##   Durbin-Watson test
##
## data:  u11
## DW = 1.1, p-value = 2e-14
## alternative hypothesis: true autocorrelation is greater than 0

##
##   Durbin-Watson test
##
## data:  u21
## DW = 1.9, p-value = 0.1
## alternative hypothesis: true autocorrelation is greater than 0
```

9.5   Time Series for Policy Analysis

Using a time series model for policy analysis, where the interpretation of parameters matters, and, therefore the accuracy of these parameters matters, raises questions about how a model satisfies the regression assumptions of exogeneity and independence of observations. Consider the finite distributed lag model

$$y_t = \alpha + \beta_0 x_t + \beta_1 x_{t-1} + ... + \beta_q x_{t-q} + e_t,$$

where

$$E(e_t | x_t, x_{t-1}, ...) = 0$$

A lag-coefficient in this model, β_s, gives the change in the conditional expectation of y_t when x_{t-s} changes by one unit, while x remains unchanged in other periods.

The order s coefficient is an s-period **delay multiplier**, and the order 0 coefficient, the immediate (contemporaneous) impact of a change in x on y, is an **impact multiplier**. If x increases by one unit today, the change in y will be $\beta_0 + \beta_1 + ... + \beta s$ after s periods; this quantity is called the s-period **interim multiplier**. The **total multiplier** is equal to the sum of all the β parameters in the model.

Example 9.13 Okun's Law

Let us look at Okun's law as an example of an FDL model. Okun's law relates the contemporaneous (time t) change in unemployment rate, Du_t, to the present level of economic growth rate, as follows:

$$u_t - u_{t-1} = -\gamma(g_t - g_N)$$

Table 9.10: The *Okun* dataset with differences and lags

g	u	lag(u,1)	diff(u,1)	lag(g,1)	lag(g,2)	lag(g,3)
0.9	6.3	NA	NA	NA	NA	NA
1.4	6.3	6.3	0.0	0.9	NA	NA
0.8	6.3	6.3	0.0	1.4	0.9	NA
2.8	6.3	6.3	0.0	0.8	1.4	0.9
-1.6	6.3	6.3	0.0	2.8	0.8	1.4
1.0	6.2	6.3	-0.1	-1.6	2.8	0.8

The econometric model to estimate this equation involves past levels of unemployment, which make it a finite distributed lag model.

$$Du_t = \alpha + \beta_0 g_t + \beta_1 g_{t-1}... + \beta_q g_{t-q} + e_t$$

This example uses Australian data, given in the file *okun5_aus*.

```
data("okun5_aus", package="POE5Rdata")
okun<-okun5_aus[,c(2,3)]
check.ts <- is.ts(okun) # "is structured as time series?"
okun.ts<-ts(okun,start=c(1978,2),end=c(2016,2),frequency=4)
okun.ts.tab <- cbind(okun.ts,
            stats::lag(okun.ts[,2], -1),
            diff(okun.ts[,2], lag=1),
            stats::lag(okun.ts[,1], -1),
            stats::lag(okun.ts[,1], -2),
            stats::lag(okun.ts[,1], -3))
kable(head(okun.ts.tab),
caption="The $Okun$ dataset with differences and lags",
col.names=c("g","u","lag(u,1)","diff(u,1)","lag(g,1)",
            "lag(g,2)","lag(g,3)"))
```

Table 9.10 shows how lags and differences work. Please note how each lag uses up an observation period. Figures 9.8 and 9.9 give time series plots for the differenced unemployment rate and for the growth rate in Australia.

```
par(cex=1.1,lwd=1.8)
plot.ts(diff(okun.ts[,2]),xlab="Year",
        ylab="Difference in Unemployment Rate")

par(cex=1.1,lwd=1.8)
plot.ts(okun.ts[,1],xlab="Year",ylab="GDP Growth Rate")
```

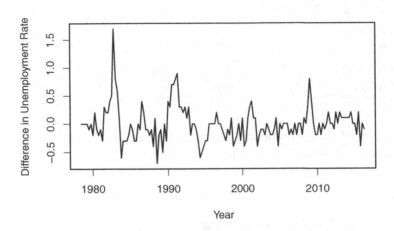

Figure 9.8 Change in Australian Unemployment Rate

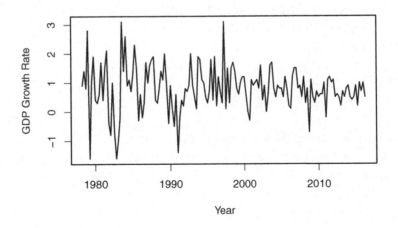

Figure 9.9 Australian GDP Growth Rate

Table 9.11: The $Okun$ Distributed Lag Model with Four Lags

term	estimate	std.error	statistic	p.value
(Intercept)	0.4100	0.0415	9.867	0.0000
L(g, 0:4)0	-0.1310	0.0244	-5.369	0.0000
L(g, 0:4)1	-0.1715	0.0240	-7.161	0.0000
L(g, 0:4)2	-0.0940	0.0240	-3.913	0.0001
L(g, 0:4)3	-0.0700	0.0239	-2.929	0.0040
L(g, 0:4)4	-0.0611	0.0238	-2.563	0.0114

Table 9.12: The $Okun$ Distributed Lag Model with Five Lags

term	estimate	std.error	statistic	p.value
(Intercept)	0.3930	0.0449	8.7458	0.0000
L(g, 0:5)0	-0.1287	0.0256	-5.0367	0.0000
L(g, 0:5)1	-0.1721	0.0249	-6.9150	0.0000
L(g, 0:5)2	-0.0932	0.0241	-3.8652	0.0002
L(g, 0:5)3	-0.0726	0.0241	-3.0118	0.0031
L(g, 0:5)4	-0.0636	0.0241	-2.6438	0.0091
L(g, 0:5)5	0.0232	0.0240	0.9663	0.3355

Tables 9.11 and 9.12 summarize the results of the linear models, with four and five lags respectively.

```
okunL4.dyn <- dynlm(d(u)~L(g, 0:4), data=okun.ts)
kable(tidy(summary(okunL4.dyn)), digits=4,
caption="The $Okun$ Distributed Lag Model with Four Lags")

okunL5.dyn <- dynlm(d(u)~L(g, 0:5), data=okun.ts)
kable(tidy(summary(okunL5.dyn)), digits=4,
caption="The $Okun$ Distributed Lag Model with Five Lags")
```

Many of the output analysis functions that we have used with the lm() function, such as summary() and coeftest() are also applicable to dynlm().

```
glL3 <- glance(okunL5.dyn)[
  c("r.squared","statistic","AIC","BIC")]
glL2 <- glance(okunL4.dyn)[
  c("r.squared","statistic","AIC","BIC")]
tabl <- rbind(as.numeric(glL2), glL3)
tabl<-cbind(Model=c("Four Lags","Five Lags"),tabl)
tabl<-data.frame(tabl)
```

Table 9.13: Statistics for Two *Okun* Models

Model	r.squared	statistic	AIC	BIC
Four Lags	0.499	28.46	-13.65	7.374
Five Lags	0.503	23.76	-11.63	12.343

Table 9.14: Multipliers for the Four-Lag *Okun* Model

	Delay Multipliers	Interim Multipliers
b0	-0.1310	-0.1310
b1	-0.1715	-0.3025
b2	-0.0940	-0.3965
b3	-0.0700	-0.4665
b4	-0.0611	-0.5276

```
kable(tabl, digits=3, caption=
      "Statistics for Two $Okun$ Models")
```

Table 9.13 compares the two FDL models of the *Okun Law* example. Most of the measures in this table point to the four- lag model as a better specification. Let us calculate the multipliers for the four lag model.

```
b<-coef(okunL4.dyn)[c(2:6)]
names(b)<-paste0("b",0:4)
S<-numeric(5)
for (s in 1:5){S[[s]]<-sum(b[1:s])}
tab<-data.frame(b,S)
names(tab)<-c("Delay Multipliers", "Interim Multipliers")
kable(tab,digits=4, align="c",
      caption="Multipliers for the Four-Lag $Okun$ Model")
```

9.6　Estimation with Serially Correlated Errors

Similar to the case of heteroskedasticity, autocorrelation in the errors does not produce biased estimates of the coefficients in linear regression, but it produces incorrect standard errors. The similarity with heteroskedasticity goes even further: with autocorrelation it is possible to calculate correct (**heteroskedasticity and autocorrelation consistent, HAC**) standard errors, known as **Newey-West** standard errors.

There are several functions in R that compute HAC standard errors, of which I choose three,

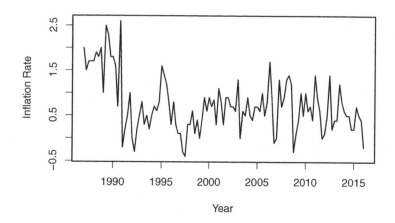

Figure 9.10 Inflation Rate in the *Phillips* Problem

all available in the sandwich package .

Example 9.14 Phillips Curve

This example uses the data set *phillips5_aus*, which gives the change in unemployment rate, du, inflation, inf, and the level of unemployment rate, u, in Australia, over the period 1987Q1 through 2016Q1. The model we want to estimate is

$$inf_t = \alpha + \beta_0 Du_t + e_t$$

```
par(cex=1.1,lwd=1.8)
data("phillips5_aus", package="POE5Rdata")
phill<-phillips5_aus[,c(2,3,4)]
phill.ts <- ts(phill,start=c(1987,1),end=c(2016,1),
               frequency=4)
inflation <- phill.ts[,"inf"]
plot(inflation, ylab="Inflation Rate", xlab="Year")
```

Figures 9.10 and 9.11 display time series plots of inflation and unemployment rates based on the *phillips5_aus* data.

```
par(cex=1.1,lwd=1.8)
Du <- diff(phill.ts[,"u"])
plot(Du, ylab="Change in Unemployment Rate", xlab="Year")
```

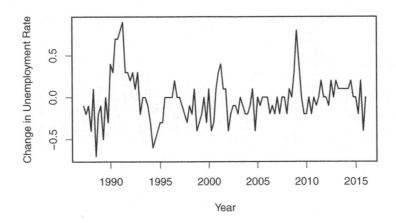

Figure 9.11 Change in Unemployment Rate, the *Phillips* Problem

Table 9.15: Summary of the *Phillips* Model

term	estimate	std.error	statistic	p.value
(Intercept)	0.721	0.055	12.998	0.000
diff(u)	-0.387	0.203	-1.906	0.059

The next code lines produce an OLS estimate of the Phillips curve equation. The results of the model are summarized in Table 9.15.

```
phill.dyn <- dynlm(inf~diff(u),data=phill.ts)
ehat <- resid(phill.dyn)
kable(tidy(phill.dyn), digits=3,
      caption="Summary of the $Phillips$ Model")
```

Figure 9.12 displays a correlogram of the residuals produced by the *Phillips* model, which indicates serial correlation in the first few lags.

```
par(cex=1.1,lwd=1.8)
resid<-residuals(phill.dyn)
acf(resid, main="")
```

Table 9.16 compares three versions of HAC standard errors for the *Phillips* equation, plus the incorrect ones from the initial equation. The differences come from different choices for the methods of calculating them.

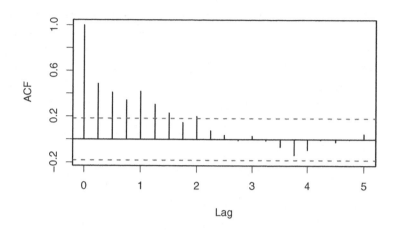

Figure 9.12 Correlogram for OLS Errors in the *Phillips* Problem

Table 9.16: Comparing Standard Errors for the Phillips model

	Incorrect	vcovHAC	NeweyWest	kernHAC
(Intercept	0.055	0.058	0.098	0.102
Du	0.203	0.264	0.296	0.282

```
library(sandwich)
ac<-acf(resid,plot=FALSE)
s0 <- coeftest(phill.dyn)
s1 <- coeftest(phill.dyn, vcov.=vcovHAC(phill.dyn))
s2 <- coeftest(phill.dyn, vcov.=NeweyWest(phill.dyn))
s3 <- coeftest(phill.dyn, vcov.=kernHAC(phill.dyn))
tbl <- data.frame(cbind(s0[c(3,4)],s1[c(3,4)],
                  s2[c(3,4)],s3[c(3,4)]))
names(tbl) <- c("Incorrect","vcovHAC", "NeweyWest", "kernHAC")
row.names(tbl) <- c("(Intercept", "Du")
kable(tbl, digits=3,
caption="Comparing Standard Errors for the Phillips model")
```

9.6.1   Estimation with AR(1) Errors

Correcting the standard errors in a model with autocorrelated errors does not make the estimator of the coefficients a minimum-variance one. Therefore, we would like to find better estimators, as we did in the case of heteroskedasticity. Let us look at models with first-order autoregressive, or **AR(1)** errors. Equation (9.9) shows the AR(1) model for the error term. The variable in this process is assumed to have zero mean and constant variance, σ_ν^2, and the errors ν_t should not be autocorrelated. In addition, the **autocorrelation coefficient**, ρ, should take values in the interval $(-1, 1)$. It can be shown that $\rho = corr(e_t, e_{t-1})$.

$$e_t = \rho e_{t-1} + \nu_t \tag{9.9}$$

The correlation coefficient for the first lag is an estimate of the coefficient ρ in the $AR(1)$ process defined in Equation (9.9), $\hat{\rho}_1 = \hat{\rho} = r_1 = 0.485$

9.7   Nonlinear Least Squares Estimation

The simple linear regression model (9.5) with AR(1) errors (9.6) can be transformed into a model having uncorrelated errors, as Equation (9.10) shows.

$$y_t = \alpha(1 - \rho) + \rho y_{t-1} + \beta_0 x_t - \rho\beta_0 x_{t-1} + \nu_t \tag{9.10}$$

Equation (9.10) is nonlinear in the coefficients, and therefore it needs special methods of estimation. After some transformation, the equation can be writtern under its nonlinear form, as Equation (9.11) shows.

$$inf_t = \alpha(1 - \rho) + \rho\, inf_{t-1} + \beta_0 Du_t - \rho\beta_0 Du_{t-1} + \nu_t \tag{9.11}$$

The next code sequence estimates the non-linear model in Equation (9.11) using the `nls()` function, which requires the data to be under a data frame form. The first few lines of code create separate variables for `inf` and `u` and their lags, then bring all of them together in a data frame. The main arguments of the `nls` function are the following: `formula`, a nonlinear function of the regression parameters, `data`, a data frame, `start`, a listof initial guess values of the parameters, and others.

```
phill.dyn <- dynlm(inf~diff(u), data=phill.ts)
# Non-linear AR(1) model with 'nls'
phill.ts.tab <- cbind(phill.ts[,"inf"],
```

```
                        phill.ts[,"u"],
                        stats::lag(phill.ts[,"inf"], -1),
                        diff(phill.ts[,"u"], lag=1),
                        stats::lag(diff(phill.ts[,2],lag=1), -1)
                        )
phill.dfr <- data.frame(phill.ts.tab)
names(phill.dfr) <- c("inf", "u", "Linf", "Du", "LDu")
phill.nls <- nls(inf~alpha*(1-rho) +
                rho*Linf +
                b0*Du -
                rho*b0*LDu,
                data=phill.dfr,
                start=list(rho=0.5, alpha=0.5, b0=-0.5))
s1 # This is `phill.dyn` with HAC errors:
```

```
##
## t test of coefficients:
##
##              Estimate Std. Error t value Pr(>|t|)
## (Intercept)    0.7214     0.0584   12.36    <2e-16 ***
## diff(u)       -0.3875     0.2638   -1.47      0.14
## ---
## Signif. codes:  0 '***' 0.001 '**' 0.01 '*' 0.05 '.' 0.1 ' ' 1
phill.dyn # The simple linear model:
```

```
##
## Time series regression with "ts" data:
## Start = 1987(2), End = 2016(1)
##
## Call:
## dynlm(formula = inf ~ diff(u), data = phill.ts)
##
## Coefficients:
## (Intercept)      diff(u)
##       0.721       -0.387
phill.nls # The 'nls' model:
```

```
## Nonlinear regression model
##   model: inf ~ alpha * (1 - rho) + rho * Linf + b0 * Du - rho * b0 * LDu
##    data: phill.dfr
```

```
##    rho  alpha      b0
## 0.5116 0.7085 0.0343
##  residual sum-of-squares: 31
##
## Number of iterations to convergence: 9
## Achieved convergence tolerance: 9.95e-06
```

```
coef(phill.nls)[["rho"]]
```

```
## [1] 0.5116
```

Comparing the nonlinear model with the two linear models (with, and without HAC standard errors) shows differences in both coefficients and standard errors. This is an indication that nonlinear estimation is a better choice than HAC standard errors. Please note that the NLS model provides an estimate of the autocorrelation coefficient, $\rho = 0.512$.

9.8   Infinite Distributed Lag (IDL) Model

The generic equation for such a model is

$$y_t = \alpha + \beta_0 x_t + \beta_1 x_{t-1} + \beta_2 x_{t-2} + \beta_3 x_{t-3} + ... + e_t$$

When the restriction of geometrical decline is imposed on the lag coefficients ($\beta_s = \lambda^s \beta_0$) and a trend is included, the infinite lag model can be transformed into the following ARDL(1,0) model:

$$y_t = \delta + \theta y_{t-1} + \beta_0 x_t + \nu_t, \ \ 0 < \lambda < 1, \tag{9.12}$$

where $\delta = \alpha(1 - \lambda)$, $\theta = \lambda$, and $\nu_t = e_t - \lambda e_{t-1}$. Once the ARDL(1,0) is estimated, the delay, interim, and total multipliers are given by the following formulas:

$$\beta_s = \beta_0 \lambda^s \tag{9.13}$$

$$\sum_{j=0}^{s} \beta_j = \frac{\beta_0(1 - \lambda^{s+1})}{1 - \lambda} \tag{9.14}$$

$$\sum_{j=0}^{\infty} \beta_j = \frac{\beta_0}{1 - \lambda} \tag{9.15}$$

Equation (9.12) should be estimated keeping in mind that its errors are serially correlated.

Example 9.16 A Consumption Function

We would like to estimate the consumption function

$$C_t = \omega + \beta Y_t^*,$$

where Y_y^* is permanent income, an infinite stream of income. As discussed above, this model can be reduced to the econometric model

$$Dcons_t = \delta + \lambda Dcons_{t-1} + \beta_0 Dy_t + \nu_t$$

The data in given in the file *cons_inc*.

```
data(cons_inc)
dt.ts<-ts(cons_inc[,c(2,4)],start=c(1959,3),
        end=c(2016,3),frequency=4)
modC<-dynlm(d(cons,1)~L(d(cons,1))+d(y,1),data=dt.ts)
tidy(modC)
```

```
##            term  estimate std.error statistic   p.value
## 1   (Intercept) 478.61146  74.19763     6.450 6.787e-10
## 2 L(d(cons, 1))   0.33690   0.05986     5.628 5.427e-08
## 3      d(y, 1)    0.09908   0.02154     4.599 7.091e-06
```

The following code sequence constructs a function that returns the multipliers corresponding to the model in Equation (9.12), using the formulas in Equations (9.13), (9.14), and (9.15). The newly created, multipliers(), function returns a list that includes the delay multipliers, the interim multipliers, and the total multipliers. The arguments of the functions are model, which is any model that accepts the R function coef(), and M, which is the number of delay or interim multipliers desired.

```
# Function to Calculate Multipliers in an Infinite Lag Model

multipliers<-function(model,M){
  mdel<-numeric(M) #creates vector of delay multipliers
  mint<-numeric(M) #creates vector of interim multipliers
  delta<-coef(model)[[1]]
  lambda<-coef(model)[[2]]
  b0<-coef(model)[[3]]
  for(s in 0:(M-1)){mdel[s+1]<-b0*lambda^s}
   for(s in 0:(M-1)){
    mint[s+1]<-(b0*(1-lambda^(s+1)))/(1-lambda)
   }
```

Table 9.17: Multipliers in Infinite Lag Model

Delay Multipliers	Interim Multipliers	Total Multiplier
0.099	0.099	0.149
0.033	0.132	0.149
0.011	0.144	0.149
0.004	0.147	0.149
0.001	0.149	0.149

```
  mtot<-b0/(1-lambda)
  lst<-list(mdel,mint,mtot)
}
```

Now, let us apply the newly created function to our *Consumption* example.

```
mList<-multipliers(modC,5) # Applying the function
dm<-mList[[1]]   # Vector of delay multipliers
im<-mList[[2]]   # Vector of interim multipliers
tm<-mList[[3]]   # Total multiplier
tab<-data.frame(dm,im,tm)
names(tab)<-c("Delay Multipliers", "Interim Multipliers",
              "Total Multiplier")
kable(tab,digits=3,align="c", caption=
        "Multipliers in Infinite Lag Model")
```

Table 9.17 shows the delay and interim multipliers for the *Consumption* model, along with the total multiplier, which is, of course, always the same.

Chapter 10

Endogeneity and Moment-Based Estimation

```
rm(list=ls()) #Removes all items in Environment!
options(digits=3)
library(AER) #for `ivreg()`
library(lmtest) #for `coeftest()` and `bptest()`.
library(broom) #for `glance(`) and `tidy()`
library(POE5Rdata) #for POE5 datasets
library(car) #for `hccm()` robust standard errors
library(sandwich)
library(knitr) #for making neat tables with `kable()`
library(stargazer)
ifelse(knitr:::is_latex_output(),
       .stargazertype <- "latex",
       .stargazertype <- "html")
```

In most data coming from natural, non-controlled phenomena, some of the independent variables are correlated with the error term in a regression model, which makes the OLS method inappropriate. Regressors (x) that are correlated with the error term are called **endogeneous**; likewise, those that are not correlated with the error term are called **exogeneous**. The remedy for the violation of the exogeneity assumption of the linear regression model is using **instrumental variables**, or **instruments**. Instruments are variables (z) that do not directly influence the response, but are correlated with the endogenous regressors in question.

Table 10.1: OLS Estimation of the $Wage$ Equation

term	estimate	std.error	statistic	p.value
(Intercept)	-0.5220	0.1986	-2.628	0.0089
educ	0.1075	0.0141	7.598	0.0000
exper	0.0416	0.0132	3.155	0.0017
I(exper^2)	-0.0008	0.0004	-2.063	0.0397

10.1   The Instrumental Variable (IV) Method

A *strong* instrument, one that is highly correlated with the endogenous regressor it concerns, reduces the variance of the estimated coefficient. Assume the multiple regression model in Equation (10.1), where regressors x_2 to x_{K-1} are exogenous and x_K is endogenous. The IV method consists in two stages: first regress x_K on all the other regressors and all the instruments and create the fitted values series, $\hat{x}_K$; second, regress the initial equation, in which x_K is replaced by $\hat{x}_K$. This procedure gives sometimes the name of **two-stage least squares**, or **2SLS** to the IV method.

$$y = \beta_1 + \beta_2 x_2 + ... + \beta_K x_K + e \tag{10.1}$$

Example 10.1 OLS Estimation of a *Wage* Equation

Consider the *wage* model in Equation (10.2) using the *mroz* data set restricted to women in the labour force.

$$log(wage) = \beta_1 + \beta_2\, educ + \beta_3\, exper + \beta_4\, exper^2 + e \tag{10.2}$$

```
data(mroz)
mroz1<-mroz[mroz$lfp==1,]
w1<-lm(log(wage)~educ+exper+I(exper^2),data=mroz1)
kable(tidy(w1), digits=4, align="c",
      caption="OLS Estimation of the $Wage$ Equation")
```

Table 10.1 displays the least squares estimates of Equation (10.2), showing that one extra year of education increases the average wage for the women in the labor force by 10.75%.

The notorious difficulty with this model is that the error term may include some unobserved attributes, such as personal ability, that determine both wage and education. Thus, the independent variable *educ* is correlated with the error term or, in other words, it is *endogenous*.

Table 10.2: OLS estimation of a Simple $Wage$ Regression

term	estimate	std.error	statistic	p.value
(Intercept)	-0.1852	0.1852	-0.9998	0.318
educ	0.1086	0.0144	7.5451	0.000

Table 10.3: IV estimation of a Simple $Wage$ Regression

	Estimate	Std..Error	t.value	Pr...t..
(Intercept)	0.7022	0.4851	1.448	0.1485
educ	0.0385	0.0382	1.008	0.3138

Example 10.2 IV Estimation of a Simple $Wage$ Equation

Consider the simple *wage* equation

$$ln(wage_i) = \beta_1 + \beta_2\, educ_i + e_i \tag{10.3}$$

The following code estimates the simple OLS model, with the results in Table 10.2; the sample is still restricted to the women in the labor force.

```
w0<-lm(log(wage)~educ,data=mroz1)
kable(tidy(w0),digits=4, align="c",
      caption="OLS estimation of a Simple $Wage$ Regression")
```

The simple OLS model indicates that an extra year of education increases the expected wage by 10.86%.

An instrument that may address the endogeneity of $educ$ in Equation (10.3) is $mothereduc$, of which we can reasonably assume that it does not directly influence the daughter's wage (it is not contemporaneously correlated with the independent variable), but it influences the daughter's education. Here is a code sequence that estimates the IV version of Equation (10.3).

```
w0iv <- ivreg(log(wage)~educ|mothereduc, data=mroz1)
tab<-data.frame(coefficients(summary(w0iv)))
kable(tab,digits=4, align="c",
      caption="IV estimation of a Simple $Wage$ Regression")
```

Table 10.3 displays the results of the IV regression, suggesting that the effect of education on the expected wage is 3.85%, about three times smaller than our previous estimate. The same table shows that the coefficient on $educ$ is, this time, not significant.

Table 10.4: First Stage in the 2SLS Model for the $Wage$ Equation

term	estimate	std.error	statistic	p.value
(Intercept)	10.1145	0.3109	32.532	0
mothereduc	0.2674	0.0309	8.663	0

Table 10.5: Second Stage in the 2SLS model for the $Wage$ Equation

term	estimate	std.error	statistic	p.value
(Intercept)	0.7022	0.5021	1.3984	0.1627
educHat	0.0385	0.0396	0.9742	0.3305

10.2　IV Estimation with Two-Stage Least Squares

Example 10.3 2SLS Model of a Simple $Wage$ Equation

Let us first carry out an explicit two-stage model of the simple *wage* equation with only one instrument, *mothereduc*. The first stage is to regress *educ* on the instrument, as Equation (10.4) shows.

$$educ = \gamma_1 + \theta_1 mothereduc + \nu_{educ} \qquad (10.4)$$

```
data("mroz", package="POE5Rdata")
mroz1 <- mroz[mroz$lfp==1,] #restricts sample to lfp=1
educ.ols <- lm(educ~mothereduc, data=mroz1)
kable(tidy(educ.ols), digits=4, align='c',caption=
  "First Stage in the 2SLS Model for the $Wage$ Equation")
```

The p-value for *mothereduc* is very low (see Table 10.4), indicating a strong correlation between this instrument and the endogenous variable *educ*. The second stage in the two-stage procedure is to create the fitted values of *educ* from the first stage (Equation (10.4)) and plug them into the model of interest, Equation (10.2) to replace the original variable *educ*.

```
educHat <- fitted(educ.ols)
wage.2sls <- lm(log(wage)~educHat, data=mroz1)
kable(tidy(wage.2sls), digits=4, align='c',caption=
  "Second Stage in the 2SLS model for the $Wage$ Equation")
```

The results of the explicit $2SLS$ procedure are shown in Table 10.5; keep in mind, however, that the standard errors calculated in this way are incorrect; the correct method is to use a dedicated software function to solve an instrumental variable model, such as `ivreg()`.

Table 10.6: A 2SLS Model for the $Wage$ Equation

	Estimate	Std..Error	t.value	Pr...t..
(Intercept)	0.5510	0.4258	1.294	0.1963
educhat	0.0505	0.0335	1.506	0.1328

Example 10.4 Using Surplus Instruments

When more than one instrument is available for an endogenous variable, the first stage in the 2SLS method can use them for obtaining a better estimate of the fitted values of the endogenous variable, as in the following equation, where z_1 and z_2 are both instruments for x:

$$x_i = \gamma_1 + \theta_1 z_{1i} + \theta_2 z_{2i} + e_i$$

In the $wage$ equation, a second instrument for $educ$ could be father's education. The next code lines estimate both stages of such a model.

```
educ.2sls1 <- lm(educ~mothereduc+fathereduc, data=mroz1)
educhat<-fitted(educ.2sls1)
wage.2sls2 <- lm(log(wage)~educhat, data=mroz1)
tab<-data.frame(coef(summary(wage.2sls2)))
kable(tab, digits=4, align='c',caption=
   "A 2SLS Model for the $Wage$ Equation")
```

The results of the 2SLS estimation with two instruments are shown in Table 10.6

10.3 IV Estimation in Multiple Regression

Example 10.5 IV/2SLS in the $Wage$ Equation

This example applies the 2SLS and IV methods to the multiple regression model of wage determination and compares the results. The instrument list in the command `ivreg` includes both the instrument itself ($mothereduc$) and all exogenous regressors, which are, so to speak, their own instruments. The vertical bar (|) separates the proper regressor list from the instrument list.

```
data("mroz", package="POE5Rdata")
mroz1 <- mroz[mroz$lfp==1,] # restricts sample to lfp=1.
mroz1.ols <- lm(log(wage)~educ+exper+I(exper^2), data=mroz1)
educ.2SLS1<- lm(educ~exper+I(exper^2)+
            fathereduc+mothereduc,data=mroz1)
educHat<-fitted(educ.2SLS1)
```

```
wage.2sls<-lm(log(wage)~educHat+exper+I(exper^2), data=mroz1)
mroz1.iv1 <- ivreg(log(wage)~educ+exper+I(exper^2)|
             exper+I(exper^2)+mothereduc+fathereduc,
             data=mroz1)
stargazer(mroz1.ols, wage.2sls, mroz1.iv1,
  title="Wage Equation: OLS, 2SLS, and IV Models Compared",
  header=FALSE,
  type=.stargazertype, # "html" or "latex" (in index.Rmd)
  keep.stat="n",   # what statistics to print
  omit.table.layout="n",
  star.cutoffs=NA,
  digits=4,
  intercept.bottom=FALSE, #moves the intercept coef to top
  column.labels=c("OLS","2SLS", "IV"),
  dep.var.labels.include = FALSE,
  model.numbers = FALSE,
  dep.var.caption="Dependent variable: wage",
  model.names=FALSE,
  star.char=NULL) #supresses the stars)
```

The table titled "Wage Equation: OLS, 2SLS, and IV Models Compared" shows that the importance of education in determining wage decreases in the IV model. It also shows that the explicit 2SLS model and the IV model yield the same coefficients (the *educ* coefficient in the IV model is equivalent to the *educHat* coefficient in 2SLS), but the standard errors are different. The correct ones are those provided by the IV model.

Example 10.6 Instrument Strength in the $Wage$ Equation

To test for weak instruments in the *wage* equation, we just test the joint significance of the instruments in an *educ* model as shown in (10.5).

$$educ = \gamma_1 + \gamma_2\, exper + \gamma_3\, exper^2 + \theta_1\, mothereduc + \theta_2\, fathereduc + \nu \qquad (10.5)$$

```
educ.ols <- lm(educ~exper+I(exper^2)+mothereduc+fathereduc,
             data=mroz1)
kable(tidy(educ.ols), digits=4,
      caption="The $Educ$ First-Stage Equation")
```

Table 10.8 collects the results of the weak instruments test equation, indicating a strong dependency of the variable *educ* on both *mothereduc* and *fathereduc*. The complete weak instruments test, though, requires testing both θ coefficients simultaneously, as the

Table 10.7: Wage Equation: OLS, 2SLS, and IV Models Compared

	Dependent variable: wage		
	OLS	2SLS	IV
Constant	−0.5220	0.0481	0.0481
	(0.1986)	(0.4198)	(0.4003)
educ	0.1075		0.0614
	(0.0141)		(0.0314)
educHat		0.0614	
		(0.0330)	
exper	0.0416	0.0442	0.0442
	(0.0132)	(0.0141)	(0.0134)
I(exper^2)	−0.0008	−0.0009	−0.0009
	(0.0004)	(0.0004)	(0.0004)
Observations	428	428	428

Table 10.8: The *Educ* First-Stage Equation

term	estimate	std.error	statistic	p.value
(Intercept)	9.1026	0.4266	21.3396	0.0000
exper	0.0452	0.0403	1.1236	0.2618
I(exper^2)	-0.0010	0.0012	-0.8386	0.4022
mothereduc	0.1576	0.0359	4.3906	0.0000
fathereduc	0.1895	0.0338	5.6152	0.0000

next code line shows.

```
linearHypothesis(educ.ols, c("mothereduc=0", "fathereduc=0"))
```

```
## Linear hypothesis test
##
## Hypothesis:
## mothereduc = 0
## fathereduc = 0
##
## Model 1: restricted model
## Model 2: educ ~ exper + I(exper^2) + mothereduc + fathereduc
##
##   Res.Df  RSS Df Sum of Sq    F Pr(>F)
## 1    425 2219
## 2    423 1759  2       461 55.4 <2e-16 ***
## ---
## Signif. codes:  0 '***' 0.001 '**' 0.01 '*' 0.05 '.' 0.1 ' ' 1
```

The test rejects the null hypothesis that both *mothereduc* and *fathereduc* coefficients are zero, indicating that at least one instrument is strong. A rule of thumb requires to soundly reject the null hypothesis at a value of the F-statistic greater than 10 or, for only one instrument, a t-statistic greater than 3.16 to make sure that an instrument is strong.

For a model to be identified the number of instruments should be at least equal to the number of endogenous variables. If there are more instruments than endogenous variables, the model is said to be **overidentified**.

10.4   Specification Tests

Since using IV when it is not necessary worsens our estimates, we would like to test whether the variables that worry us are indeed endogenous. This problem is addressed by the **Hausman test for endogeneity**, where the null hypothesis is $H_0 : Cov(x, e) = 0$. Thus, rejecting the null hypothesis indicates the existence of endogeneity and the need for instrumental variables.

The test for the validity of instruments (whether the instruments are correlated with the error term) can only be performed for the *extra* instruments, which are those in excess of the number of endogenous variables. This test is sometimes called a test for **overidentifying restrictions**, or the **Sargan** test. The null hypothesis is that the covariance between the instrument and the error term is zero, $H_0 : Cov(z, e) = 0$. Thus, rejecting the null indicates that at least one of the extra instruments is not valid.

R automatically performs these three tests and reports the results in the output to the ivreg function.

```
summary(mroz1.iv1, diagnostics=TRUE)
```

```
##
## Call:
## ivreg(formula = log(wage) ~ educ + exper + I(exper^2) | exper +
##      I(exper^2) + motheduc + fatheduc, data = mroz1)
##
## Residuals:
##     Min      1Q  Median      3Q     Max
## -3.0986 -0.3196  0.0551  0.3689  2.3493
##
## Coefficients:
##              Estimate Std. Error t value Pr(>|t|)
## (Intercept)  0.048100   0.400328    0.12   0.9044
## educ         0.061397   0.031437    1.95   0.0515 .
## exper        0.044170   0.013432    3.29   0.0011 **
## I(exper^2)  -0.000899   0.000402   -2.24   0.0257 *
##
## Diagnostic tests:
##                   df1 df2 statistic p-value
## Weak instruments    2 423     55.40  <2e-16 ***
## Wu-Hausman          1 423      2.79   0.095 .
## Sargan              1  NA      0.38   0.539
## ---
## Signif. codes:  0 '***' 0.001 '**' 0.01 '*' 0.05 '.' 0.1 ' ' 1
##
## Residual standard error: 0.675 on 424 degrees of freedom
## Multiple R-Squared: 0.136,   Adjusted R-squared: 0.13
## Wald test: 8.14 on 3 and 424 DF,  p-value: 0.0000279
```

The results for the wage equation are as follows:

- Weak instruments test: rejects the null, meaning that at least one instrument is strong
- (Wu-)Hausman test for endogeneity: barely rejects the null that the variable of concern is uncorrelated with the error term, indicating that *educ* is marginally endogenous
- Sargan overidentifying restrictions: does not reject the null, meaning that the extra instruments are valid (are uncorrelated with the error term).

10.5   Cragg-Donald F-Test for Weak Instruments

The test for weak instruments might be unreliable with more than one endogenous regressor, though, because there is indeed one F-statistic for each endogenous regressor. An alternative is the **Cragg-Donald** test based on the statistic shown in Equation (10.6), where N is the number of observations, L is the number of external instruments, and r_B is the lowest **canonical correlation** (a measure of the correlation between the endogenous and the exogenous variables, calculated by the function cancor() in R).

$$F = \frac{N - L}{L} \frac{r_B^2}{1 - r_B^2} \tag{10.6}$$

Let us look at the *hours* equation with two endogenous variables, mtr and $educ$, and two external instruments, $mothereduc$ and $fathereduc$. One of the two exogenous regressors, $nwifeinc$, is the family income net of the wife's income; the other exogenous regressor, mtr, is the wife's marginal tax rate. Equation (10.7) shows this model; the data set is *mroz*, restricted to women that are in the labor force.

$$hours = \beta_1 + \beta_2\, mtr + \beta_3\, educ + \beta_4\, kidsl6 + \beta_5\, nwifeinc + e \tag{10.7}$$

The next code sequence uses the R function cancor() to calculate the lowest of two canonical correlations, r_B, which is needed for the Cragg-Donald F-statistic in Equation (10.6).

```
data("mroz", package="POE5Rdata")
mroz1 <- mroz[which(mroz$wage>0),]
nwifeinc <- (mroz1$faminc-mroz1$wage*mroz1$hours)/1000
L<-2
N<-nrow(mroz1)
x1 <- resid(lm(mtr~kidsl6+nwifeinc, data=mroz1))
x2 <- resid(lm(educ~kidsl6+nwifeinc, data=mroz1))
z1 <-resid(lm(mothereduc~kidsl6+nwifeinc, data=mroz1))
z2 <-resid(lm(fathereduc~kidsl6+nwifeinc, data=mroz1))
X <- cbind(x1,x2)
Y <- cbind(z1,z2)
rB <- min(cancor(X,Y)$cor)
CraggDonaldF <- ((N-L)/L)*(rB^2/(1-rB^2))
```

The result is the Cragg-Donald $F = 0.1013$, which is much smaller than the critical value of 4.58 given in Table 10A.1 of the textbook. This test does not reject the null hypothesis of weak instruments, contradicting my previous result.

Chapter 11

Simultaneous Equations Models

```
rm(list=ls()) #Removes all items in Environment!
options(digits=3)
library(systemfit)
library(broom) #for `glance(`) and `tidy()`
library(POE5Rdata) #for POE5 datasets
library(knitr) #for kable()
library(dplyr)
library(stargazer)
ifelse(knitr:::is_latex_output(),
       .stargazertype <- "latex",
       .stargazertype <- "html")
```

New package: `systemfit` (Henningsen and Hamann, 2015).

Simultaneous equations are models with more than one response variable, where the solution is determined by an equilibrium among opposing forces. The econometric problem is similar to the endogenous variable one that we have studied in the previous chapter because the mutual interaction between dependent variables can be considered a form of endogeneity. The typical example of an economic simultaneous equation problem is the demand and supply model, where price and quantity are interdependent and are determined by the interaction between demand and supply.

Usually, an economic model such as demand and supply includes several of the dependent (endogenous) variables in each equation. This arrangement is called the **structural form** of the model. If the structural form is transformed such that each equation shows one dependent variable as a function of only exogenous independent variables, the new form is called the **reduced form**. The reduced form can be estimated by least squares, while the structural form cannot because it includes endogenous variables on its right-hand side.

The **necessary condition for identification** requires that, for the problem to have a solution each equation in the structural form of the system should miss at least an exogenous variable that is present in other equations.

Simultaneous equations are the object of package systemfit in R, with the function systemfit(), which requires the following main arguments: formula= a list describing the equations of the system; method= the desired (appropriate) method of estimation, which can be one of "OLS", "WLS", "SUR", "2SLS", "W2SLS", or "3SLS" (we have only studied OLS, WLS, and 2SLS so far); inst= a list of instrumental variables under the form of one-sided model formulas; all the exogenous variables in the system must be in this list.

Example 11.1 Supply and Demand for Truffles

This example uses the data set $truffles$, where q is quantity of truffles traded, p is the market price, ps is the price of a substitute, di is income, and pf is a measure of costs of production. The structural demand and supply equations (Equations (11.1) and (11.2)) are formulated based on economic theory; quantity and price are endogenous, and all the other variables are considered exogenous.

$$q = \alpha_1 + \alpha_2 p + \alpha_3 ps + \alpha_4 di + e_d \tag{11.1}$$

$$q = \beta_1 + \beta_2 p + \beta_3 pf + e_s \tag{11.2}$$

```
data("truffles", package="POE5Rdata")
D <- q~p+ps+di
S <- q~p+pf
sys <- list(D,S)
instr <- ~ps+di+pf
truff.sys <- systemfit(sys, inst=instr,
                method="2SLS", data=truffles)
summary(truff.sys)

##
## systemfit results
## method: 2SLS
##
##         N DF SSR detRCov OLS-R2 McElroy-R2
## system 60 53 692    49.8  0.439      0.807
##
##       N DF   SSR   MSE RMSE    R2 Adj R2
```

```
## eq1 30 26 631.9 24.30 4.93 -0.024 -0.142
## eq2 30 27  60.6  2.24 1.50  0.902  0.895
##
## The covariance matrix of the residuals
##        eq1  eq2
## eq1 24.30 2.17
## eq2  2.17 2.24
##
## The correlations of the residuals
##        eq1   eq2
## eq1 1.000 0.294
## eq2 0.294 1.000
##
##
## 2SLS estimates for 'eq1' (equation 1)
## Model Formula: q ~ p + ps + di
## Instruments: ~ps + di + pf
##
##                Estimate Std. Error t value Pr(>|t|)
## (Intercept)    -4.279      5.544     -0.77   0.4471
## p              -0.374      0.165     -2.27   0.0315 *
## ps              1.296      0.355      3.65   0.0012 **
## di              5.014      2.284      2.20   0.0372 *
## ---
## Signif. codes:  0 '***' 0.001 '**' 0.01 '*' 0.05 '.' 0.1 ' ' 1
##
## Residual standard error: 4.93 on 26 degrees of freedom
## Number of observations: 30 Degrees of Freedom: 26
## SSR: 631.917 MSE: 24.305 Root MSE: 4.93
## Multiple R-Squared: -0.024 Adjusted R-Squared: -0.142
##
##
## 2SLS estimates for 'eq2' (equation 2)
## Model Formula: q ~ p + pf
## Instruments: ~ps + di + pf
##
##              Estimate Std. Error t value Pr(>|t|)
## (Intercept) 20.0328     1.2231     16.4   1.6e-15 ***
## p            0.3380     0.0249     13.6   1.4e-13 ***
## pf          -1.0009     0.0825    -12.1   1.9e-12 ***
## ---
```

Table 11.1: Reduced Form for Quantity of Truffles

term	estimate	std.error	statistic	p.value
(Intercept)	7.8951	3.2434	2.434	0.0221
ps	0.6564	0.1425	4.605	0.0001
di	2.1672	0.7005	3.094	0.0047
pf	-0.5070	0.1213	-4.181	0.0003

Table 11.2: Reduced Form for Price of Truffles

term	estimate	std.error	statistic	p.value
(Intercept)	-32.512	7.9842	-4.072	0.0004
ps	1.708	0.3509	4.868	0.0000
di	7.603	1.7243	4.409	0.0002
pf	1.354	0.2985	4.536	0.0001

```
## Signif. codes:  0 '***' 0.001 '**' 0.01 '*' 0.05 '.' 0.1 ' ' 1
##
## Residual standard error: 1.498 on 27 degrees of freedom
## Number of observations: 30 Degrees of Freedom: 27
## SSR: 60.555 MSE: 2.243 Root MSE: 1.498
## Multiple R-Squared: 0.902 Adjusted R-Squared: 0.895
```

The output of the `systemfit()` function shows the estimates by structural equation: eq1 is the demand function, where, as expected, price has a negative sign, and eq2 is the supply equation, with a positive sign for price.

By evaluating the reduced form equation using OLS, one can determine the effects of changes in exogenous variables on the **equilibrium** market price and quantity, while the structural equations show the effects of such changes on the quantity demanded, respectively on the quantity supplied. Estimating the structural equations by such methods as 2SLS is, in fact, estimating the market demand and supply curves, which is extremely useful for economic analysis. Estimating the reduced forms, while being useful for prediction, does not allow for deep analysis - it only gives the equilibrium point, not the whole curves.

```
Q.red <- lm(q~ps+di+pf, data=truffles)
kable(tidy(Q.red), digits=4,
      caption="Reduced Form for Quantity of Truffles")

P.red <- lm(p~ps+di+pf, data=truffles)
kable(tidy(P.red), digits=4,
      caption="Reduced Form for Price of Truffles")
```

Tables 11.1 and 11.2 show that all the exogenous variables have significant effects on the equilibrium quantity and price and have the expected signs.

Example 11.2 Supply and Demand at Fulton Fish Market

The *fultonfish* data set provides another demand and supply example where the simultaneous equations method can be applied. The purpose of this example is to emphasize that the exogenous variables that are key for identification must be statistically significant. Otherwise, the structural equation that needs to be identified by those variables cannot be reliably estimated. The remaining equations in the structural system are, however, not affected.

$$log(quan) = \alpha_1 + \alpha_2 log(price) + \alpha_3 mon + \alpha_4 tue + \alpha_4 wed + \alpha_5 thu + e_D \qquad (11.3)$$

$$log(quan) = \beta_1 + \beta_2 log(price) + \beta_3 stormy + e_S \qquad (11.4)$$

In the *fultonfish* example, the endogenous variables are *lprice*, the log of price, and *lquan*; the exogenous variables are the indicator variables for the day of the week, and whether the catching day was stormy. The identification variable for the demand equation is *stormy*, which will only show up in the supply equation; the identification variables for the supply equation will be *mon, tue, wed,* and *thu.*

$$log(q) = \pi_{11} + \pi_{21} mon + \pi_{31} tue + \pi_{41} wed + \pi_{51} thu + \pi_{61} stormy + \nu_1 \qquad (11.5)$$

$$log(p) = \pi_{12} + \pi_{22} mon + \pi_{32} tue + \pi_{42} wed + \pi_{52} thu + \pi_{62} stormy + \nu_2 \qquad (11.6)$$

Now, let us consider the reduced form equations, Equations (11.5) and (11.6). Since the endogenous variable that appears in the right-hand side of the structural equations (Equations (11.3) and (11.4)) is *price*, the *price* reduced equation (Equation (11.6)) is essential for evaluating the identification state of the model. If the weekday indicators are all insignificant, the supply equation cannot be identified; if *stormy* turns out insignificant, the demand equation cannot be identified; if the weekday indicators are insignificant but *stormy* is significant the supply is not identified, but the demand is; if at least one weekday indicator turns out significant but *stormy* turns out insignificant, the demand equation is not identified but the supply equation is. Equations (11.3) and (11.4) display the structural demand and supply equations for the *fultonfish* example.

Table 11.3: Reduced Q Equation for the Fulton Fish Example

term	estimate	std.error	statistic	p.value
(Intercept)	8.8101	0.1470	59.9225	0.0000
mon	0.1010	0.2065	0.4891	0.6258
tue	-0.4847	0.2011	-2.4097	0.0177
wed	-0.5531	0.2058	-2.6875	0.0084
thu	0.0537	0.2010	0.2671	0.7899
stormy	-0.3878	0.1437	-2.6979	0.0081

Table 11.4: Reduced P Equation for the Fulton Fish Example

term	estimate	std.error	statistic	p.value
(Intercept)	-0.2717	0.0764	-3.5569	0.0006
mon	-0.1129	0.1073	-1.0525	0.2950
tue	-0.0411	0.1045	-0.3937	0.6946
wed	-0.0118	0.1069	-0.1106	0.9122
thu	0.0496	0.1045	0.4753	0.6356
stormy	0.3464	0.0747	4.6387	0.0000

```
data("fultonfish", package="POE5Rdata")
fishQ.ols <- lm(lquan~mon+tue+wed+thu+stormy,
                data=fultonfish)
kable(tidy(fishQ.ols), digits=4, caption=
    "Reduced $Q$ Equation for the Fulton Fish Example")

fishP.ols <- lm(lprice~mon+tue+wed+thu+stormy,
                data=fultonfish)
kable(tidy(fishP.ols), digits=4,caption=
    "Reduced $P$ Equation for the Fulton Fish Example")
```

The relevant equation for evaluating identification is shown in Table 11.4, which is the price reduced equation. The results show that the weekday indicators are not significant, which will make the 2SLS estimation of the supply equation unreliable; the coefficient on *stormy* is significant, thus the estimation of the (structural) demand equation will be reliable. The following code sequence and output show the 2SLS estimates of the demand and supply (the structural) equations.

```
fish.D <- lquan~lprice+mon+tue+wed+thu
fish.S <- lquan~lprice+stormy
fish.eqs <- list(fish.D, fish.S)
```

```
fish.ivs <- ~mon+tue+wed+thu+stormy
fish.sys <- systemfit(fish.eqs, method="2SLS",
              inst=fish.ivs, data=fultonfish)
summary(fish.sys)
```

```
##
## systemfit results
## method: 2SLS
##
##          N  DF SSR detRCov OLS-R2 McElroy-R2
## system 222 213 110   0.107  0.094     -0.598
##
##        N  DF  SSR   MSE  RMSE    R2 Adj R2
## eq1 111 105 52.1 0.496 0.704 0.139  0.098
## eq2 111 108 57.5 0.533 0.730 0.049  0.032
##
## The covariance matrix of the residuals
##       eq1   eq2
## eq1 0.496 0.396
## eq2 0.396 0.533
##
## The correlations of the residuals
##       eq1   eq2
## eq1 1.000 0.771
## eq2 0.771 1.000
##
##
## 2SLS estimates for 'eq1' (equation 1)
## Model Formula: lquan ~ lprice + mon + tue + wed + thu
## Instruments: ~mon + tue + wed + thu + stormy
##
##              Estimate Std. Error t value Pr(>|t|)
## (Intercept)    8.5059     0.1662   51.19   <2e-16 ***
## lprice        -1.1194     0.4286   -2.61    0.010 *
## mon           -0.0254     0.2148   -0.12    0.906
## tue           -0.5308     0.2080   -2.55    0.012 *
## wed           -0.5664     0.2128   -2.66    0.009 **
## thu            0.1093     0.2088    0.52    0.602
## ---
## Signif. codes:  0 '***' 0.001 '**' 0.01 '*' 0.05 '.' 0.1 ' ' 1
```

```
##
## Residual standard error: 0.704 on 105 degrees of freedom
## Number of observations: 111 Degrees of Freedom: 105
## SSR: 52.09 MSE: 0.496 Root MSE: 0.704
## Multiple R-Squared: 0.139 Adjusted R-Squared: 0.098
##
##
## 2SLS estimates for 'eq2' (equation 2)
## Model Formula: lquan ~ lprice + stormy
## Instruments: ~mon + tue + wed + thu + stormy
##
##              Estimate Std. Error t value Pr(>|t|)
## (Intercept)  8.62835   0.38897    22.18   <2e-16 ***
## lprice       0.00106   1.30955     0.00    1.00
## stormy      -0.36325   0.46491    -0.78    0.44
## ---
## Signif. codes:  0 '***' 0.001 '**' 0.01 '*' 0.05 '.' 0.1 ' ' 1
##
## Residual standard error: 0.73 on 108 degrees of freedom
## Number of observations: 111 Degrees of Freedom: 108
## SSR: 57.522 MSE: 0.533 Root MSE: 0.73
## Multiple R-Squared: 0.049 Adjusted R-Squared: 0.032
```

In the output of the 2SLS estimation, eq1 is the demand equation, and eq2 is the supply. As we have seen the demand equation is identified, i.e., reliable, while the supply equation is not. A solution might be to find better instruments, other than the weekdays for the demand equation. Finding valid instruments is, however, a difficult task in many problems.

Example 11.3 The *Klein* Macroeconomic Model

This model involves three equations: aggregate consumption, cn, investment, i, and wages in the private sector, w_1. The data come from the data set *klein*. The structural equations are

$$cn_t = \alpha_1 + \alpha_2(w_{1t} + w_{2t}) + \alpha_3 p_t + \alpha_4 p_{t-1} + e_{1t}$$

$$i_t = \beta_1 + \beta_2 p_t + \beta_3 p_{t-1} + \beta_4 k_{t-1} + e_2$$

$$w_{1t} = \gamma_1 + \gamma_2 E_t + \gamma_3 E_{t-1} + \gamma_4 time + e_{3t}$$

```
data(klein)
klein$Lp<-dplyr::lag(klein$p,1)
klein$Lk<-klein$klag
klein$Le<-dplyr::lag(klein$e,1)
```

Table 11.5: Estimated Structural Equations in the $Klein$ Problem

	Estimate	Std. Error	t value	Pr($>$|t|)
eq1_(Intercept)	15.9611	1.3105	12.1790	0.0000
eq1_I(w1 + w2)	0.8096	0.0403	20.0649	0.0000
eq1_p	0.1819	0.0916	1.9859	0.0634
eq1_Lp	0.0843	0.0910	0.9264	0.3672
eq2_(Intercept)	24.0347	11.3615	2.1154	0.0486
eq2_cn	0.3507	0.0861	4.0716	0.0007
eq2_Lk	-0.2080	0.0594	-3.5007	0.0026
eq3_(Intercept)	1.4342	1.2724	1.1272	0.2753
eq3_e	0.4403	0.0324	13.5770	0.0000
eq3_Le	0.1463	0.0374	3.9074	0.0011
eq3_time	0.1268	0.0321	3.9445	0.0010

```
klein<-klein[-1,]
CN<-cn~I(w1+w2)+p+Lp
I<-i~cn+Lk
W1<-w1~e+Le+time
streq<-list(CN,I,W1)
instr<- ~w2+p+e+Lp+Le+Lk
strSys<-systemfit(streq,inst=instr, method="2SLS",
                data=klein)
sSys<-summary(strSys)
kable(coef(sSys), digits=4, align="c", caption=
  "Estimated Structural Equations in the $Klein$ Problem")
```

Table 11.5 collects the estimated coefficients in the structural model of the *Klein* problem. The next code lines estimate the reduced-form equations, with the results shown in the table titled "Reduced Equations in the *Klein* Model."

```
CNr<-lm(cn~w2+p+e+Lp+Le+Lk+time, data=klein)
Ir <-lm(i~w2+p+e+Lp+Le+Lk+time, data=klein)
W1r<-lm(w1~w2+p+e+Lp+Le+Lk+time, data=klein)
tab<-rbind(tidy(CNr), tidy(Ir), tidy(W1r))

stargazer(CNr, Ir, W1r,
  title="Reduced Equations in the $Klein$ Model",
  header=FALSE,
  type=.stargazertype, # "html" or "latex" (in index.Rmd)
```

```
#keep.stat="n",   # what statistics to print
omit.table.layout="n",
star.cutoffs=NA,
digits=3,
intercept.bottom=FALSE, #moves the intercept coef to top
column.labels=c("Demand","Investment", "Wage"),
dep.var.labels.include = TRUE,
model.numbers = FALSE,
dep.var.caption="",
model.names=FALSE)
```

Table 11.6: Reduced Equations in the *Klein* Model

	cn Demand	i Investment	w1 Wage
Constant	10.460 (9.377)	−1.330 (11.310)	3.511 (12.220)
w2	0.655 (0.667)	−0.360 (0.804)	−0.857 (0.869)
p	0.526 (0.117)	0.244 (0.141)	−0.015 (0.152)
e	0.198 (0.069)	0.241 (0.083)	0.493 (0.090)
Lp	0.121 (0.139)	0.475 (0.167)	−0.029 (0.181)
Le	0.105 (0.073)	−0.255 (0.088)	0.095 (0.096)
Lk	0.057 (0.036)	−0.036 (0.043)	0.014 (0.047)
time	0.257 (0.208)	−0.039 (0.251)	0.372 (0.271)
Observations	21	21	21
R^2	0.995	0.974	0.990
Adjusted R^2	0.993	0.959	0.985
Residual Std. Error (df = 13)	0.593	0.715	0.773
F Statistic (df = 7; 13)	380.700	68.660	188.400

Chapter 12

Nonstationary Time Series

```
rm(list=ls()) #Removes all items in Environment!
options(digits=3)
library(tseries) # for ADF unit root tests
library(dynlm)
library(nlWaldTest) # for the `nlWaldtest()` function
library(lmtest) #for `coeftest()` and `bptest()`.
library(broom) #for `glance(`) and `tidy()`
library(POE5Rdata) #for POE5 datasets
library(car) #for `hccm()` robust standard errors
library(sandwich)
library(knitr) #for kable()
library(forecast)
library(stargazer)
library(dplyr)
.stargazertype <- "html"
if (knitr:::is_latex_output()) {.stargazertype <- "latex"}
```

New package: tseries (Trapletti and Hornik, 2016).

12.1 Stationary and Nonstationary Variables

A time series is nonstationary if its distribution, in particular its mean, variance, or timewise covariance change over time. Nonstationary time series cannot be used in regression models because they may create **spurious regression**, a false relationship due to, for instance, a

215

common trend in otherwise unrelated variables. Two or more nonstationary series can still be part of a regression model if they are **cointegrated**, that is, they are in a stationary relationship of some sort.

In this chapter, we are concerned with testing time series for nonstationarity and finding out how we can transform nonstationary time series such that we can still use them in regression analysis. Before examining the ways of identifying and treating nonstationarity, let us visualize some potentially nonstationary series.

Example 12.1 Visualizing U.S. Economic Time Series

The data set *gdp5* gives U.S. GDP over the period of 1984Q1 through 2016Q1; the data set *usdata* includes monthly data on the variables inflation, federal funds rate, and bond rate in the U.S. over the period of August, 1954, through December, 2016. The next code plots these variables and their changes to reveal their trends and to show how differencing eliminates their trends and reveals their short-term variation. Trends and apparent changes in volatility should raise suspicion about non-stationarity in a time series. Figure 12.1 shows the plots.

```
data(gdp5)
data(usdata5)
gdp<-ts(gdp5$gdp,start=c(1984,1),end=c(2016,4),frequency=4)
usa.ts <- ts(usdata5, start=c(1954,8), end=c(2016,12),
       frequency=12)
par(cex=1.4,mar=c(4,4,2,1),lwd=1.6)
ts.plot(gdp,xlab="(a) Real GDP ($trillion)", ylab="")
ts.plot(diff(gdp,1), xlab="(b) Change in GDP", ylab="")
ts.plot(usa.ts[,"infn"],xlab="(c) Inflation Rate", ylab="")
ts.plot(diff(usa.ts[,"infn"]),
        xlab="(d) Change in Inflation", ylab="")
ts.plot(usa.ts[,"ffr"],
        xlab="Federal Funds Rate in Percent", ylab="")
ts.plot(diff(usa.ts[,"ffr"]),
        xlab="(f) Change in Federal Funds", ylab="")
ts.plot(usa.ts[,"br"],
        xlab="(g) Three-Year Bond Rate, Percent", ylab="")
ts.plot(diff(usa.ts[,"br"]),
        xlab="Chang in the Bond Rate", ylab="")
```

After plotting a time series, inspecting the graphs and some summary statistics could reveal interesting patterns in the data. Table 12.1 presents the head of the *usdata5* file.

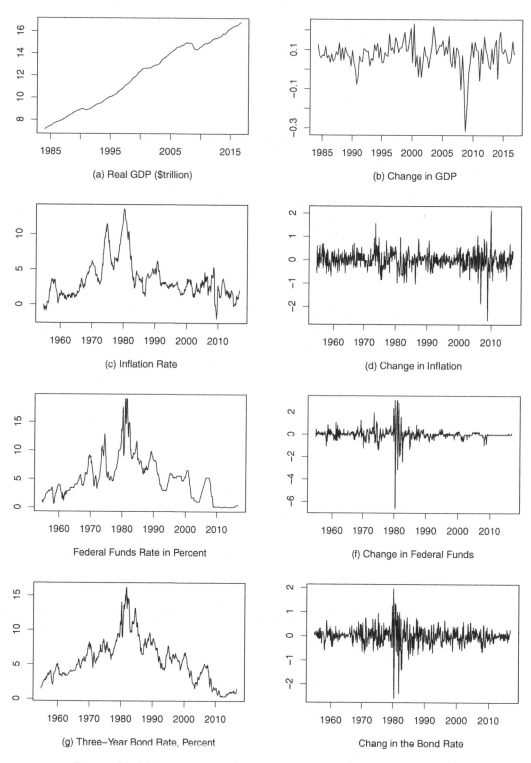

Figure 12.1 Various Time Series to Illustrate Nonstationarity

Table 12.1: Head of the *usdata5* Time Series Data

Bond Rate	Funds Rate	Inflation Rate
1.49	1.22	0.0000
1.60	1.06	-0.2980
1.72	0.85	-0.8571
1.75	0.83	-0.2610
1.81	1.28	-0.3729
1.99	1.39	-0.6330

```
usa.ts.df<-data.frame(b=usa.ts[,2],f=usa.ts[,3],inf=usa.ts[,4])
kable(head(usa.ts.df), align="c",
      col.names=c("Bond Rate","Funds Rate","Inflation Rate"),
      caption="Head of the $usdata5$ Time Series Data")
```

A symptom of nonstationarity is a significant difference in means between two periods. Using the function `window()`, The following code splits the *gdp5* and *usdata5* time series in two periods and calculates the partial means for these periods. The results suggest that the difference in means may be important.

```
mean(window(gdp, from=c(1984,2),end=c(2000,3)))
```

```
## [1] 9.521
```

```
mean(window(gdp, from=c(2000,4),end=c(2016,4)))
```

```
## [1] 12.06
```

```
mean(window(usa.ts[,"infn"], from=c(1954,8),end=c(1985,10)))
```

```
## [1] 4.416
```

```
mean(window(usa.ts[,"infn"], from=c(1985,11),end=c(2016,12)))
```

```
## [1] 3.506
```

The correlogram is another tool that can be used for studying the stationarity properties of a time series. Nonstationary series often display serial correlations for many lags. Let us draw the correlograms for the *gdp* and change in *gdp* series. Figure 12.2 shows these two correlograms, which appear to support our previous suspicion that the *gdp* series seems to entail a stronger nonstationarity problem than its change does.

```
par(cex=1.6, lwd=2)
Acf(gdp, main="", xlab="(a) GDP", ylab="")
```

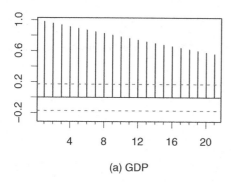 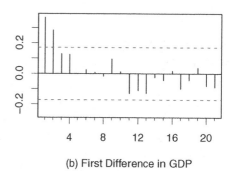

Figure 12.2 ACF Correlograms for the *gdp5* Data Set

```
Acf(diff(gdp), main="", xlab="(b) First Difference in GDP", ylab="")
```

12.2 Deterministic Trend

Nonstationary time series that become stationary after removing a deterministic (persistent) trend are said to be **trend stationary**. A linear trend term in a time series model is one that includes the time variable, as Equation (12.1) shows.

$$y_t = c_1 + c_2 t + u_t \tag{12.1}$$

Removing the trend from the variable y amounts to constructing a new variable, $\tilde{y}$, given by

$$\tilde{y}_t = y_t - (\hat{c}_1 + \hat{c}_2 t), \tag{12.2}$$

where $\hat{c}_1$ and $\hat{c}_2$ are estimated using Equation (12.1). When y ans x are both trend stationary, we can estimate their relationship simply by including the trend (time) term when regressing y on x.

$$y_t = \alpha_1 + \alpha_2 t + \beta x_t + e_t \tag{12.3}$$

The same method of a trend term can be applied in an ARDL model.

$$y_t = \alpha_1 + \alpha_2 t + \sum_{s=1}^{p} \theta_s y_{t-s} + \sum_{r=0}^{q} \delta_r x_{t-r} + e_t \qquad (12.4)$$

Besides the linear trend model, another possible model of a deterministic trend is the **constant percentage rate**,

$$y_t = y_{t-1} + a_2 y_{t-1},$$

or, in percentage,

$$100 \times \left(\frac{y_t - y_{t-1}}{y_{t-1}} \right) = 100 a_2$$

Since the percentage change in y is the difference in its logs, a model of constant percentage trend is

$$ln(y_t) = a_1 + a_2 t + u_t$$

Example 12.2 A Deterministic Trend for Wheat Yield

The file $toody5$ contains annual data on wheat yield in Toodyay Shire, from 1950 to 1997. The following code draws the wheat yield and rainfall variables along with their linear trend.

```
data(toody5)
yield<-ts(toody5$y, start=1950, end=1997,frequency=1)
rain<-ts(toody5$rain, start=1950, end=1997,frequency=1)
wheat<-ts.union(yield,rain)
par(cex=1.6,lwd=1.8,mar=c(3,4,3,2))
ts.plot(log(wheat[,1]),main="",
        ylab="Ln(Yield)",xlab=NULL)
abline(lm(log(wheat[,1])~time(wheat), data=wheat))
ts.plot(wheat[,2], main="",ylab="Rain",xlab=NULL)
abline(lm(wheat[,2]~time(wheat), data=wheat))
```

Assume a constant growth rate trend for yield, $ln(yield) = a_1 + a_2 t + u_t$, and decreasing returns to scale in the $rain$ factor. These assumption translate in the following model:

$$ln(yield_t) = a_1 + a_2 t + \beta_1 rain_t + \beta_2 rain_t^2 + e_t$$

The following code lines estimate this model on the assumption that all the series involved are trend stationary. Table 12.2 collects the results.

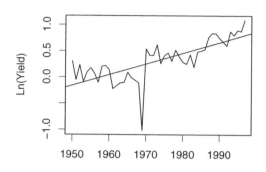 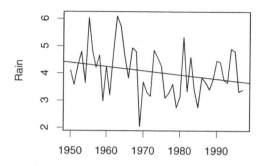

Figure 12.3 Wheat Yield Series and Trends

Table 12.2: Estimates of the $Ln(Yield)$ Equation

term	estimate	std.error	statistic	p.value
(Intercept)	-2.5101	0.5944	-4.223	0.0001
t	0.0197	0.0025	7.822	0.0000
rain	1.1490	0.2904	3.957	0.0003
I(rain^2)	-0.1344	0.0346	-3.883	0.0003

```
t<-1:NROW(toody5)
wheat<-dynlm(log(yield)~t+rain+I(rain^2))
kable(tidy(wheat),digits=4,align="c",
caption="Estimates of the $Ln(Yield)$ Equation")
```

The intercept in Table 12.2 is based on having the time origin at t=1; if we did not define the time origin (see the variable t in the above code), then the constant term in the estimated equation would have been different.

12.3 First-Order Autoregressive Model, AR(1)

Time series with a stochastic trend can be modeled with an autoregressive equation, AR(1). An AR(1) **stochastic process** is defined by Equation (12.5), where the error term is sometimes called "innovation" or "shock."

$$y_t = \rho y_{t-1} + \nu_t, \quad |\rho| < 1 \tag{12.5}$$

The AR(1) process is stationary if $|\rho| < 1$; when $\rho = 1$, the process is called **random walk**. The next code piece plots various AR(1) processes, with or without a constant, with or without trend (time as a term in the random process equation), with ρ less or equal to 1. The generic equation used to draw the diagrams is given in Equation (12.6). Figure 12.4 shows the results.

$$y_t = \alpha + \lambda t + \rho y_{t-1} + \nu_t \tag{12.6}$$

```
par(cex=1.4,mar=c(4,4,2,1),lwd=1.8)
N <- 500
a <- 1
l <- 0.01
rho <- 0.7
set.seed(246810)
v <- ts(rnorm(N,0,1))
y <- ts(rep(0,N))
for (t in 2:N){
  y[t]<- rho*y[t-1]+v[t]
}
plot(y,type='l', main="y[t]=rho*y[t-1]+v[t]",ylab="")
abline(h=0)
y <- ts(rep(0,N))
for (t in 2:N){
  y[t]<- a+rho*y[t-1]+v[t]
}
plot(y,type='l', main="y[t]=a+rho*y[t-1]+v[t]",ylab="")
abline(h=0)
y <- ts(rep(0,N))
for (t in 2:N){
  y[t]<- a+l*time(y)[t]+rho*y[t-1]+v[t]
}
plot(y,type='l', main=
    "y[t]=a+l*time(y)[t]+rho*y[t-1]+v[t]",
    ylab="")
abline(h=0)
y <- ts(rep(0,N))
for (t in 2:N){
  y[t]<- y[t-1]+v[t]
}
plot(y,type='l', main="y[t]=y[t-1]+v[t]",ylab="")
```

```
abline(h=0)
a <- 0.1
y <- ts(rep(0,N))
for (t in 2:N){
  y[t]<- a+y[t-1]+v[t]
}
plot(y,type='l', main="y[t]=a+y[t-1]+v[t]",ylab="")
abline(h=0)
y <- ts(rep(0,N))
for (t in 2:N){
  y[t]<- a+1*time(y)[t]+y[t-1]+v[t]
}
plot(y,type='l', main=
        "y[t]=a+1*time(y)[t]+y[t-1]+v[t]",ylab="")
abline(h=0)
```

12.4   Consequences of Stochastic Trends

Nonstationarity can lead to **spurious regression**, an apparent relationship between variables that are, in reality, not related.

Example 12.3 Two Random Walks

The following code sequence generates two independent random walk processes, y and x, and regresses y on x. The two time series and their scatter plot are shown in Figure 12.5.

```
T <- 1000
s<-300
set.seed(1357)
y <- ts(rep(0,T))
vy <- ts(rnorm(T))
for (t in 2:T){y[t] <- y[t-1]+vy[t]}

set.seed(4365)
x <- ts(rep(0,T))
vx <- ts(rnorm(T))
for (t in 2:T){x[t] <- x[t-1]+vx[t]}

x <- ts(x[s:T])
y <- ts(y[s:T])
```

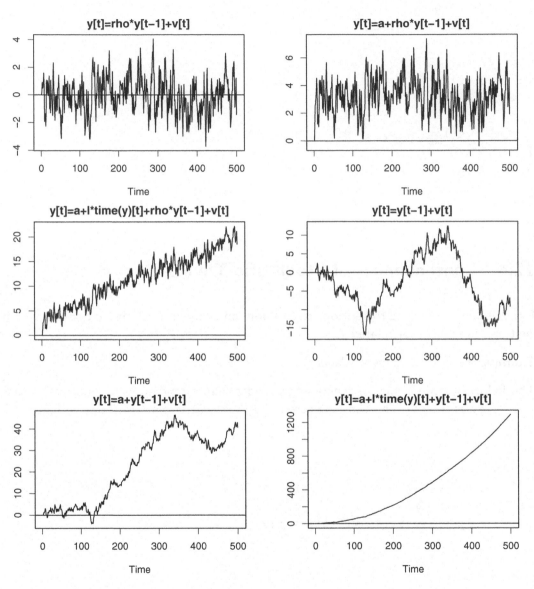

Figure 12.4 Artificially Generated AR(1) Processes with $rho = 0.7$

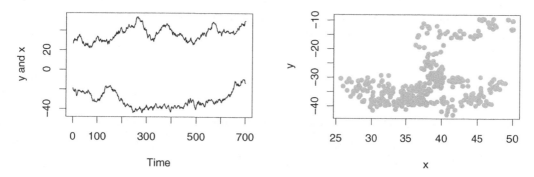

Figure 12.5 Artificially Generated Independent Random Variables

Table 12.3: Spurious Regression Results

term	estimate	std.error	statistic	p.value
(Intercept)	-53.338	2.614	-20.404	0
x	0.567	0.068	8.315	0

```
par(cex=1.6,mar=c(4,4,2,2))
ts.plot(y,x, ylab="y and x",lwd=1.6)
plot(x[s:T],y[s:T],col="darkgrey",
     xlab="x",ylab="y",pch=16,alpha=0.7)
```

It is difficult to asses, just examining the graphs, whether there is an apparent relationship between the two variables. Let us regress y on x and analyse the results.

```
spurious.ols <- lm(y~x, subset=s:T)
kable(tidy(spurious.ols), digits=3,
      caption="Spurious Regression Results")
```

The summary output of the regression, which is displayed in Table 12.3, shows a strong correlation between the two variables, though they have been generated independently. (Not any two randomly generated processes need to create spurious regression, though.)

12.5 Unit Root Tests for Stationarity

The Dickey-Fuller test for stationarity is based on an AR(1) process as defined in Equation (12.5); if our time series seems to display a constant and trend, the basic equation is the one in Equation (12.6). According to the Dickey-Fuller test, a time series is nonstationary when $\rho = 1$, which makes the AR(1) process a random walk. The null and alternative hypotheses of the test is given in Equation (12.7).

$$H_0 : |\rho| = 1, \quad H_A : |\rho| < 1 \tag{12.7}$$

The basic AR(1) equations mentioned above are transformed, for the purpose of the DF test, into Equation (12.8), with the transformed hypothesis shown in Equation (12.9). Rejecting the DF null hypothesis implies that our time series is stationary.

$$\Delta y_t = \alpha + \gamma y_{t-1} + \lambda t + \nu_t \tag{12.8}$$

$$H_0 : \gamma = 0, \quad H_A : \gamma < 0 \tag{12.9}$$

An augmented DF test includes several lags of the variable tested; the number of lags to include can be assessed by examining the correlogram of the variable. The DF test can be of three types: with no constant and no trend, with constant and no trend, and, finally, with constant and trend. It is important to specify which DF test we want because the critical values are different for the three different types of the test. One decides which test to perform by examining a time series plot of the variable and determine if an imaginary regression line would have an intercept and a slope.

Example 12.4 ADF Test with Intercept and No Trend

Let us apply the DF test to the *ffr* series in the *usdata5* data set.

```
par(cex=1.6,mar=c(4,4,1,2),lwd=1.6)
usa.ts <- ts(usdata5, start=c(1954,8), end=c(2016,12),
      frequency=12)
ts.plot(usa.ts[,"ffr"])
Acf(usa.ts[,"ffr"], main="")
```

The time series plot in Figure 12.6 indicates both intercept and trend for our series, while the correlogram suggests including 10 lags in the DF test equation. Suppose we choose $\alpha = 0.05$ for the DF test. The adf.test function does not require specifying whether the test should be conducted with constant or trend, and if no value for the number of lags is given (the argument for the number of lags is k), R will calculate a value for it. I would recommend always taking a look at the series' plot and correlogram.

```
adf.test(usa.ts[,"ffr"], k=10)
```

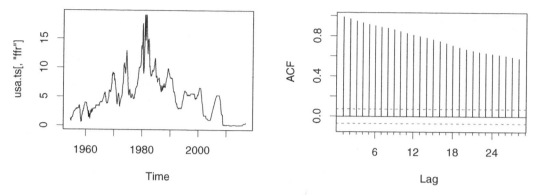

Figure 12.6 A Plot and Correlogram for Series ffr in Data Set $usdata5$

```
##
##   Augmented Dickey-Fuller Test
##
## data:  usa.ts[, "ffr"]
## Dickey-Fuller = -2.7, Lag order = 10, p-value = 0.3
## alternative hypothesis: stationary
```

The result of the test is a p-value greater than our chosen significance level of 0.05; therefore, we cannot reject the null hypothesis of nonstationarity.

```
par(cex=1.6,mar=c(4,4,1,2),lwd=1.6)
plot(usa.ts[,"br"])
Acf(usa.ts[,"br"], main="")
adf.test(usa.ts[,"br"], k=10)
```

```
##
##   Augmented Dickey-Fuller Test
##
## data:  usa.ts[, "br"]
## Dickey-Fuller = -2.1, Lag order = 10, p-value = 0.5
## alternative hypothesis: stationary
```

Here is a code to reproduce the results in the textbook. The results are collected in Tables 12.4 and 12.5.

```
f <- usa.ts[,"ffr"]
f.dyn <- dynlm(d(f)~L(f)+L(d(f))+L(d(f),2))
kable(tidy(f.dyn), digits=4, align='c',
      caption="Checking Federal Funds Rate for Stationarity")
```

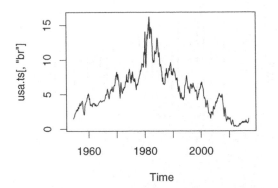 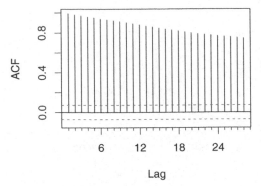

Figure 12.7 Plot and Correlogram for Series *br* in Data Set *usdata5*

Table 12.4: Checking Federal Funds Rate for Stationarity

term	estimate	std.error	statistic	p.value
(Intercept)	0.0580	0.0290	1.999	0.0460
L(f)	-0.0118	0.0048	-2.475	0.0135
L(d(f))	0.4443	0.0361	12.301	0.0000
L(d(f), 2)	-0.1471	0.0363	-4.050	0.0001

```
b <- usa.ts[,"br"]
b.dyn <- dynlm(d(b)~L(b)+L(d(b))+L(d(b),2))
kable(tidy(b.dyn), digits=4, align='c',
      caption="Checking Bond Rate for Stationarity")
```

Example 12.5 ADF Test with Intercept and Trend

We would like to test stationarity for the *gdp* series in the *gdp5* data set, for which we follow the same steps as before, beginning with a plot and correlogram of the series.

```
par(cex=1.4,mar=c(4,4,1,2),lwd=1.5)
data(gdp5)
```

Table 12.5: Checking Bond Rate for Stationarity

term	estimate	std.error	statistic	p.value
(Intercept)	0.0343	0.0235	1.459	0.1450
L(b)	-0.0064	0.0037	-1.695	0.0904
L(d(b))	0.4257	0.0356	11.946	0.0000
L(d(b), 2)	-0.2297	0.0358	-6.425	0.0000

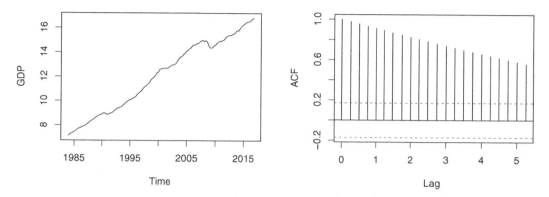

Figure 12.8 Plot and Correlogram of GDP

Table 12.6: GDP Model with Intercept and Trend

term	estimate	std.error	statistic	p.value
(Intercept)	0.266	0.114	2.329	0.021
trend(gdp)	0.010	0.005	1.970	0.051
L(gdp)	-0.033	0.017	-1.999	0.048
L(d(gdp, 1))	0.312	0.087	3.576	0.000
L(d(gdp), 2)	0.202	0.088	2.284	0.024

```
gdp<-ts(gdp5[,2], start=c(1984,1), end=c(2016,4),frequency=4)
ts.plot(gdp, ylab="GDP")
acf(gdp, main="")
```

Figure 12.8 indicates that the gdp series could be modeled with trend and intercept. The following code lines create such a model, where the time and intercept terms may differ from the textbook because R treats the trend variable differently. The slope estimates and their statistics, however, are the same.

```
gdp.ct<-dynlm(d(gdp)~trend(gdp)+L(gdp)+
              L(d(gdp,1))+L(d(gdp),2))
kable(tidy(gdp.ct), digits=3, align="c",caption=
       "GDP Model with Intercept and Trend")
```

Table 12.6 displays the results of the GDP model with intercept and trend, with the co-efficient of gdp_{t-1}, the "unit-root" term, coming out insignificant when compared to the Dickey-Fuller critical value, τ. The same conclusion of non-stationarity of the GDP series can be reached using R's adf.test function.

```
adf.test(gdp)
```

```
##
##   Augmented Dickey-Fuller Test
##
## data:   gdp
## Dickey-Fuller = -1.9, Lag order = 5, p-value = 0.6
## alternative hypothesis: stationary
```

12.6   Order of Integration

A concept that is closely related to stationarity is **order of integration**, which is how many times we need to difference a series until it becomes stationary. A series is **I(0)**, that is, integrated of order 0 if it is already stationary (it is stationary *in levels*, not in differences); a series is **I(1)** if it is nonstationary in levels, but stationary in its first differences.

```
par(cex=1.4,mar=c(4,4,1,2),lwd=1.5)
df <- diff(usa.ts.df$f)
plot(df, ylab="Difference in $ffr$")
Acf(df, main="")
adf.test(df, k=2)
```

```
##
##   Augmented Dickey-Fuller Test
##
## data:   df
## Dickey-Fuller = -15, Lag order = 2, p-value = 0.01
## alternative hypothesis: stationary
```

```
par(cex=1.4,mar=c(4,4,1,2),lwd=1.5)
db <- diff(usa.ts.df$b)
plot(db, ylab="Difference in $br$")
Acf(db, main="")
adf.test(db, k=1)
```

```
##
##   Augmented Dickey-Fuller Test
##
## data:   db
## Dickey-Fuller = -20, Lag order = 1, p-value = 0.01
## alternative hypothesis: stationary
```

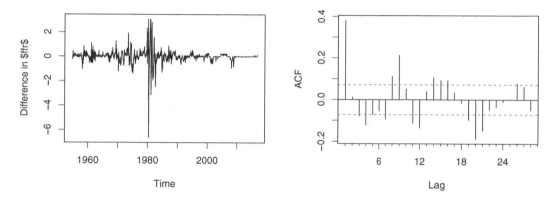

Figure 12.9 Plot and Correlogram for Series $diff(ffr)$ in Data Set $usdata5$

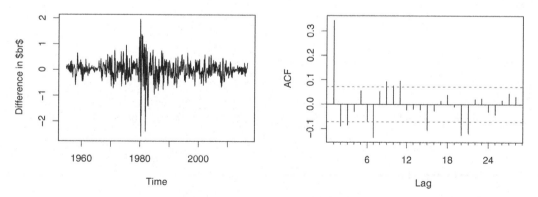

Figure 12.10 Plot and Correlogram for Series diff(br) in Data Set $usdata5$

Both the plots and the DF tests indicate that the *ffr* and *br* series are stationary in first differences, which makes each of them integrated of order 1. The next code sequence reproduces the results in the textbook. Please note the term (-1) in the dynlm command; it tells R that we do not want an intercept in our model. Figures 12.9 and 12.10 show plots of the differenced *ffr* and *br* series, respectively.

```
df.dyn <- dynlm(d(df)~L(df)+d(L(df))-1)
db.dyn <- dynlm(d(db)~L(db)+d(L(db))-1)
tidy(df.dyn)
```

```
##         term estimate std.error statistic   p.value
## 1    L(df)  -0.7148   0.04025    -17.76 4.189e-59
## 2 d(L(df))   0.1568   0.03621      4.33 1.692e-05
```

```
tidy(db.dyn)
```

```
##         term estimate std.error statistic   p.value
## 1    L(db)  -0.8105   0.04086   -19.837 1.272e-70
## 2 d(L(db))   0.2347   0.03565     6.582 8.751e-11
```

Function ndiffs() in the package forecast is a convenient way of determining the order of integration in a series. The arguments of this function are x, a time series, alpha, the significance level of the test (0.05 by default), test= one of "kpss", "adf", or "pp", which indicates the unit root test to be used (we have only studied the "adf" test), and max.d= maximum number of differences. The output of this function is an integer, which is the order of integration of the time series.

```
ndiffs(f)
```

```
## [1] 1
```

```
ndiffs(b)
```

```
## [1] 1
```

As we have already found, the orders of integration for both *ffr* and *br* are 1.

12.7   Cointegration

Two series are cointegrated when their trends are not too far apart and are in some sense similar. This vague statement, though, can be made precise by conducting a cointegration test, which tests whether the residuals from regressing one series on the other one are stationary. If they are, the series are cointegrated. Thus, a cointegration test is in fact a Dickey-Fuller stationarity test on residuals, and its null hypothesis is of noncointegration.

Table 12.7: Cointegration Test Between ffr and br

term	estimate	std.error	statistic	p.value
L(ehat.fb)	-0.0817	0.0148	-5.526	0
L(d(ehat.fb))	0.2234	0.0355	6.285	0
L(d(ehat.fb), 2)	-0.1770	0.0361	-4.905	0

In other words, we would like to reject the null hypothesis in a cointegration test, as we wanted in a stationarity test.

Let us apply this method to determine the state of cointegration between the series *ffr* and *br* in data set *usdata5*.

```
fb.dyn <- dynlm(b~f)
ehat.fb <- resid(fb.dyn)
output <- dynlm(d(ehat.fb)~L(ehat.fb)+L(d(ehat.fb))+
                L(d(ehat.fb),2)-1)
kable(tidy(output), digits=4,align="c",
  caption="Cointegration Test Between $ffr$ and $br$")

foo<-tidy(output)
```

The relevant statistic in Table 12.7 is $\tau = -5.526$, which is less than the absolute value of -3.37, the relevant critical value for the cointegration test. In conclusion, we reject the null hypothesis that the residuals have unit roots, therefore the series are cointegrated.

R has a special function to perform cointegration tests, function po.test in package tseries. (The name comes from the method it uses, which is called "Phillips-Ouliaris.") The main argument of the function is a matrix having in its first column the dependent variable of the cointegration equation and the independent variables in the other columns. Let me illustrate its application in the case of the same series *br* and *ffr*.

```
bfx <- as.matrix(cbind(b,f), demean=FALSE)
po.test(bfx)
```

```
##
##   Phillips-Ouliaris Cointegration Test
##
## data:  bfx
## Phillips-Ouliaris demeaned = -61, Truncation lag parameter = 7,
## p-value = 0.01
```

The PO test rejects the null of no cointegration, confirming our previous result.

12.8   The Error Correction Model

A relationship between cointegrated I(1) variables is a long run relationship, while a relationship between I(0) variables is a short run one. The short run error correction model combines, in some sense, short run and long run effects. Starting from an ARDL(1,1) model in Equation (12.10) and assuming that there is a steady state (long run) relationship between y and x, one can derive the **error correction** model in Equation (12.11), where more lagged differences of x may be necessary to eliminate autocorrelation.

$$y_t = \delta + \theta_1 y_{t-1} + \delta_0 x_t + \delta_1 x_{t-1} + \nu_t \tag{12.10}$$

$$\Delta y_t = -\alpha(y_{t-1} - \beta_1 - \beta_2 x_{t-1}) + \delta_0 \Delta x_t + \nu_t \tag{12.11}$$

Example 12.9 ECM for Federal Fund and Bond Rates

In the case of the US bonds and funds example, the error correction model can be constructed as in Equation (12.12).

$$\Delta b_t = -\alpha(b_{t-1} - \beta_1 - \beta_2 f_{t-1}) + \delta_0 \Delta f_t + \delta_1 \Delta f_{t-1} + \nu_t \tag{12.12}$$

The R function that estimates a nonlinear model such as the one in Equation (12.12) is nls, which requires three main arguments: a `formula`, which is the regression model to be estimated written using regular text mathematical operators, a `start=` list of guessed or otherwise approximated values of the estimated parameters to initiate a Gauss-Newton numerical optimization process, and `data=` a data frame, list, or environment data source. Please note that `data` cannot be a matrix.

In the next code sequence, the initial values of the parameters have been determined by estimating Equation (12.10) with b and f replacing y and x.

```
b.ols <- dynlm(L(b)~L(f))
b1ini <- coef(b.ols)[[1]]
b2ini <- coef(b.ols)[[2]]
d.ols <- dynlm(b~L(b)+f+L(f))
aini <- 1-coef(d.ols)[[2]]
d0ini <- coef(d.ols)[[3]]
d1ini <- coef(d.ols)[[4]]
Db <- diff(b)
Df <- diff(f)
Lb <- stats::lag(b,-1)
```

Table 12.8: Parameter Estimates in the Error Correction Model

term	estimate	std.error	statistic	p.value
a	0.0512	0.0117	4.377	0.0000
b1	1.3058	0.3627	3.600	0.0003
b2	0.8369	0.0595	14.070	0.0000
d0	0.3940	0.0238	16.553	0.0000
d1	-0.0757	0.0237	-3.199	0.0014

Table 12.9: Stationarity test Within the Error Correction Model

term	estimate	std.error	statistic	p.value
L(ehat, 1)	-0.0825	0.0148	-5.559	0
L(d(ehat), 1)	0.2244	0.0355	6.315	0
L(d(ehat), 2)	-0.1758	0.0361	-4.870	0

```
Lf <- stats::lag(f,-1)
LDf <- stats::lag(diff(f),-1)
bfset <- data.frame(ts.union(cbind(b,f,Lb,Lf,Db,Df,LDf)))
formula <- Db ~ -a*(Lb-b1-b2*Lf)+d0*Df+d1*LDf
bf.nls <- nls(formula, na.action=na.omit, data=bfset,
          start=list(a=aini, b1=b1ini, b2=b2ini,
                 d0=d0ini, d1=d1ini))
kable(tidy(bf.nls), caption=
  "Parameter Estimates in the Error Correction Model")
```

The error correction model can also be used to test the two series for cointegration. All we need to do is to test the errors of the correction part embedded in Equation (12.12) for stationarity. The estimated errors are given by Equation (12.13).

$$\hat{e}_{t-1} = b_{t-1} - \beta_1 - \beta_2 f_{t-1} \tag{12.13}$$

```
ehat <- bfset$Lb-coef(bf.nls)[[2]]-
  coef(bf.nls)[[3]]*bfset$Lf
ehat <- ts(ehat)
ehat.adf <- dynlm(d(ehat)~L(ehat,1)+
             L(d(ehat),1)+L(d(ehat),2)-1)
kable(tidy(ehat.adf), caption=
"Stationarity test Within the Error Correction Model")
```

```
foo <- tidy(ehat.adf)
```

To test for cointegration, one should compare the t-ratio of the lagged term shown as 'statistic' in Table 12.9, $\tau = -5.559$ to the critical value of -3.37. The result is to reject the null of no cointegration, which means the series are cointegrated.

In conclusion, the error correction model allows using both I(0) and I(1) series in the same equation if they are cointegrated.

12.9   Regression When There Is No Cointegration

We have established that non-stationary, but cointegrated I(1) series can coexist in the same regression model, but what if the series are I(1) but not cointegrated? The general answer is to transform the nonstationary variables into stationary ones. We have already done this in the case of trend-stationary variables by including a trend term in the regression. Now we look at **differencing** as a way of dealing with nonstationarity.

Example 12.10 Consumption Function in First Differences

The data in this example come from the data set *cons_inc* and cover the period of 1985Q1 to 2016Q3. First, let us draw the two series and show them in Figure 12.11.

```
data(cons_inc)
cons<-ts(cons_inc$cons, start=c(1959,3),
         end=c(2016,3), frequency=4)
incm<-ts(cons_inc$y, start=c(1959,3),
          end=c(2016,3),frequency=4)
cons<-window(cons,start=c(1985,1),end=c(2016,3))
incm<-window(incm,start=c(1985,1),end=c(2016,3))
par(cex=1.6,mar=c(4,4,1,2),lwd=1.5)
ts.plot(cons,ylab="Consumption",xlab=NULL)
ts.plot(incm, ylab="Disposable Income",xlab=NULL)
```

The plots show trends in both variables. Therefore, we include a trend in the Dickey-Fuller test equations.

```
dc<-dynlm(d(cons)~trend(cons)+L(cons)+d(L(cons)))
dy<-dynlm(d(incm)~trend(cons)+L(incm)+d(L(incm)))
stargazer(dc,dy,
  header=FALSE,
  title="Consumption and Income in Differences",
  type=.stargazertype,#"html" or "latex" (in index.Rmd)
```

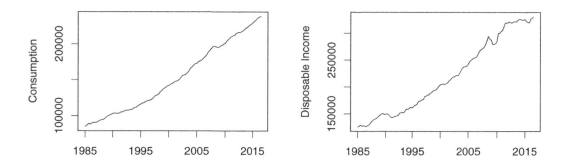

Figure 12.11 Consumption and Income in Levels

```
#  keep.stat="n",  # what statistics to print
   omit.table.layout="n",
   star.cutoffs=NA,
   report="vct*",
   digits=3,
#  single.row=TRUE,
   intercept.bottom=FALSE, #moves intercept to top
   column.labels=c("Consumption","Income"),
   dep.var.labels.include = TRUE,
   model.numbers = FALSE,
   dep.var.caption="Dependent variables: Differences",
   model.names=FALSE,
   star.char=NULL) #supresses the stars
```

The table titled "Consumption and Income in Differences" shows t-values that are within the acceptance interval, indicating that the null hypothesis of trend non-stationarity cannot be rejected. But are these two series cointegrated? A cointegration test regresses consumption on income and tests if the residuals of this regression are stationary. Since we have previously determined that the two series are not trend stationary, we include a trend term in the cointegration regression. For a time series y, the R function dynlm accepts three ways of including a trend term. First, the argument trend(y) constructs a time variable using the formula (1:N)/frequency(y). Second, trend(series, scale=TRUE) constructs a time index equal to 1:N. Finally, the argument time(y) uses the original time index.

```
cns<-dynlm(cons~trend(cons)+incm)
ehat<-residuals(cns)
dehat<-dynlm(d(ehat)~L(ehat)+L(d(ehat))-1)
```

Table 12.10: Consumption and Income in Differences

	Dependent variables: Differences	
	d(cons) Consumption	d(incm) Income
Constant	2,181.000 t = 2.638	5,271.000 t = 2.636
trend(cons)	139.900 t = 2.319	355.100 t = 2.404
L(cons)	−0.023 t = −1.989	
d(L(cons))	0.248 t = 2.854	
L(incm)		−0.045 t = −2.277
d(L(incm))		0.252 t = 2.912
Observations	125	125
R^2	0.174	0.108
Adjusted R^2	0.154	0.085
Residual Std. Error (df = 121)	796.500	2,549.000
F Statistic (df = 3; 121)	8.515	4.864

Table 12.11: Consumption – Income Cointegration Test

term	estimate	std.error	statistic	p.value
L(ehat)	-0.121	0.041	-2.930	0.004
L(d(ehat))	0.263	0.089	2.944	0.004

Table 12.12: Consumption–Income Equation in Differences

term	estimate	std.error	statistic	p.value
(Intercept)	772.471	129.013	5.988	0.000
d(incm)	0.056	0.028	2.027	0.045
L(d(cons))	0.292	0.086	3.419	0.001

```
tab<-tidy(dehat)
kable(tab, digits=3, align="c", caption=
    "Consumption -- Income Cointegration Test")
```

The results of our cointegration test are collected in Table 12.11, where the relevant statistic is $\tau = -2.93$. Comparing this with the critical value of $\tau_{0.05} = -3.42$, we conclude that we cannot reject the null hypothesis of non-cointegration.

Since the consumption and income series are neither trend stationary nor cointegrated, we shall regress consumption on income in first differences (you may test the first differences to find that they are stationary).

```
dcons<-dynlm(d(cons)~d(incm)+L(d(cons)))
kable(tidy(dcons), digits=3, align="c", caption=
    "Consumption--Income Equation in Differences")
```

Chapter 13

VEC and VAR Models

```
rm(list=ls()) #Removes all items in Environment!
library(tseries) # for `adf.test()`
library(dynlm) #for function `dynlm()`
library(vars) # for function `VAR()`
library(nlWaldTest) # for the `nlWaldtest()` function
library(lmtest) #for `coeftest()` and `bptest()`.
library(broom) #for `glance(`) and `tidy()`
library(POE5Rdata) #for POE5 data sets
library(car) #for `hccm()` robust standard errors
library(sandwich)
library(knitr) #for `kable()`
library(forecast)
```

New package: vars (Pfaff, 2013).

When there is no good reason to assume a one-way causal relationship between two time series variables we may think of their relationship as one of mutual interaction. The concept of "vector," as in vector error correction, refers to a number of series in such a model.

13.1 VEC and VAR Models

Equations (13.1) and (13.2) show a generic **vector autoregression** model of order 1, VAR(1), which can be estimated if the series are both I(0). If they are I(1) and not cointegrated, the same equations need to be estimated in first differences.

$$y_t = \beta_{10} + \beta_{11}y_{t-1} + \beta_{12}x_{t-1} + \nu_t^y \tag{13.1}$$

$$x_t = \beta_{20} + \beta_{21}y_{t-1} + \beta_{22}x_{t-1} + \nu_t^x \tag{13.2}$$

If the two variables in Equations (13.1) and (13.2) are cointegrated, their cointegration relationship should be taken into account in the model, since it is valuable information; such a model is called **vector error correction**. The cointegration relationship is, remember, as shown in Equation (13.3), where the error term has been proven to be stationary.

$$y_t = \beta_0 + \beta_1 x_t + e_t \tag{13.3}$$

13.2   Estimating a VEC Model

The simplest method is a two-step procedure. First, estimate the cointegrating relationship given in Equation (13.3) and create the lagged residual series $\hat{e}_{t-1} = y_{t-1} - b_0 - b_1 x_{t-1}$. Second, estimate Equations (13.4) and (13.5) by OLS.

$$\Delta y_t = \alpha_{10} + \alpha_{11} + \hat{e}_{t-1} + \nu_t^y \tag{13.4}$$

$$\Delta x_t = \alpha_{20} + \alpha_{21} + \hat{e}_{t-1} + \nu_t^x \tag{13.5}$$

Example 13.1 VEC Model for GDP

The following example uses the data set gdp, which includes GDP series for Australia and USA for the period 1970Q1 to 2000Q4. First, we plot the series and determine their order of integration.

```
data("gdp", package="POE5Rdata")
gdp <- ts(gdp, start=c(1970,1), end=c(2000,4),
          frequency=4)
par(cex=1.2,lwd=1.8)
ts.plot(gdp[,"usa"],gdp[,"aus"], type="l",
        lty=c(1,2), col=c(1,1))
legend("topleft", border=NULL,
       legend=c("Real GDP (USA)","Real GDP (AUS)"),
       lty=c(1,2), col=c(1,1))
```

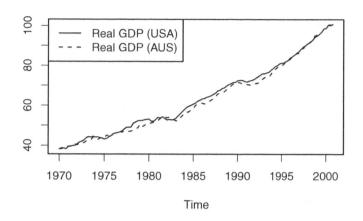

Figure 13.1 Australian and USA GDP Series from Dataset *gdp*

Figure 13.1 represents the two series in levels, revealing a common trend and, therefore, suggesting that the series are nonstationary.

```
adf.test(gdp[,"usa"])
```

```
##
##   Augmented Dickey-Fuller Test
##
## data:  gdp[, "usa"]
## Dickey-Fuller = -0.91, Lag order = 4, p-value = 0.9
## alternative hypothesis: stationary
```

```
adf.test(gdp[,"aus"])
```

```
##
##   Augmented Dickey-Fuller Test
##
## data:  gdp[, "aus"]
## Dickey-Fuller = -0.61, Lag order = 4, p-value = 1
## alternative hypothesis: stationary
```

```
adf.test(diff(gdp[,"usa"]))
```

```
##
##   Augmented Dickey-Fuller Test
```

Table 13.1: The Results of the Cointegration Equation

term	estimate	std.error	statistic	p.value
usa	0.985	0.002	594.8	0

```
##
## data:  diff(gdp[, "usa"])
## Dickey-Fuller = -4.3, Lag order = 4, p-value = 0.01
## alternative hypothesis: stationary

adf.test(diff(gdp[,"aus"]))
```

```
##
##   Augmented Dickey-Fuller Test
##
## data:  diff(gdp[, "aus"])
## Dickey-Fuller = -4.4, Lag order = 4, p-value = 0.01
## alternative hypothesis: stationary
```

The stationarity tests indicate that both series are I(1), Let us now test them for cointegration, using Equations (13.6) and (13.7).

$$aus_t = \beta_1 usa_t + e_t \qquad\qquad (13.6)$$

$$\hat{e}_t = aus_t - \beta_1 usa_t \qquad\qquad (13.7)$$

```
cint1.dyn <- dynlm(aus~usa-1, data=gdp)
kable(tidy(cint1.dyn), digits=3,
   caption="The Results of the Cointegration Equation")

ehat <- resid(cint1.dyn)
cint2.dyn <- dynlm(d(ehat)~L(ehat)-1)
tidy(cint2.dyn)
```

```
##       term estimate std.error statistic p.value
## 1 L(ehat)  -0.1279   0.04428    -2.889 0.00457
```

Our test rejects the null hypothesis of no cointegration (the critical value is -2.76), meaning that the series are cointegrated. Figure 13.2 shows the residuals in the cointegration equation.

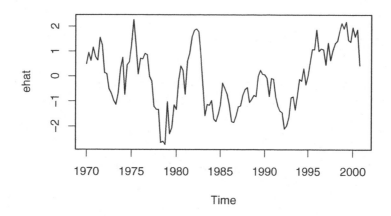

Figure 13.2 Residuals of the GDP Cointegrating Equation

```
par(cex=1.2,lwd=1.6)
plot(ehat)
```

With cointegrated series we can construct a VEC model to better understand the causal relationship between the two variables.

```
vecaus<- dynlm(d(aus)~L(ehat), data=gdp)
vecusa <- dynlm(d(usa)~L(ehat), data=gdp)
tidy(vecaus)
```

```
##            term estimate std.error statistic   p.value
## 1 (Intercept)   0.4917   0.05791      8.491 6.125e-14
## 2     L(ehat)  -0.0987   0.04752     -2.077 3.989e-02
```

```
tidy(vecusa)
```

```
##            term estimate std.error statistic   p.value
## 1 (Intercept)  0.50988   0.04668    10.9237 9.508e-20
## 2     L(ehat)  0.03025   0.03830     0.7898 4.312e-01
```

The coefficient on the error correction term ($\hat{e}_{t-1}$) is significant for Australia, suggesting that changes in the US economy do affect Australian economy; the error correction coefficient in the US equation is not statistically significant, suggesting that changes in Australia do not influence American economy. To interpret the sign of the error correction coefficient, one should remember that $\hat{e}_{t-1}$ measures the deviation of Australian economy from its cointegrating level of 0.985 of the US economy (see Equations (13.6) and (13.7) and the value of β_1 in Table 13.1).

13.3   Estimating a VAR Model

The VAR model can be used when the variables under study are I(1) but not cointegrated. The model is the one in Equations (13.1) and (13.2), but in differences, as specified in Equations (13.8) and (13.9).

$$\Delta y_t = \beta_{11}\Delta y_{t-1} + \beta_{12}\Delta x_{t-1} + \nu_t^{\Delta y} \tag{13.8}$$

$$\Delta x_t = \beta_{21}\Delta y_{t-1} + \beta_{22}\Delta x_{t-1} + \nu_t^{\Delta x} \tag{13.9}$$

Example 13.2 VAR Model for Consumption and Income

Let us look at the income-consumption relationship based on the $fred5$ dataset, where consumption and income are already in logs, and the period is 1986Q1 to 2015Q2. Figure 13.3 shows that the two series both have a trend.

```
data("fred5", package="POE5Rdata")
fred <- ts(fred5, start=c(1986,1),end=c(2015,2),
           frequency=4)
par(cex=1.1,lwd=1.6)
ts.plot(fred[,"consn"],fred[,"y"], type="l",
        lty=c(1,2), col=c(1,1))
legend("topleft", border=NULL,
       legend=c("Personal Consumption",
           "Personal Disposable Income"),
       lty=c(1,2), col=c(1,1))
```

Are the two series cointegrated?

```
par(cex=1.5,mar=c(4,4,1,2),lwd=1.6)
Acf(fred[,"consn"],main=NULL)
Acf(fred[,"y"],main=NULL)
adf.test(fred[,"consn"])
```

```
##
##   Augmented Dickey-Fuller Test
##
```

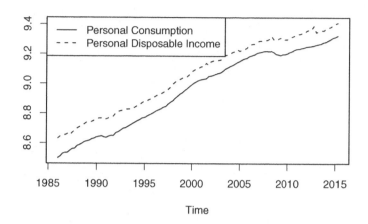

Figure 13.3 Logs of Income and Consumption, Data Set *Fred5*

```
## data:  fred[, "consn"]
## Dickey-Fuller = -1.5, Lag order = 4, p-value = 0.8
## alternative hypothesis: stationary
adf.test(fred[,"y"])
```

```
##
##   Augmented Dickey-Fuller Test
##
## data:  fred[, "y"]
## Dickey-Fuller = -0.54, Lag order = 4, p-value = 1
## alternative hypothesis: stationary
adf.test(diff(fred[,"consn"]))
```

```
##
##   Augmented Dickey-Fuller Test
##
## data:  diff(fred[, "consn"])
## Dickey-Fuller = -3.3, Lag order = 4, p-value = 0.07
## alternative hypothesis: stationary
adf.test(diff(fred[,"y"]))
```

```
##
```

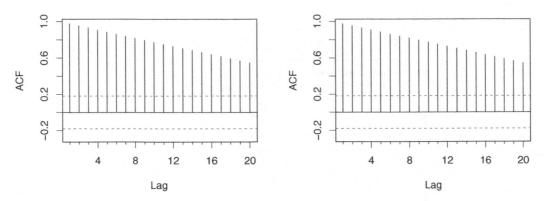

Figure 13.4 Correlograms for the Series c and y, Dataset $fred$

```
##   Augmented Dickey-Fuller Test
##
## data:  diff(fred[, "y"])
## Dickey-Fuller = -5, Lag order = 4, p-value = 0.01
## alternative hypothesis: stationary

cointcy <- dynlm(consn~y, data=fred5)
ehat <- resid(cointcy)
adf.test(ehat)
```

```
##
##   Augmented Dickey-Fuller Test
##
## data:  ehat
## Dickey-Fuller = -2.8, Lag order = 4, p-value = 0.2
## alternative hypothesis: stationary
```

Figure 13.4 shows a long serial correlation sequence; therefore, I will let R calculate the lag order in the ADF test. As the results of the above adf and cointegration tests show, the series are both I(1) but they fail the cointegration test (the series are not cointegrated.) (Please remember that the `adf.test` function uses a constant and trend in the test equation; therefore, the critical values are not the same as in the textbook.)

```
library(vars)
Dc <- diff(fred[,"consn"])
Dy <- diff(fred[,"y"])
varmat <- as.matrix(cbind(Dc,Dy))
varfit <- VAR(varmat) # `VAR()` from package `vars`+
summary(varfit)
```

```
##
## VAR Estimation Results:
## =========================
## Endogenous variables: Dc, Dy
## Deterministic variables: const
## Sample size: 116
## Log Likelihood: 856.789
## Roots of the characteristic polynomial:
## 0.452 0.395
## Call:
## VAR(y = varmat)
##
##
## Estimation results for equation Dc:
## ===================================
## Dc = Dc.l1 + Dy.l1 + const
##
##         Estimate Std. Error t value Pr(>|t|)
## Dc.l1 0.348192    0.086589    4.02    0.0001 ***
## Dy.l1 0.131345    0.052067    2.52    0.0130 *
## const 0.003671    0.000753    4.87   3.6e-06 ***
## ---
## Signif. codes:  0 '***' 0.001 '**' 0.01 '*' 0.05 '.' 0.1 ' ' 1
##
##
## Residual standard error: 0.00474 on 113 degrees of freedom
## Multiple R-Squared: 0.211,   Adjusted R-squared: 0.197
## F-statistic: 15.1 on 2 and 113 DF,  p-value: 1.55e-06
##
##
## Estimation results for equation Dy:
## ===================================
## Dy = Dc.l1 + Dy.l1 + const
##
##         Estimate Std. Error t value Pr(>|t|)
## Dc.l1   0.58954    0.14892    3.96   0.00013 ***
## Dy.l1  -0.29094    0.08955   -3.25   0.00153 **
## const   0.00438    0.00130    3.38   0.00098 ***
## ---
## Signif. codes:  0 '***' 0.001 '**' 0.01 '*' 0.05 '.' 0.1 ' ' 1
##
```

```
##
## Residual standard error: 0.00814 on 113 degrees of freedom
## Multiple R-Squared: 0.156,    Adjusted R-squared: 0.141
## F-statistic: 10.4 on 2 and 113 DF,   p-value: 0.0000712
##
##
##
## Covariance matrix of residuals:
##            Dc         Dy
## Dc 0.0000224 0.0000100
## Dy 0.0000100 0.0000663
##
## Correlation matrix of residuals:
##         Dc     Dy
## Dc 1.000 0.259
## Dy 0.259 1.000
```

Function VAR(), which is part of the package vars (Pfaff, 2013), accepts the following main arguments: y= a matrix containing the endogenous variables in the VAR model, p= the desired lag order (default is 1), and exogen= a matrix of exogenous variables. (VAR is a more powerful instrument than I imply here; please type ?VAR() for more information.)

The results of a VAR model are more useful in analyzing the time response to shocks in the variables, which is the topic of the next section.

13.4   Impulse Responses and Variance Decompositions

Impulse responses are best represented in graphs showing the responses of a VAR endogenous variable in time. Figure 13.5 shows the impulse response diagrams for the income-consumption example considered in the previous section.

```
impresp <- irf(varfit)

plot(impresp , plot.type="m", names="Cons",
     main="", mar=c(gap=0.4, 5.1, gap=0.4, 2.1),
     lwd=1.6)
```

The interpretation of Figure 13.5 is straightforward: an impulse (shock) to Dc at time zero has large effects the next period, but the effects become smaller and smaller as the time passes. The dotted lines show the 95% interval estimates of these effects. The VAR function prints the values corresponding to the impulse response graphs.

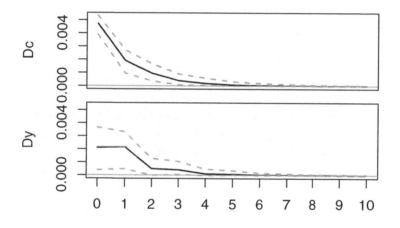

95 % Bootstrap CI, 100 runs

Figure 13.5 Impulse Response Diagrams for c and y, Data Set $fred5$

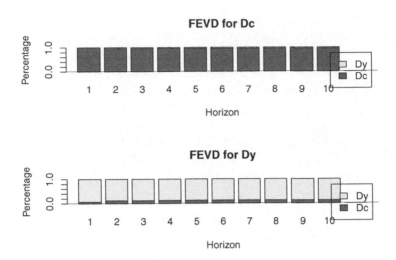

Figure 13.6 Forecast Variance Decomposition for the Series c and y

```
plot(fevd(varfit)) # `fevd()` is in package `vars`
```

Forecast variance decomposition estimates the contribution of a shock in each variable to the response in both variables. Figure 13.6 shows that almost 100 percent of the variance in Dc is caused by Dc itself, while only about 80 percent in the variance of Dy is caused by Dy and the rest is caused by Dc. The R function fevd() in package vars allows forecast variance decomposition.

Chapter 14

Time-Varying Volatility and ARCH Models

```
rm(list=ls()) #Removes all items in Environment!
library(rugarch) #for GARCH models
library(tseries) # for `adf.test()`
library(dynlm) #for function `dynlm()`
library(vars) # for function `VAR()`
library(nlWaldTest) # for the `nlWaldtest()` function
library(lmtest) #for `coeftest()` and `bptest()`.
library(broom) #for `glance(`) and `tidy()`
library(POE5Rdata) #for POE5 datasets
library(car) #for `hccm()` robust standard errors
library(sandwich)
library(knitr) #for `kable()`
library(forecast)
```

New package: rugarch (Ghalanos, 2015).

The **autoregressive conditional heteroskedasticity** (ARCH) model concerns time series with time-varying heteroskedasticity, where variance is conditional on the information existing at a given time.

14.1   The ARCH Model

The ARCH model assumes that the conditional mean of the error term in a time series model is constant (zero), unlike the nonstationary series we have discussed so far, but its conditional variance is not. Such a model can be described as in Equations (14.1), (14.2) and (14.3).

$$y_t = \beta_0 + e_t \tag{14.1}$$

$$e_t | I_{t-1} \sim N(0, h_t) \tag{14.2}$$

$$h_t = \alpha_0 + \alpha_1 e_{t-1}^2, \quad \alpha_0 > 0, \ 0 \le \alpha_1 < 1 \tag{14.3}$$

Equations (14.4) and (14.5) give both the test model and the hypotheses to **test for ARCH effects** in a time series, where the residuals $\hat{e}_t$ come from regressing the variable y_t on a constant, such as (14.1), or on a constant plus other regressors; the test shown in Equation (14.4) may include several lag terms, in which case the null hypothesis in Equation (14.5) would be that all of them are jointly insignificant.

$$\hat{e}_t^2 = \gamma_0 + \gamma_1 \hat{e}_{t-1}^2 + ... + \gamma_q e_{t-q}^2 + \nu_t \tag{14.4}$$

$$H_0 : \gamma_1 = ... = \gamma_q = 0 \quad H_A : \gamma_1 \ne 0 \text{ or } ...\gamma_q \ne 0 \tag{14.5}$$

The null hypothesis is that there are no ARCH effects. The test statistic is

$$(T - q)R^2 \sim \chi_{(1-\alpha, q)}^2$$

Example 14.1

Figure 14.1 displays time series plots for four stock price series in U.S., Australia, U.K., and Japan for the period 1988M1 to 2015M12. The plots show sharp changes and time-varying volatility.

```
data(returns5)
par(cex=1.5,mar=c(4,4,1,1))
ts.plot(returns5$nasdaq, ylab="nasdaq")
ts.plot(returns5$allords, ylab="allords")
ts.plot(returns5$ftse, ylab="ftse")
ts.plot(returns5$nikkei, ylab="nikkei")
```

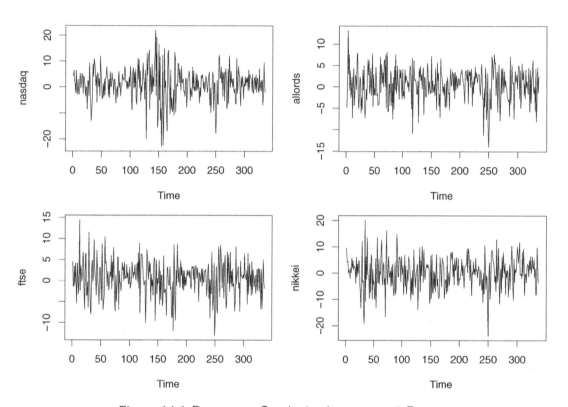

Figure 14.1 Returns to Stocks in the *returns*5 Dataset

Based on the same data, Figure 14.2 shows histograms of the four stock markets, with superimposed approximate unconditional distributions (dotted lines) and equivalent standard distributions (solid lines).

```
par(cex=1.5,mar=c(4,4,1,1),lwd=1.5)
hist(returns5$nasdaq, breaks=20,prob=TRUE,
    col="lightgrey",
    xlab="Nasdaq", main="")
curve(dnorm(x, mean=mean(returns5$nasdaq),
          sd=sd(returns5$nasdaq)), add=TRUE)
lines(density(returns5$nasdaq, adjust=2),
    col="blue", lwd=2, lty=5)
hist(returns5$allords, breaks=20,prob=TRUE,
    col="lightgrey",
    xlab="Allords", main="")
curve(dnorm(x, mean=mean(returns5$allords),
          sd=sd(returns5$allords)), add=TRUE)
lines(density(returns5$allords, adjust=2),
    col="blue", lwd=2, lty=5)
hist(returns5$ftse, breaks=20,prob=TRUE,
    col="lightgrey",
    xlab="Ftse", main="")
curve(dnorm(x, mean=mean(returns5$ftse),
          sd=sd(returns5$ftse)), add=TRUE)
lines(density(returns5$ftse, adjust=2),
    col="blue", lwd=2, lty=5)
hist(returns5$nikkei, breaks=20,prob=TRUE,
    col="lightgrey",
    xlab="Nikkei", main="")
curve(dnorm(x, mean=mean(returns5$nikkei),
          sd=sd(returns5$nikkei)), add=TRUE)
lines(density(returns5$nikkei, adjust=2),
    col="blue", lwd=2, lty=5)
```

Example 14.2 ARCH Simulation

This example simulates an ARCH process using Equations (14.1), (14.2), and (14.3), for different values of the parameters β_0, α_0, and α_1. First, let us construct a function, which I will name archSim, with the arguments N=number of desired observations, beta0, alpha0, and alpha1. The function starts with drawing a value for e_1 from a standard normal distribution.

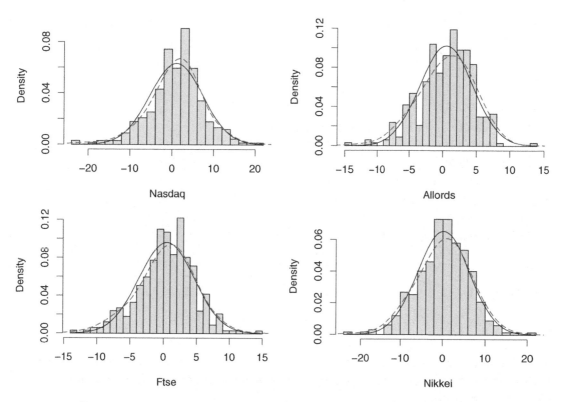

Figure 14.2 Histograms and Distributions for the *returns5* Dataset

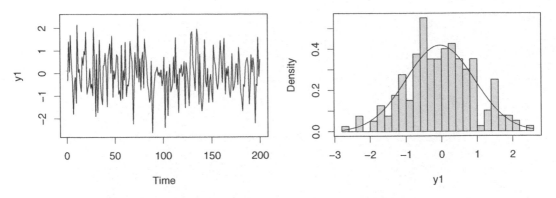

Figure 14.3 ARCH Simulation for $\beta_0 = 0$, $\alpha_0 = 1$, and $\alpha_1 = 0$

```
#    Function for ARCH Simulation
archSim<-function(N,beta0,alpha0,alpha1){
 u<-numeric(N)
 h<-numeric(N)
 set.seed(24689)
 u[1]<-rnorm(1,0,1)
 for(t in 2:200){
  h[t]<-alpha0+alpha1*u[t-1]^2
  u[t]<-rnorm(1,mean=0,sd=sqrt(h[t]))
  }
 y<-beta0+u
 return(y)
}
```

Here, I apply the newly constructed function, `archSim`, to simulate a constant-variance arch process. Figure 14.3 displays the result, which serves for comparison with the varying volatility graph in Figure 14.4.

```
par(cex=1.5,mar=c(4,4,1,1),lwd=1.5)
y1<-archSim(N=200,beta0=0,alpha0=1,alpha1=0)
ts.plot(y1)
hist(y1,breaks=20,prob=TRUE,main="",col="lightgrey")
box(bty="o")
curve(dnorm(x,mean=mean(y1),sd=sd(y1)),add=TRUE)
```

The next code plots a variable-variance time series. One can see that this distribution contains more observations in the tails than the one in Figure 14.3.

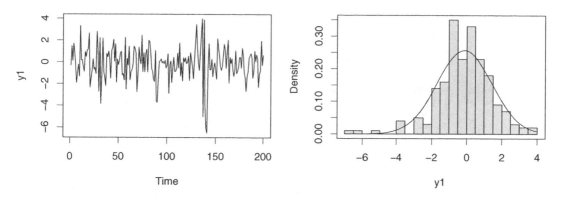

Figure 14.4 ARCH Simulation for $\beta_0 = 0$, $\alpha_0 = 1$, and $\alpha_1 = 0.8$

```
par(cex=1.5,mar=c(4,4,1,1),lwd=1.5)
y1<-archSim(N=200,beta0=0,alpha0=1,alpha1=0.8)
ts.plot(y1)
hist(y1,breaks=20,prob=TRUE,main="",col="lightgrey")
curve(dnorm(x,mean=mean(y1),sd=sd(y1)),add=TRUE)
box(bty="o")
```

Example 14.3 Testing for ARCH in BYD Lighting

The following example uses the dataset *byd*, which contains 500 generated observations on the returns to shares in BrightenYourDay Lighting. Figure 14.5 shows a time series plot of the data and histogram.

```
par(cex=1.5,mar=c(4,4,1,1),lwd=1.5)
data(byd)
rTS <- ts(byd$r)
plot.ts(rTS)
hist(rTS, main="", breaks=20, freq=FALSE,
     col="grey", xlab="Histogram of Returns of BYD Lighting")
box(bty="o")
```

Let us first perform, step by step, the ARCH test described in Equations (14.4) and (14.5), on the variable r from data set r.

```
byd.mean <- dynlm(rTS~1)
tidy(byd.mean)
```

```
##           term estimate std.error statistic  p.value
## 1 (Intercept)    1.078     0.053     20.35 1.833e-67
```

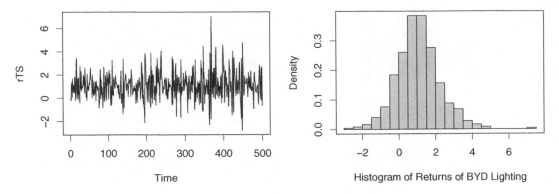

Figure 14.5 Level and Histogram of Variable *byd*

```
ehatsq <- ts(resid(byd.mean)^2)
byd.ARCH <- dynlm(ehatsq~L(ehatsq))
tidy(byd.ARCH)
```

```
##          term estimate std.error statistic   p.value
## 1 (Intercept)   0.9083   0.12440     7.301 1.141e-12
## 2   L(ehatsq)   0.3531   0.04198     8.410 4.387e-16
```

```
T <- nobs(byd.mean)
q <- length(coef(byd.ARCH))-1
Rsq <- glance(byd.ARCH)[[1]]
LM <- (T-q)*Rsq
alpha <- 0.05
Chicr <- qchisq(1-alpha, q)
```

The result is the LM statistic, equal to 62.16, which is to be compared to the critical chi-squared value with $\alpha = 0.05$ and $q = 1$ degrees of freedom; this value is $\chi^2_{(0.95,1)} = 3.84$; this indicates that the null hypothesis is rejected, concluding that the series has ARCH effects.

The function garch() in the tseries package becomes an ARCH model when used with the order= argument equal to c(0,1). This function can be used to estimate and plot the variance h_t defined in Equation (14.3), as shown in the following code and in Figure 14.6.

```
byd.arch <- garch(rTS,c(0,1), trace=FALSE)
sbydarch <- summary(byd.arch)
coef(byd.arch)
```

```
##      a0      a1
```

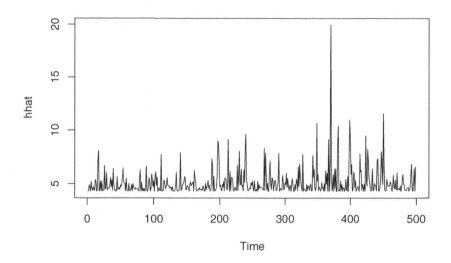

Figure 14.6 Estimated ARCH(1) Variance for the *byd* Data Set

```
## 2.1523 0.1592
```

```
hhat <- ts(2*byd.arch$fitted.values[-1,1]^2)
plot.ts(hhat)
```

14.2   The GARCH Model

GARCH(p,q), or Generalized ARCH(q), can be reduced to the form shown in Equation (14.6), where p is the number of lagged h terms and q is the number of e^2 terms.

$$h_t = \delta + \alpha_1 e_{t-1}^2 + \beta_1 h_{t-1} \tag{14.6}$$

Example 14.6 GARCH Model for the BYD Data Set

This example uses the R package rugarch (Ghalanos, 2015), which describes all the GARCH models in the accompanying documentation. The first (following) code sequence demonstrates the use of the ugarchspec (univariate GARCH specification) and garchFit functions with the sGARCH (standard GARCH) model, with the following notations:

- The estimated mean of the series is μ

- ARCH(q) parameters are α_1, α_2, ...
- GARCH(p) parameters are β_1, β_2, ...
- Variance parameter is ω (equivalent to δ in Equation (14.6))

```
# Using package `rugarch` for GARCH models
library(rugarch)
garchSpec <- ugarchspec(
          variance.model=list(model="sGARCH",
                                    garchOrder=c(1,1)),
          mean.model=list(armaOrder=c(0,0)),
          distribution.model="std")
garchFit <- ugarchfit(spec=garchSpec, data=rTS)
tidy(coef(garchFit))
```

```
## # A tibble: 5 x 2
##    names         x
##    <chr>      <dbl>
## 1 mu          1.05
## 2 omega       0.397
## 3 alpha1      0.495
## 4 beta1       0.241
## 5 shape     100.0
```

Figure 14.7 shows the (constant) mean and the variance of the return series given by the sGARCH model.

```
par(cex=1.5,mar=c(4,4,1,1),lwd=1.5)
rhat <- garchFit@fit$fitted.values
plot.ts(rhat)
hhat <- ts(garchFit@fit$sigma^2)
plot.ts(hhat)
```

The next code lines show the use of the family GARCH model (`fGARCH`), "Threshold" submodel, with the following notations:

- ARCH(q) parameters are α_1, α_2, ...
- Asymmetry1(q) (rotation) parameters are η_{11}, η_{12}, ...
- Asymmetry2 (q) (shift) parameters are η_{21}, η_{22}, ...
- Asymmetry Power parameter is δ

```
# tGARCH
garchMod <- ugarchspec(variance.model=list(model="fGARCH",
                            garchOrder=c(1,1),
                            submodel="TGARCH"),
```

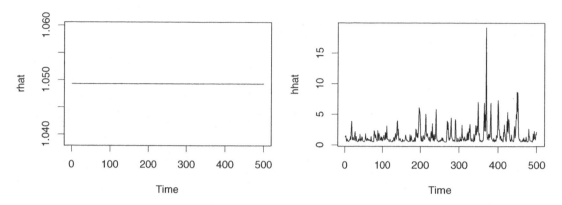

Figure 14.7 Standard GARCH Model (sGARCH) With Data Set *byd*

```
          mean.model=list(armaOrder=c(0,0)),
          distribution.model="std")
garchFit <- ugarchfit(spec=garchMod, data=rTS)
tidy(coef(garchFit))
```

```
## # A tibble: 6 x 2
##    names        x
##    <chr>    <dbl>
## 1 mu       0.987
## 2 omega    0.352
## 3 alpha1   0.391
## 4 beta1    0.375
## 5 eta11    0.339
## 6 shape  100.0
```

Figure 14.8 shows the (constant) mean and the variance of the return series given by the fGARCH model and TGARCH submodel.

```
par(cex=1.5,mar=c(4,4,1,1),lwd=1.5)
rhat <- garchFit@fit$fitted.values
plot.ts(rhat)
hhat <- ts(garchFit@fit$sigma^2)
plot.ts(hhat)
```

The next code and Figure 14.9 show the (constant) mean and the variance of the return series given by the fGARCH model and APARCH submodel.

```
# GARCH-in-mean
par(cex=1.5,mar=c(4,4,1,1),lwd=1.5)
```

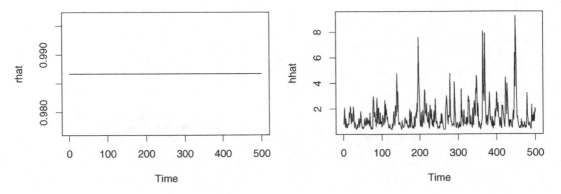

Figure 14.8 The fGARCH Model with Dataset *byd*

```
garchMod <- ugarchspec(
        variance.model=list(model="fGARCH",
                            garchOrder=c(1,1),
                            submodel="APARCH"),
        mean.model=list(armaOrder=c(0,0),
                        include.mean=TRUE,
                        archm=TRUE,
                        archpow=2
                        ),
        distribution.model="std"
                        )
garchFit <- ugarchfit(spec=garchMod, data=rTS)
tidy(coef(garchFit))
```

```
## # A tibble: 8 x 2
##    names        x
##    <chr>    <dbl>
## 1 mu       0.821
## 2 archm    0.193
## 3 omega    0.369
## 4 alpha1   0.443
## 5 beta1    0.287
## 6 eta11    0.186
## 7 lambda   1.90
## 8 shape  100.0
```

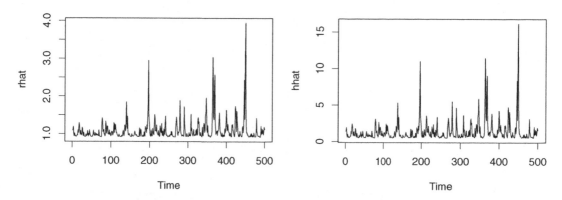

Figure 14.9 A Version of the GARCH-in-mean Model with Dataset *byd*

```
rhat <- garchFit@fit$fitted.values
plot.ts(rhat)
hhat <- ts(garchFit@fit$sigma^2)
plot.ts(hhat)
```

Predictions can be obtained using the function ugarchboot() from the package ugarch.

Chapter 15

Panel Data Models

```
rm(list=ls()) #Removes all items in Environment!
library(plm)
library(tseries) # for `adf.test()`
library(dynlm) #for function `dynlm()`
library(vars) # for function `VAR()`
library(nlWaldTest) # for the `nlWaldtest()` function
library(lmtest) #for `coeftest()` and `bptest()`.
library(broom) #for `glance(`) and `tidy()`
library(POE5Rdata) #for POE5Rdata data +sets
library(car) #for `hccm()` robust standard errors
library(sandwich)
library(knitr) #for `kable()`
library(forecast)
library(systemfit)
library(AER)
library(stargazer)
.stargazertype <- "html"
if (knitr:::is_latex_output()) {.stargazertype <- "latex"}
```

New package: plm (Croissant and Millo, 2015).

Panel data gathers information about several individuals (cross-sectional **units**) over several **periods**. The panel is **balanced** if all units are observed in all periods; if some units are missing in some periods, the panel is **unbalanced**. Equation (15.1) gives the form of a pooled panel data model, where the subscript $i = 1, ..., N$ denotes an individual (cross sectional unit), and $t = 1, ..., T$ denotes the time period, or longitudinal unit. The total number of observations in the panel is $N \times T$.

$$y_{it} = \beta_1 + \beta_2 x_{2it} + ... + \beta_K x_{Kit} + e_{it} \qquad (15.1)$$

15.1   Organizing the Data as a Panel

A **wide** panel has the cross-sectional dimension (N) much larger than the longitudinal dimension (T); when the opposite is true, we have a **long** panel. Normally, the same units are observed in all periods; when this is not the case and each period samples mostly other units, the result is not a proper panel data, but a **pooled cross-sections** model.

This manual uses the panel data package plm(), which also gives the possibility of organizing the data under the form of a panel. Panel data sets can be organized in mainly two forms: the **long** form has a column for each variable and a row for each individual-period; the **wide** form has a column for each variable-period and a row for each individual. Most panel data methods require the long form, but many data sources provide one wide-form table for each variable; assembling the data from different sources into a long form data frame is often not a trivial matter.

Example 15.1 A Microeconomic Panel

The next code sequence creates a panel structure for the data set *nls_panel* using the function pdata.frame of the plm package and displays a small part of this data set. Please note how the selection of the rows and columns to be displayed is done, using the compact operator $\%in\%$ and arrays such as c(1:6, 14:15). Table 15.1 shows this sample.

```
library(xtable)
data("nls_panel", package="POE5Rdata")
nlspd <- pdata.frame(nls_panel, index=c("id", "year"))
smpl <- nlspd[nlspd$id %in% c(1,2),c(1:6, 14:15)]
tbl <- xtable(smpl)
kable(tbl, digits=4, align="c",
      caption="A Data Sample")
```

Function pdim() extracts the dimensions of the panel data:

```
pdim(nlspd)
```

```
## Balanced Panel: n = 716, T = 5, N = 3580
```

Table 15.1: A Data Sample

	id	year	lwage	hours	age	educ	union	exper
1-82	1	82	1.808	38	30	12	1	7.667
1-83	1	83	1.863	38	31	12	1	8.583
1-85	1	85	1.789	38	33	12	1	10.180
1-87	1	87	1.847	40	35	12	1	12.180
1-88	1	88	1.856	40	37	12	1	13.622
2-82	2	82	1.281	48	36	17	0	7.577
2-83	2	83	1.516	43	37	17	0	8.385
2-85	2	85	1.930	35	39	17	0	10.385
2-87	2	87	1.919	42	41	17	1	12.039
2-88	2	88	2.201	42	43	17	1	13.211

15.2 The Panel Data Regression Function

Equation (15.2) shows the typical panel data regression model, where u_i is a time-invariant individual random error (unobserved heterogeneity), and e_{it} is an individual and time specific random error.

$$y_{it} = \beta_1 + \beta_2 x_{2it} + \alpha_1 w_{1i} + (u_i + e_{it}) = \beta_1 + \beta_2 x_{2it} + \alpha_1 w_{1i} + \nu_{it} \qquad (15.2)$$

Panel data models can be estimated in R using the plm() function, as the following code sequence illustrates.

```
wage.pooled <- plm(lwage~educ+exper+I(exper^2)+
  tenure+I(tenure^2)+black+south+union,
  model="pooling", data=nlspd)
kable(tidy(wage.pooled), digits=3,
        caption="Pooled Model")
```

The plm() function accepts the following main arguments, where the parameters shown as vectors c(...), such as effect and model can only take one value at a time out of the provided list.

```
plm(formula, data, subset, na.action, effect = c("individual", "time",
"twoways"), model = c("within", "random", "ht", "between", "pooling",
"fd"),...)
```

```
tbl <- tidy(coeftest(wage.pooled, vcov=vcovHC(wage.pooled,
                type="HC0",cluster="group")))
```

Table 15.2: Pooled Model

term	estimate	std.error	statistic	p.value
(Intercept)	0.477	0.056	8.487	0.000
educ	0.071	0.003	26.567	0.000
exper	0.056	0.009	6.470	0.000
I(exper^2)	-0.001	0.000	-3.176	0.002
tenure	0.015	0.004	3.394	0.001
I(tenure^2)	0.000	0.000	-1.886	0.059
black	-0.117	0.016	-7.426	0.000
south	-0.106	0.014	-7.465	0.000
union	0.132	0.015	8.839	0.000

Table 15.3: Pooled *wage* Model With Cluster Robust Standard Errors

term	estimate	std.error	statistic	p.value
(Intercept)	0.47660	0.08441	5.646	0.00000
educ	0.07145	0.00549	13.015	0.00000
exper	0.05569	0.01129	4.932	0.00000
I(exper^2)	-0.00115	0.00049	-2.334	0.01963
tenure	0.01496	0.00711	2.104	0.03545
I(tenure^2)	-0.00049	0.00041	-1.187	0.23532
black	-0.11671	0.02808	-4.156	0.00003
south	-0.10600	0.02701	-3.924	0.00009
union	0.13224	0.02703	4.893	0.00000

```
kable(tbl, digits=5, caption=
"Pooled $wage$ Model With Cluster Robust Standard Errors")
```

15.3 Fixed Effects Models

Fixed effects models address endogeneity situations, situations in which unobservable individual attributes are correlated with the independent variables.

Table 15.4: OLS Estimate of the *chemical* Production Function

term	estimate	std.error	statistic	p.value
(Intercept)	5.8745	0.2107	27.885	0
lcapital	0.2536	0.0354	7.155	0
llabor	0.4264	0.0577	7.391	0

The Difference Estimator: $T = 2$

Assume a panel data with only two time periods, $t = 1, 2$, and the following model, where individual attributes are correlated with the regressor x.

$$y_{it} = \beta_1 + \beta_2 x_{2it} + \alpha_1 w_{1i} + u_i + e_1 \qquad (15.3)$$

Taking differences between the two time periods, Equation (15.3) becomes

$$\Delta y_i = \beta_2 \Delta x_{i2} + \Delta e_i \qquad (15.4)$$

where the endogenous individual attributes have been dropped in the process of differencing but β_2, the parameter of interest, has been preserved. This estimator is called the **difference** estimator.

Example 15.2 The Difference Estimator for a Production Function

The data set is *chemical2* restricted to years 2005-2006, and the equation to be estimated is

$$ln(sales_{it}) = \beta_1 + \beta_2 ln(capital_{it}) + \beta_3 ln(labor_{it}) + u_i + e_{it} \qquad (15.5)$$

```
data(chemical2)
chem.two<-chemical2[chemical2$year%in%c(2005,2006),]
chem.ols<-lm(lsales~lcapital+llabor, data=chem.two)
kable(tidy(chem.ols), digits=4, align="c", caption=
  "OLS Estimate of the $chemical$ Production Function")
```

Table 15.4 shows the results of the OLS estimates of the model in Equation (15.5).

The next code lines estimate a difference model originating in the same model as in Equation (15.5). The safest way to run such a model is to use R's function plm in the plm package with the argument fd, which stands for *first differences*.

Table 15.5: Difference Estimate of the *chemical* Production Function

term	estimate	std.error	statistic	p.value
lcapital	0.0384	0.0507	0.7566	0.4502
llabor	0.3097	0.0755	4.1041	0.0001

```
data(chemical2)
chem2.pnl<-pdata.frame(chemical2,index=c("firm","year"))
smpl<-sample(chem2.pnl[chem2.pnl$year %in% c(2005,2006),1:5])
chem2.plm<-plm(lsales~lcapital+llabor-1, data=smpl, model="fd")
kable(tidy(chem2.plm), digits=4, align='c', caption=
"Difference Estimate of the $chemical$ Production Function")
```

Table 15.5 collects the results of the *difference* model.

15.3.1 The Within Estimator

The **within estimator** is similar to the difference estimator, except the difference is between a variable and its mean over all time periods. Its advantage over the difference estimator is, then, that it allows for more than two time periods. The relevant equation is

$$\tilde{y}_{it} = \beta_2 \tilde{x}_{2it} + \tilde{e}_{it} \tag{15.6}$$

where $\tilde{y}_{it} = y_{it} - \bar{y}_{i\cdot}$ and $\tilde{x}_{2it} = x_{2it} - \bar{x}_{2i\cdot}$.

Example 15.5 Within Transformation with $T = 3$

Consider the data set *chemical2* with sales data for years 2004-2006. The *within* model can be estimated using the `plm` function with the `model` argument set to "within."

```
data(chemical2)
dat.pnl<-pdata.frame(chemical2)
chem.wthn<-plm(lsales~lcapital+llabor,data=dat.pnl,
               model="within",effect="time")
tidy(chem.wthn)
```

```
##       term estimate std.error statistic  p.value
## 1 lcapital  0.08887   0.03321     2.676 7.753e-03
## 2    llabor  0.35224   0.05067     6.952 1.485e-11
```

Table 15.6: Fixed Effects Test: Ho:'No Individual Heterogeneity'

df1	df2	statistic	p.value	method	alternative
199	398	22.71	0	F test for time effects	significant effects

15.3.2 Least Squares Dummy Variable Model (Fixed Effects Model)

A **dummy variable** (or **fixed effects**) model includes a dummy variable for each individual in the panel. This model is equivalent to the *within* model discussed above. The *fixed effects* model requires testing for unobserved heterogeneity, or individual differences. The hypotheses to be tested are

H_0 : "All coefficients of the dummy variables are zero", and
H_A : "At least a coefficient of a dummy variable is not zero"

Example 15.6 Fixed Effects Estimator with $T = 3$

This example uses the same *chemical2* data set as before and the results of the estimate should be the same. In fact, the R code to estimate a *fixed effects* model is the same as for the *within* one.

Testing if fixed effects are necessary is to compare the fixed effects model chem.wthn with the pooled model chem.ols. The function pFtest() does this comparison, as in the following code lines.

```
data(chemical2)
dat.pnl<-pdata.frame(chemical2)
chem.wthn<-plm(lsales~lcapital+llabor,data=dat.pnl,
            model="within",effect="time")
chem.ols<-lm(lsales~lcapital+llabor,data=dat.pnl)
tst<- pFtest(chem.wthn, chem.ols)
kable(tidy(tst), caption=
        "Fixed Effects Test: Ho:'No Individual Heterogeneity'")
```

Table 15.6 shows that the null hypothesis of no fixed effects is rejected.

15.4 Panel Data Regression Error Assumptions

Example 15.7 Pooled OLS with Cluster-Robust Standard Errors

This example compares pooled OLS with and without cluster standard errors using the data set *chemical3*. Cluster standard errors should not be used without further research when N

Table 15.7: OLS and Pooled Estimates with Alternative Standard Errors

	Conventional	Heteroskedastic	ClusterRobust
(Intercept)	0.0828	0.0890	0.1423
lcapital	0.0153	0.0179	0.0273
llabor	0.0225	0.0257	0.0390

Table 15.8: Fixed Effects Estimates with Alternative Standard Errors

	Conventional	ClusterRobust
lcapital	0.0195	0.0273
llabor	0.0307	0.0458

is not large or when T is large.

```
data(chemical3)
chm3.ols<-lm(lsales~lcapital+llabor, data=chemical3)
Conventional<-sqrt(diag(vcov(chm3.ols)))
Heteroskedastic<-sqrt(diag(vcovHC(chm3.ols, type = "HC0")))
chm3.plm<-plm(lsales~lcapital+llabor,
           model="pooling", data=chemical3)
ClusterRobust<-sqrt(diag(vcovHC(chm3.plm, type = "HC0",
           cluster="time")))
tab<-data.frame(Conventional, Heteroskedastic, ClusterRobust)
kable(tab,digits=4, align='c', caption=
   "OLS and Pooled Estimates with Alternative Standard Errors")
```

Table 15.7 shows that the cluster-robust standard errors are greater than both OLS conventional and heteroskedasticity-robust ones.

Example 15.8 Fixed Effects with Cluster-Robust Standard Errors

```
dat.pnl<-pdata.frame(chemical3,index=c("firm","year"))
chem3.fe<-plm(lsales~lcapital+llabor,model="within",data=dat.pnl)
Conventional<-sqrt(diag(vcov(chem3.fe)))
ClusterRobust<-sqrt(diag(vcovHC(chem3.fe,type="HC0",
                              cluster="group")))
tab<-data.frame(Conventional, ClusterRobust)
kable(tab,digits=4, align='c', caption=
   "Fixed Effects Estimates with Alternative Standard Errors")
```

Table 15.8 compares the conventional standard errors to the cluster robust errors in a fixed effects model.

Table 15.9: Random Effects with Alternative Standard Errors

	Coefficients	FGLS	Cluster
(Intercept)	6.1718	0.1142	0.1427
lcapital	0.2393	0.0147	0.0221
llabor	0.4140	0.0220	0.0327

15.5 Random Effects

We have seen that the *fixed effects* model is appropriate when the unobserved heterogeneity term, u_i, is correlated with the independent variables; When this is not the case, we can use either OLS, or, when OLS is not precise enough, the **random effects** model.

Example 15.9 Random Effects Estimation of a Production Function

This example uses the data set *chemical3*. The same function we used for fixed effects can be used for random effects, but setting the argument model= to 'random' and selecting the random.method as one out of four possibilities: "swar" (default), "amemiya", "walhus", or "nerlove". Table 15.9 shows the coefficients of the random effects model and compares the FGLS to the cluster robust standard errors.

```
data(chemical3)
dat.pnl<-pdata.frame(chemical3,index=c("firm","year"))
chem3.rnd<-plm(lsales~lcapital+llabor,data=dat.pnl,model="random",
            ramdom.method="swar")
Coefficients<-coef(chem3.rnd)
FGLS<-sqrt(diag(vcov(chem3.rnd)))
Cluster<-sqrt(diag(vcovHC(chem3.rnd,type="HC0",cluster="group")))
tab<-data.frame(Coefficients,FGLS,Cluster)
kable(tab,digits=4,align='c',
    caption="Random Effects with Alternative Standard Errors")
```

Example 15.10 Random Effects of a *wage* Equation

```
data("nls_panel", package="POE5Rdata")
nlspd <- pdata.frame(nls_panel, index=c("id", "year"))
wage.within <- plm(lwage~exper+I(exper^2)+tenure+I(tenure^2)+
                south+union, data=nlspd, model="within")
wage.random <- plm(lwage~educ+exper+I(exper^2)+
                tenure+I(tenure^2)+black+south+union,
                data=nlspd, random.method="swar",
                model="random")
```

```
stargazer(wage.within,wage.random,
  header=FALSE,
  title="Fixed and Random Effects in the $wage$ Equation",
  type=.stargazertype, # "html" or "latex" (in index.Rmd)
  keep.stat="n",   # what statistics to print
  omit.table.layout="n",
  star.cutoffs=NA,
#  report="vct*",
  digits=4,
#  single.row=TRUE,
  intercept.bottom=FALSE, #moves the intercept coef to top
  column.labels=c("Fixed Effects","Random Effects"),
  dep.var.labels.include = TRUE,
  model.numbers = FALSE,
  dep.var.caption="Dependent variables: Log(wage)",
  model.names=FALSE,
  star.char=NULL) #supresses the stars
```

Testing for random effects amounts to testing the hypothesis that there are no differences among individuals, which implies that the individual-specific random variable has zero variance. Equation (15.7) shows the hypothesis to be tested.

$$H_0 : \sigma_u^2 = 0, \quad H_A : \sigma_u^2 > 0 \tag{15.7}$$

The random effects test function is $plmtest()$, which takes as its main argument the pooling model (indeed it extracts the residuals from the pooling object). The $effects$ argument should be set equal to "time" for testing random effects.

```
ChemReTest <- plmtest(chm3.plm, effect="time")
tab<-tidy(ChemReTest)[c(1,2,4)]
kable(tab, caption=
        "A Random Effects Test for the $chemical3$ Equation")
```

Table 15.11 shows that the null hypothesis of zero variance in individual-specific errors is rejected; therefore, heterogeneity among individuals may be significant.

15.5.1 Hausman Test for Endogeneity in Random Effects Model

Random effects estimator are reliable under the assumption that individual characteristics (heterogeneity) are exogenous, that is, they are independent with respect to the regressors

Table 15.10: Fixed and Random Effects in the *wage* Equation

| | Dependent variables: Log(wage) | |
| | lwage | |
	Fixed Effects	Random Effects
Constant		0.5339
		(0.0799)
educ		0.0733
		(0.0053)
exper	0.0411	0.0436
	(0.0066)	(0.0064)
I(exper^2)	−0.0004	−0.0006
	(0.0003)	(0.0003)
tenure	0.0139	0.0142
	(0.0033)	(0.0032)
I(tenure^2)	−0.0009	−0.0008
	(0.0002)	(0.0002)
black		−0.1167
		(0.0302)
south	−0.0163	−0.0818
	(0.0361)	(0.0224)
union	0.0637	0.0802
	(0.0143)	(0.0132)
Observations	3,580	3,580

Table 15.11: A Random Effects Test for the *chemical3* Equation

statistic	p.value	alternative
44.06	0	significant effects

Table 15.12: Hausman Endogeneity Test for the *chemical3* Model

statistic	p.value	parameter	method	alternative
98.82	0	2	Hausman Test	one model is inconsistent

in the random effects equation.

Example 15.12 Hausman Endogeneity Test in the *chemical3* Equation

The same Hausman test for endogeneity we have already used in another chapter can be used here as well, with the null hypothesis that individual random effects are exogenous. The test function `phtest()` compares the fixed effects and the random effects models. This example tests the *chemical3* random effects model for endogeneity; the null hypothesis is that there is no correlation between the unobserved heterogeneity term and any of the regressors.

```
data(chemical3)
dat.pnl<-pdata.frame(chemical3,index=c("firm","year"))
chem3.within<-plm(lsales~lcapital+llabor,model="within",data=dat.pnl)
chem3.random<-plm(lsales~lcapital+llabor,model="random",data=dat.pnl)
test<-phtest(chem3.within, chem3.random)
kable(tidy(test), digits=4, align='c',
caption="Hausman Endogeneity Test for the $chemical3$ Model")
```

The results of the test are collected in Table 15.12 and show that the test rejects the null hypothesis, indicating the presence of endogeneity in the model.

Example 15.13 Hausman Test in the *wage* Equation

The next code lines estimate the random effects model and performs the Hausman endogeneity test.

```
data(nls_panel)
nlspd <- pdata.frame(nls_panel, index=c("id", "year"))
wage.within<-plm(lwage~exper+I(exper^2)+tenure+I(tenure^2)+
                south+union, data=nlspd, model="within")
wage.random <- plm(lwage~educ+exper+I(exper^2)+
            tenure+I(tenure^2)+black+south+union,
            data=nlspd, random.method="swar", model="random")
test<-phtest(wage.within, wage.random)
kable(tidy(test), digits=4, align='c', caption=
 "Hausman Test for the Random Effects $wage$ Model")
```

Table 15.13 shows a low p-value of the test, which indicates that the null hypothesis saying

Table 15.13: Hausman Test for the Random Effects *wage* Model

statistic	p.value	parameter	method	alternative
20.73	0.0021	6	Hausman Test	one model is inconsistent

that the individual random effects are exogenous is rejected, which makes the random effects equation inconsistent. In this case the fixed effects model is the correct solution. (The number of parameters in Table 15.13 is given for the time-varying variables only.)

15.5.2 A Regression-Based Hausman Test

The regular Hausman test is based on homoskedasticity assumptions and can yield negative test statistics. These inconveniences can be overcome by the Mundlak version of the test, which is based on a regression model of the form

$$y_{it} = \delta_1 + \beta_2 x_{2it} + \alpha_1 w_{1i} + \gamma_2 \bar{x}_{2i} + (c_i + e_{it}) \tag{15.8}$$

where $\bar{x}_{2i}$ is the time average of the independent variable.

Example 15.14 The Mundlak Approach for the *chemical3* Model

```
library(dplyr)
data(chemical3)
dat.pnl<-pdata.frame(chemical3,index=c("firm","year"))

# Calculate time averages and merge them to data set
dat.pnl<-dat.pnl%>%
  group_by(firm)%>%
  summarize(lcapbar=mean(lcapital),
            llbar=mean(llabor))%>%
  left_join(dat.pnl,.,by="firm")

# Run the two regressions
formula<-lsales~lcapital+llabor+lcapbar+llbar
chem3.OLS<-plm(formula,
  model="pooling",data=dat.pnl)
chem3.RE<-plm(formula,
  model="random",effect="time",data=dat.pnl)

# Retrieve standard errors
```

Table 15.14: Mundlack Regressions for the *chemical3* Model

	coef.chem3.OLS.	Cluster.OLS	Conventional.RE	Cluster.RE
C	5.4553	0.14824	0.13713	0.14824
lcapital	0.1160	0.02732	0.01955	0.02732
llabor	0.2689	0.04577	0.03067	0.04577
lcapital bar	0.2223	0.04121	0.03338	0.04121
llabor bar	0.1095	0.06213	0.05010	0.06213
Mundlak test	NA	56.71820	96.99674	56.71820

```
Cluster.OLS<-sqrt(diag(vcovHC(
  chem3.OLS,type="HC0",cluster="time")))
Conventional.RE<-sqrt(diag(vcov(chem3.RE)))
Cluster.RE<-sqrt(diag(vcovHC(
  chem3.RE,type="HC0",cluster="time")))

# Perform the Mundlak test
H0<-c("lcapbar=0","llbar=0")
chi.OLS<-linearHypothesis(
  chem3.OLS,H0,vcov=vcovHC(chem3.RE,
    type="HC0",cluster="time"))[2,3]
chi.REconv<-linearHypothesis(chem3.RE,H0)[2,3]
chi.REclus<-linearHypothesis(
  chem3.RE,H0,vcov=vcovHC(chem3.RE,
  type="HC0",cluster="time"))[2,3]
Mundlak.test<-c(NA,chi.OLS,chi.REconv,chi.REclus)

# Collect and print the results
tab<-data.frame(coef(chem3.OLS),
    Cluster.OLS, Conventional.RE, Cluster.RE)
tab<-rbind(tab,Mundlak.test)
row.names(tab)<-c("C","lcapital","llabor",
  "lcapital bar", "llabor bar", "Mundlak test")
kable(tab, digits=5, align='c', caption=
 "Mundlack Regressions for the $chemical3$ Model")
```

Table 15.14 shows the results of the Mundlak approach to endogeneity test for the production function model.

Table 15.15: Hausman-Taylor Estimates for the *wage* Equation

term	estimate	std.error	statistic	p.value
(Intercept)	-0.48189	0.34457	-1.399	0.16195
educ	0.15191	0.02729	5.565	0.00000
exper	0.03658	0.00858	4.264	0.00002
I(exper^2)	-0.00033	0.00036	-0.917	0.35912
tenure	0.01572	0.00389	4.037	0.00005
I(tenure^2)	-0.00077	0.00024	-3.185	0.00145
black	-0.04164	0.03782	-1.101	0.27086
south	-0.07384	0.04412	-1.674	0.09417
union	0.09615	0.01562	6.157	0.00000

15.5.3 The Hausman–Taylor Estimator

While the fixed effects model solves the problem of correlation between the error term and the regressors, it does not allow time-invariant variables such as *educ* or *black* in the *wage* equation. Since the problem of the random effects model is endogeneity, one can use instrumental variables methods when time-invariant regressors must be in the model.

The *Hausman-Taylor* estimator uses instrumental variables in a random effects model; it assumes four categories of regressors: time-varying exogenous, time-varying endogenous, time-invariant exogenous, and time-invariant endogenous. The number of time-varying variables must be at least equal to the number of time-invariant ones. In our *wage* model, suppose *exper*, *tenure* and *union* are time-varying exogenous, *south* is time-varying endogenous, *black* is time-invariant exogenous, and *educ* is time-invariant endogenous. The same plm() function allows carrying out Hausman-Taylor estimation by setting model= "ht".

Let us use this method for the *wage* equation, using the *nls_panel* data set.

```
wage.HT <- plm(lwage~educ+exper+I(exper^2)+
    tenure+I(tenure^2)+black+south+union |
    exper+I(exper^2)+tenure+I(tenure^2)+union+black,
    data=nlspd, model="ht")
kable(tidy(wage.HT), digits=5, caption=
    "Hausman-Taylor Estimates for the $wage$ Equation")
```

Table 15.15 shows the results of the Hausman-Taylor estimation, with the largest changes taking place for *educ* and *black*.

Chapter 16

Qualitative and LDV Models

```
rm(list=ls()) #Removes all items in Environment!
library(nlWaldTest) # for the `nlWaldtest()` function
library(lmtest) #for `coeftest()` and `bptest()`.
library(broom) #for `glance(`) and `tidy()`
library(POE5Rdata) #for PoE4 datasets
library(car) #for `hccm()` robust standard errors
library(sandwich)
library(knitr) #for `kable()`
library(forecast)
library(AER)
library(xtable)
library(stargazer)
library(MCMCpack)
.stargazertype <- "html"
if (knitr:::is_latex_output()) {
  .stargazertype <- "latex"}
```

16.1 The Linear Probability Model

Suppose the response variable is binary, such that $y_i = 1$ if individual i chooses to buy a house and $y_i = 0$ if individual i chooses not to buy. The linear probability model has the general form shown in Equation (16.1), where $E(y_i|\mathbf{x}_i)$ gives the probability that the response variable, y_i, is equal to 1; therefore, a predicted value of y is a prediction for the probability that $y = 1$.

Table 16.1: Linear Probability Model for the $auto$ Problem

term	estimate	std.error	statistic	p.value
(Intercept)	0.4848	0.0714	6.785	0
dtime	0.0703	0.0129	5.467	0

$$p(\mathbf{x}_i) = E(y_i|\mathbf{x}_i) + e = \beta_1 + \beta_2 x_{i2} + \ldots + \beta_K x_{iK} \tag{16.1}$$

Example 16.2 Linear Probability Model: The $auto$ Equation

In the data set *transportation*, $auto = 1$ if an individual drives to work, and $auto = 0$ if the individual rides the bus. The explanatory variable is the difference in travel time between traveling by car and traveling by bus.

```
data(transport)
auto.ols<-lm(auto~dtime,data=transport)
kable(tidy(auto.ols), digits=4,align='c', caption=
  "Linear Probability Model for the $auto$ Problem")
```

The results in Table 16.1 show that an increase in the time difference by 10 minutes increases the probability of choosing $auto$ by 0.07.

16.2   The Probit Model

The **probit** model assumes a nonlinear relationship between the response variable and regressors, this relationship being the cumulative distribution function of the normal distribution (see Equation (16.2) and Figure 16.1, left).

$$p = P[y = 1] = E(y|x) = \Phi(\beta_1 + \beta_2 x) \tag{16.2}$$

The slope of the regression curve is not constant, but is given by the standard normal density function (Figure 16.1, right); the slope can be calculated using Equation (16.3).

$$\frac{dp}{dx} = \phi(\beta_1 + \beta_2 x)\beta_2 \tag{16.3}$$

Predictions of the probability that $y = 1$ are given by Equation (16.4).

$$\hat{p} = \Phi(\hat{\beta}_1 + \hat{\beta}_2 x) \tag{16.4}$$

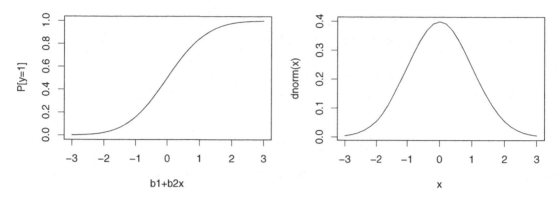

Figure 16.1 The Shape of the Probit Function

Table 16.2: The *auto* Problem, Estimated by Probit

term	estimate	std.error	statistic	p.value
(Intercept)	-0.0644	0.4007	-0.1608	0.8722
dtime	0.3000	0.1029	2.9154	0.0036

```
par(cex=1.5,mar=c(4,4,1,1),lwd=1.5)
x <- seq(-3,3, .2)
plot(x, pnorm(x), type="l", xlab="b1+b2x", ylab="P[y=1]")
plot(x, dnorm(x), type="l")
```

Example 16.4 Probit Model for the *auto* Problem

The R function to estimate a probit model is glm, with the family argument equal to binomial(link="probit"). The glm function has the following general structure:

glm(formula, family, data, ...)

```
data("transport", package="POE5Rdata")
auto.probit <- glm(auto~dtime, family=binomial(link="probit"),
                   data=transport)
kable(tidy(auto.probit), digits=4, align='c', caption=
        "The $auto$ Problem, Estimated by Probit")
```

Equation (16.3) can be used to calculate partial effects of an increase in *dtime* by one unit (10 minutes). The following code lines calculate this effect at $dtime = 0, 2,$ and 3 (time difference of 0, 20, and 30 minutes).

```
xdtime <- data.frame(dtime=c(0,2,3))
predLinear <- predict(auto.probit, xdtime,
            data=transport, type="link")
DpDdtime <- coef(auto.probit)[[2]]*dnorm(predLinear)
DpDdtime
```

```
##       1       2       3
## 0.11943 0.10369 0.08442
```

Predictions can be calculated using the function `predict`, which has the following general form:

> predict(object, newdata = NULL, type = c("link", "response", "terms"), se.fit
> = FALSE, dispersion = NULL, terms = NULL, na.action = na.pass, ...)

The optional argument `newdata` must be a data frame containing the new values of the regressors for which the prediction is desired; if missing, prediction is calculated for all observations in the sample.

Here is how to calculate the predicted probability of choosing *auto* when the time difference is of 0, 20, and 30 minutes ($dtime = 3$):

```
xdtime <- data.frame(dtime=c(0,2,3))
predProbit <- predict(auto.probit, xdtime,
            data=transport, type="response")
predProbit
```

```
##      1      2      3
## 0.4743 0.7039 0.7983
```

The marginal effect at the average predicted value can be determined as follows:

```
avgPredLinear <- predict(auto.probit, type="link")
avgPred <- mean(dnorm(avgPredLinear))
AME <- avgPred*coef(auto.probit)[[2]]
AME
```

```
## [1] 0.04841
```

16.3   The Logit Model for Binary Choice

This is very similar to the *probit* model, with the difference that **logit** uses the logistic function Λ to link the linear expression $\beta_1 + \beta_2 x$ to the probability that the response

Table 16.3: Logit Estimates for the *coke* Problem

term	estimate	std.error	statistic	p.value
(Intercept)	1.9230	0.3258	5.902	0.00000
pratio	-1.9957	0.3146	-6.344	0.00000
disp_coke	0.3516	0.1585	2.218	0.02657
disp_pepsi	-0.7310	0.1678	-4.356	0.00001

variable is equal to 1. Equations (16.5) and (16.6) give the defining expressions of the *logit* model (the two expressions are equivalent).

$$p = \Lambda(\beta_1 + \beta_2 x) = \frac{1}{1 + exp(-(\beta_1 + \beta_2 x))} \tag{16.5}$$

$$p = \frac{exp(\beta_1 + \beta_2 x)}{1 + exp(\beta_1 + \beta_2 x)} \tag{16.6}$$

Equation (16.7) gives the marginal effect of a change in the regressor x_k on the probability that $y = 1$.

$$\frac{\partial p}{\partial x_k} = \beta_k \Lambda(1 - \Lambda) \tag{16.7}$$

Example 16.6 Logit Estimates for the *coke* Problem

The data set *coke* collects data on the choices of either coke or pepsi by 1140 individuals, as well as whether coke or pepsi was on display at the time of choice.

```
data("coke", package="POE5Rdata")
coke.logit <- glm(coke~pratio+disp_coke+disp_pepsi,
            data=coke, family=binomial(link="logit"))
kable(tidy(coke.logit), digits=5, align="c",
      caption="Logit Estimates for the $coke$ Problem")
```

Table 16.3 shows the results of the logit model; the table titled "Three Binary Choice Models for the *coke* Problem" shows the LPM, probit, and logit estimates side by side.

```
coke.LPM <- lm(coke~pratio+disp_coke+disp_pepsi,
            data=coke)
coke.probit <- glm(coke~pratio+disp_coke+disp_pepsi,
            data=coke, family=binomial(link="probit"))
stargazer(coke.LPM, coke.probit, coke.logit,
```

```
header=FALSE,
title="Three Binary Choice Models for the $coke$ Problem",
type=.stargazertype,
keep.stat="n",digits=4, single.row=FALSE,
intercept.bottom=FALSE,
model.names=FALSE,
column.labels=c("LPM","probit","logit"),
omit.table.layout="n")
```

Table 16.4: Three Binary Choice Models for the *coke* Problem

	Dependent variable:		
		coke	
	LPM	probit	logit
	(1)	(2)	(3)
Constant	0.8902***	1.1080***	1.9230***
	(0.0655)	(0.1925)	(0.3258)
pratio	−0.4009***	−1.1459***	−1.9957***
	(0.0613)	(0.1839)	(0.3146)
disp_coke	0.0772**	0.2172**	0.3516**
	(0.0344)	(0.0962)	(0.1585)
disp_pepsi	−0.1657***	−0.4473***	−0.7310***
	(0.0356)	(0.1010)	(0.1678)
Observations	1,140	1,140	1,140

Prediction and marginal effects for the *logit* model can be determined using the same predict function as for the *probit* model, and Equation (16.7) for marginal effects. In the following code fragment, the function table counts and compares the true and predicted outcomes.

```
tble <- data.frame(table(true=coke$coke,
            predicted=round(fitted(coke.logit))))
kable(tble, align='c', caption="Accuracy of the Logit Model")
```

Table 16.5 shows that true and predicted results coincide in 754 cases out of the total of

Table 16.5: Accuracy of the Logit Model

true	predicted	Freq
0	0	507
1	0	263
0	1	123
1	1	247

1140. The choices of 0 or 1 have been determined by rounding the predicted probabilities yielded by the *logit* model.

The usual functions for hypothesis testing such as anova, coeftest, waldtest and linearHypothesis are available for these models as well.

```
Hnull <- "disp_coke+disp_pepsi=0"
linearHypothesis(coke.logit, Hnull)
```

```
## Linear hypothesis test
##
## Hypothesis:
## disp_coke  + disp_pepsi = 0
##
## Model 1: restricted model
## Model 2: coke ~ pratio + disp_coke + disp_pepsi
##
##   Res.Df Df Chisq Pr(>Chisq)
## 1    1137
## 2    1136  1  5.61      0.018 *
## ---
## Signif. codes:  0 '***' 0.001 '**' 0.01 '*' 0.05 '.' 0.1 ' ' 1
```

The above code tests the hypothesis that the effects of displaying coke and displaying pepsi have equal but opposite effects, a null hypothesis that is being rejected by the test. Here is another example, testing the null hypothesis that displaying coke and pepsi have (jointly) no effect on an individual's choice. This hypothesis is also rejected.

```
Hnull <- c("disp_coke=0", "disp_pepsi=0")
linearHypothesis(coke.logit, Hnull)
```

```
## Linear hypothesis test
##
## Hypothesis:
## disp_coke = 0
```

Table 16.6: Linear Probability IV, the $labor force$ Problem

	Estimate	Std. Error	t value	Pr($>$|t|)
(Intercept)	0.5919	0.2359	2.509	0.0123
educ	0.0388	0.0164	2.359	0.0186
exper	0.0394	0.0059	6.728	0.0000
I(exper^2)	-0.0006	0.0002	-3.030	0.0025
kidsl6	-0.2712	0.0338	-8.012	0.0000
age	-0.0177	0.0023	-7.531	0.0000

```
## disp_pepsi = 0
##
## Model 1: restricted model
## Model 2: coke ~ pratio + disp_coke + disp_pepsi
##
##    Res.Df Df Chisq Pr(>Chisq)
## 1    1138
## 2    1136  2    19    0.000076 ***
## ---
## Signif. codes:  0 '***' 0.001 '**' 0.01 '*' 0.05 '.' 0.1 ' ' 1
```

Example 16.9 LPM with Endogenous Regressors: the $labour force$ Problem

In the data set $mroz$, the variable *lfp* is equal to 1 if a woman is in the labor force and 0 otherwise. Let us consider $education$ endogenous and estimate a linear probability model using $mothereduc$ as an instrument for $educ$.

```
data(mroz)
lfp.livr<-ivreg(lfp~educ+exper+I(exper^2)+kidsl6+age|
          exper+I(exper^2)+kidsl6+age+mothereduc, data=mroz)
ivout<- summary(lfp.livr)$coefficients
kable(ivout,digits=4, align='c',
 caption="Linear Probability IV, the $labor force$ Problem")
```

Table 16.6 shows the results of the Linear Probability Model with $mothereduc$ as an instrumental variable for $educ$.

```
ivdiag<-summary(lfp.livr, diagnostics=TRUE)$diagnostics
kable(ivdiag,digits=4,align='c',
      caption="The $labor force$ Problem: IV Diagnostic")
```

Table 16.7 displays the instrumental variable regression diagnostics, which show that the null hypothesis of endogeneity cannot be rejected.

Table 16.7: The *laborforce* Problem: IV Diagnostic

	df1	df2	statistic	p-value
Weak instruments	1	747	165.1000	0.0000
Wu-Hausman	1	746	0.2097	0.6472
Sargan	0	NA	NA	NA

16.4 Multinomial Logit

A relatively common R function that fits multinomial logit models is `multinom` in the `nnet` package.

Example16.12 Multinomial Logit for the *psechoice* Problem

Let us use the data set *nels_small* for an example of how `multinom` works. The variable *grades* in this data set is an index, with best grades represented by lower values of *grade*. We try to explain the choice of a secondary institution (*psechoice*) only by the high school grade. The variable *pschoice* can take one of three values:

- *psechoice* = 1 no college,
- *psechoice* = 2 two year college
- *psechoice* = 3 four year college

```
library(nnet)
data("nels_small", package="POE5Rdata")
nels.multinom <- multinom(psechoice~grades, data=nels_small)

## # weights:  9 (4 variable)
## initial  value 1098.612289
## iter  10 value 875.313116
## final  value 875.313099
## converged

summary(nels.multinom)

## Call:
## multinom(formula = psechoice ~ grades, data = nels_small)
##
## Coefficients:
##    (Intercept)  grades
## 2       2.505  -0.3086
## 3       5.770  -0.7062
##
```

```
## Std. Errors:
##    (Intercept)  grades
## 2       0.4184 0.05229
## 3       0.4043 0.05293
##
## Residual Deviance: 1751
## AIC: 1759
```

The output from function `multinom` gives coefficient estimates for each level of the response variable *psechoice*, except for the first level, which is the benchmark.

```
medGrades <- median(nels_small$grades)
fifthPercentileGrades <-
  quantile(nels_small$grades, .05)
newdat <- data.frame(grades=c(medGrades,fifthPercentileGrades))
pred <- predict(nels.multinom, newdat, "probs")
pred
```

```
##                 1          2         3
##     0.18101808 0.28557312 0.5334088
## 5% 0.01781764 0.09662199 0.8855604
```

The above code lines show how the usual function `predict` can calculate the predicted probabilities of choosing any of the three secondary education levels for two arbitrary grades: one at the median grade in the sample, and the other at the top fifth percent.

16.5   The Conditional Logit Model

In the multinomial logit model all individuals face the same external conditions and each individual's choice is only determined by an individual's circumstances or preferences. The **conditional logit model** allows for individuals to face individual-specific external conditions, such as the price of a product.

Example 16.13 Conditional Logit Soft Drink Choice

Suppose we want to study the effect of price on an individual's decision about choosing one of three brands of soft drinks:

1. pepsi
2. seven up
3. coke

In the conditional logit model, the probability that individual i chooses brand j is given by Equation (16.8).

$$p_{ij} = \frac{exp(\beta_{1j} + \beta_2 price_{ij})}{exp(\beta_{11} + \beta_2 price_{i1}) + exp(\beta_{12} + \beta_2 price_{i2}) + exp(\beta_{13} + \beta_2 price_{i3})} \quad (16.8)$$

In Equation (16.8) not all parameters β_{11}, β_{12}, and β_{13} can be estimated, and therefore one will be set equal to zero. Unlike in the multinomial logit model, the coefficient on the independent variable *price* is the same for all choices, but the value of the independent variable is different for each individual.

R offers several alternatives that allow fitting conditional logit models, one of which is the function MCMCmnl() from the package MCMCpack (others are, for instance, clogit() in the survival package and mclogit() in the mclogit package). The following code is adapted from (Adkins, 2014).

```
data("cola", package="POE5Rdata")
N <- nrow(cola)
N3 <- N/3
price1 <- cola$price[seq(1,N,by=3)]
price2 <- cola$price[seq(2,N,by=3)]
price3 <- cola$price[seq(3,N,by=3)]

bchoice <- rep("1", N3)
for (j in 1:N3){
    if(cola$choice[3*j-1]==1) bchoice[j] <- "2"
    if(cola$choice[3*j]==1) bchoice[j] <- "3"
 }
cola.clogit <- MCMCmnl(bchoice ~
    choicevar(price1, "b2", "1")+
    choicevar(price2, "b2", "2")+
    choicevar(price3, "b2", "3"),
    baseline="3", mcmc.method="IndMH")

## Calculating MLEs and large sample var-cov matrix.
## This may take a moment...
## Inverting Hessian to get large sample var-cov matrix.

sclogit <- summary(cola.clogit)
tabMCMC <- as.data.frame(sclogit$statistics)[,1:2]
row.names(tabMCMC)<- c("b2","b11","b12")
```

Table 16.8: Conditional Logit Estimates for the *cola* Problem

	Mean	SD
b2	-2.2991	0.1382
b11	0.2839	0.0610
b12	0.1037	0.0621

```
kable(tabMCMC, digits=4, align="c", caption=
 "Conditional Logit Estimates for the $cola$ Problem")
```

Table 16.8 shows the estimated parameters β_{ij} in Equation (16.8), with choice 3 (coke) being the baseline, which makes β_{13} equal to zero. Using the βs in Table 16.8, let us calculate the probability that individual i chooses *pepsi* and *sevenup* for some given values of the prices that individual i faces. The calculations follow the formula in Equation (16.8), with $\beta_{13} = 0$. Of course, the probability of choosing the baseline brand, in this case Coke, must be such that the sum of all three probabilities is equal to 1.

```
pPepsi <- 1 # prices
pSevenup <- 1.25
pCoke <- 1.10
b13 <- 0
b2  <- tabMCMC$Mean[1]
b11 <- tabMCMC$Mean[2]
b12 <- tabMCMC$Mean[3]

# The probability that individual i chooses Pepsi:
PiPepsi <- exp(b11+b2*pPepsi)/
           (exp(b11+b2*pPepsi)+exp(b12+b2*pSevenup)+
                           exp(b13+b2*pCoke))
# The probability that individual i chooses Sevenup:
PiSevenup <- exp(b12+b2*pSevenup)/
           (exp(b11+b2*pPepsi)+exp(b12+b2*pSevenup)+
                           exp(b13+b2*pCoke))
# The probability that individual i chooses Coke:
PiCoke <- 1-PiPepsi-PiSevenup
```

The calculated probabilities are:

- $p_{i,\,pepsi} = 0.483$
- $p_{i,\,sevenup} = 0.227$
- $p_{i,\,coke} = 0.289$

Table 16.9: Ordered Probit Estimates for the *nels* Problem

	Mean	SD
(Intercept)	2.9542	0.1478
grades	-0.3074	0.0193
gamma2	0.8616	0.0487

The three probabilities are different for different individuals because different individuals face different prices; in a more complex model other regressors may be included, some of which may reflect individual characteristics.

16.6 Ordered Choice Models

The order of choices in these models is meaningful, unlike the multinomial and conditional logit model we have studied so far. The following example explains the choice of higher education, when the choice variable is *psechoice* and the only regressor is *grades*; the data set, *nels_small*, is already known to us.

The R package MCMCpack is again used here, with its function MCMCoprobit().

```
nels.oprobit <- MCMCoprobit(psechoice ~ grades,
                data=nels_small, mcmc=10000)
sOprobit <- summary(nels.oprobit)
tabOprobit <- sOprobit$statistics[, 1:2]
kable(tabOprobit, digits=4, align="c", caption=
  "Ordered Probit Estimates for the $nels$ Problem")
```

Table 16.9 gives the ordered probit estimates. The results from MCMCoprobit can be translated into the textbook notations as follows:

- $\mu_1 = -(\text{Intercept})$
- $\beta = \text{grades}$
- $\mu_2 = \text{gamma2} - (\text{Intercept})$

The probabilities for each choice can be calculated as in the next code fragment:

```
mu1 <- -tabOprobit[1]
b <- tabOprobit[2]
mu2 <- tabOprobit[3]-tabOprobit[1]
xGrade <- c(mean(nels_small$grades),
            quantile(nels_small$grades, 0.05))
```

```
# Probabilities:
prob1 <- pnorm(mu1-b*xGrade)
prob2 <- pnorm(mu2-b*xGrade)-pnorm(mu1-b*xGrade)
prob3 <- 1-pnorm(mu2-b*xGrade)

# Marginal effects:
Dp1DGrades <- -pnorm(mu1-b*xGrade)*b
Dp2DGrades <- (pnorm(mu1-b*xGrade)-pnorm(mu2-b*xGrade))*b
Dp3DGrades <- pnorm(mu2-b*xGrade)*b
```

For instance, the marginal effect of *grades* on the probability of attending a four-year college for a student with average grade and for a student in the top 5 percent are, respectively, -0.143 and -0.031.

16.7   Models for Count Data

Such models use the Poisson distribution function, of the (count) variable y, as shown in Equations (16.9) and (16.10).

$$f(y) = P(Y = y) = \frac{e^{-\lambda}\lambda^y}{y!} \tag{16.9}$$

$$E(y) = \lambda = exp(\beta_1 + \beta_2 x)y = \beta_1 \tag{16.10}$$

Example 16.15 A Count Model for Doctor Visits

```
data(rwm88_small)
docs.count <- glm(docvis~age+female+public,
                  family= "poisson",
                  na.action=na.omit,
                  data=rwm88_small)
kable(tidy(docs.count), digits=4, align='c',
caption="A Poisson Model for the $Doctor$ Problem")

library(AER)
dispersiontest(docs.count)

##
##  Overdispersion test
##
```

Table 16.10: A Poisson Model for the *Doctor* Problem

term	estimate	std.error	statistic	p.value
(Intercept)	-0.0030	0.0918	-0.0328	0.9738
age	0.0116	0.0015	7.8037	0.0000
female	0.1283	0.0335	3.8265	0.0001
public	0.5726	0.0680	8.4234	0.0000

```
## data:   docs.count
## z = 3.8583, p-value = 5.708e-05
## alternative hypothesis: true dispersion is greater than 1
## sample estimates:
## dispersion
##    9.866489
```

Table 16.10 shows the output of a count model to explain the number of doctor visits based on an individual's age, gender, and access to public health insurance. The function dispersiontest in package AER tests the validity of the Poisson distribution based on this distribution's characteristic that its mean is equal to its variance. The null hypothesis of the test is *equidispersion*; rejecting the null hypothesis questions the validity of the model. Our example fails the overdispersion test.

16.8 The Tobit, or Censored Data Model

Censored data include a large number of observations for which the dependent variable takes one, or a limited number of values. An example is the *mroz* data, where about 43 percent of the women observed are not in the labor force, therefore their market hours worked are zero. Figure 16.2 shows the histogram of the variable *wage* in the data set *mroz*.

```
data(mroz)
hist(mroz$hours, breaks=20, col="grey", main="",
     xlab="Hours Worked")
box(byd="o")
```

A censored model is based on the idea of a **latent**, or unobserved variable that is not censored, and is explained via a probit model, as shown in Equation (16.11).

$$y_i^* = \beta_1 + \beta_2 x_i + e_i \tag{16.11}$$

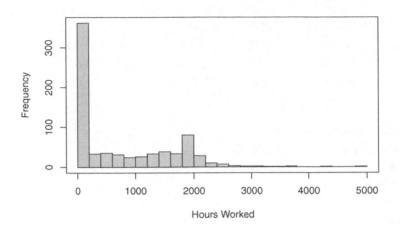

Figure 16.2 Histogram for the Variable *wage* in the *mroz* Data Set

The observable variable, y, is zero for all y^* that are less or equal to zero and is equal to y^* when y^* is greater than zero. The model for censored data is called **Tobit**, and is described by Equation (16.12).

$$P(y = 0) = P(y* \leq 0) = 1 - \Phi[(\beta_1 + \beta_2 x)/\sigma] \qquad (16.12)$$

The marginal effect of a change in x on the observed variable y is given by Equation (16.13).

$$\frac{\partial E(y|x)}{\partial x} = \beta_2 \Phi \left(\frac{\beta_1 + \beta_2 x}{\sigma} \right) \qquad (16.13)$$

```
library(AER)
mroz.tobit <- tobit(hours~educ+exper+age+kids16,
                    data=mroz)
sMrozTobit <- summary(mroz.tobit)
sMrozTobit
```

```
##
## Call:
## tobit(formula = hours ~ educ + exper + age + kids16, data = mroz)
##
## Observations:
##          Total  Left-censored     Uncensored Right-censored
```

```
##              753           325            428              0
##
## Coefficients:
##                Estimate Std. Error z value Pr(>|z|)
## (Intercept) 1349.8763    386.2991    3.49  0.00048 ***
## educ          73.2910     20.4746    3.58  0.00034 ***
## exper         80.5353      6.2878   12.81  < 2e-16 ***
## age          -60.7678      6.8882   -8.82  < 2e-16 ***
## kids16       -918.9181    111.6607   -8.23  < 2e-16 ***
## Log(scale)     7.0332      0.0371  189.57  < 2e-16 ***
## ---
## Signif. codes:  0 '***' 0.001 '**' 0.01 '*' 0.05 '.' 0.1 ' ' 1
##
## Scale: 1134
##
## Gaussian distribution
## Number of Newton-Raphson Iterations: 4
## Log-likelihood: -3.83e+03 on 6 Df
## Wald-statistic:  243 on 4 Df, p-value: <2e-16
```

The following code lines calculate the marginal effect of education on hours for some given values of the regressors.

```
xEduc <- 12.29
xExper <- 10.63
xAge <- 42.54
xKids <- 1
bInt <- coef(mroz.tobit)[[1]]
bEduc <- coef(mroz.tobit)[[2]]
bExper <- coef(mroz.tobit)[[3]]
bAge <- coef(mroz.tobit)[[4]]
bKids <- coef(mroz.tobit)[[5]]
bSigma <- mroz.tobit$scale
Phactor <- pnorm((bInt+bEduc*xEduc+bExper*xExper+
          bAge*xAge+bKids*xKids)/bSigma)
DhoursDeduc <- bEduc*Phactor
```

The calculated marginal effect is 26.606. (The function censReg() from package censReg can also be used for estimating Tobit models; this function gives the possibility of calculating marginal effects using the function margEff().)

16.9 The Heckit, or Sample Selection Model

The models are useful when the sample selection is not random, but whether an individual is in the sample depends on individual characteristics. For example, when studying wage determination for married women, some women are not in the labor force, therefore their wages are zero.

The model to use in such situation is **Heckit**, which involves two equations: the **selection equation**, given in Equation (16.14), and the linear **equation of interest**, as in Equation (16.15).

$$z_i^* = \gamma_1 + \gamma_2 w_i + u_i \tag{16.14}$$

$$y_i = \beta_1 + \beta_2 x_i + e_i \tag{16.15}$$

Estimates of the β coefficients can be obtained by using least squares on the model in Equation (16.16), where λ_i is calculated using the formula in Equation (16.17).

$$y_i = \beta_1 + \beta_2 x_i + \beta_\lambda \lambda_i + \nu_i \tag{16.16}$$

$$\lambda_i = \frac{\phi(\gamma_1 + \gamma_2 w_i)}{\Phi(\gamma_1 + \gamma_2 w_i)} \tag{16.17}$$

The amount λ given by Equation (16.17) is called the **inverse Mills ratio**.

The Heckit procedure involves two steps, estimating both the selection equation and the equation of interest. Function selection() in the sampleSelection package performs both steps; therefore, it needs both equations among its arguments. (The selection equation is, in fact, a *probit* model.)

```
library(sampleSelection)
wage.heckit <- selection(lfp~age+educ+I(kids618+kids16)+mtr,
                         log(wage)~educ+exper,
                         data=mroz, method="ml")
summary(wage.heckit)


## ---------------------------------------------
## Tobit 2 model (sample selection model)
## Maximum Likelihood estimation
## Newton-Raphson maximisation, 4 iterations
```

```
## Return code 2: successive function values within tolerance limit
## Log-Likelihood: -913.5
## 753 observations (325 censored and 428 observed)
## 10 free parameters (df = 743)
## Probit selection equation:
##                       Estimate Std. Error t value Pr(>|t|)
## (Intercept)            1.53798    0.61889    2.49   0.0132 *
## age                   -0.01346    0.00603   -2.23   0.0259 *
## educ                   0.06278    0.02180    2.88   0.0041 **
## I(kids618 + kids16)   -0.05108    0.03276   -1.56   0.1194
## mtr                   -2.20864    0.54620   -4.04 0.000058 ***
## Outcome equation:
##               Estimate Std. Error t value Pr(>|t|)
## (Intercept)    0.64622    0.23557    2.74   0.0062 **
## educ           0.06646    0.01657    4.01 0.000067 ***
## exper          0.01197    0.00408    2.93   0.0035 **
##     Error terms:
##           Estimate Std. Error t value Pr(>|t|)
## sigma      0.8411     0.0430     19.6   <2e-16 ***
## rho       -0.8277     0.0391    -21.2   <2e-16 ***
## ---
## Signif. codes:  0 '***' 0.001 '**' 0.01 '*' 0.05 '.' 0.1 ' ' 1
## ---------------------------------------------
```

Bibliography

Adkins, L. (2014). *Using gretl for Principles of Econometrics, 4th Edition*. Number 1412.

Allaire, J., Cheng, J., Xie, Y., McPherson, J., Chang, W., Allen, J., Wickham, H., Atkins, A., and Hyndman, R. (2016). *rmarkdown: Dynamic Documents for R*. R package version 0.9.6.

Colonescu, C. (2017). *POE5Rdata: R Data for Principles of Econometrics by Hill, Griffiths, and Lim, 5-th Edition*. R package version 0.1.0.

Cookson, T. (2011). *Shadenorm, An R function to shade areas under the normal distribution*.

Croissant, Y. and Millo, G. (2015). *plm: Linear Models for Panel Data*. R package version 1.5-12.

Dahl, D. B. (2016). *xtable: Export Tables to LaTeX or HTML*. R package version 1.8-2.

Dissanayake, A. and Wijekoon, P. (2016). *lrmest: Different Types of Estimators to Deal with Multicollinearity*. R package version 3.0.

Fox, J. and Weisberg, S. (2016). *car: Companion to Applied Regression*. R package version 2.1-2.

Fox, J., Weisberg, S., Friendly, M., and Hong, J. (2016). *effects: Effect Displays for Linear, Generalized Linear, and Other Models*. R package version 3.1-1.

Ghalanos, A. (2015). *rugarch: Univariate GARCH Models*. R package version 1.3-6.

Grolemund, G. and Wickham, H. (2016). *R for Data Science*.

Henningsen, A. and Hamann, J. D. (2015). *systemfit: Estimating Systems of Simultaneous Equations*. R package version 1.1-18.

Hill, R., Griffiths, W., and Lim, G. (2018). *Principles of Econometrics, Fifth Edition*. Wiley.

Hlavac, M. (2015). *stargazer: Well-Formatted Regression and Summary Statistics Tables*. R package version 5.2.

Hothorn, T., Zeileis, A., Farebrother, R. W., and Cummins, C. (2015). *lmtest: Testing Linear Regression Models*. R package version 0.9-34.

Hyndman, R. (2016). *forecast: Forecasting Functions for Time Series and Linear Models*. R package version 7.1.

Kleiber, C. and Zeileis, A. (2015). *AER: Applied Econometrics with R*. R package version 1.2-4.

Komashko, O. (2016). *nlWaldTest: Wald Test of Nonlinear Restrictions and Nonlinear CI*. R package version 1.1.3.

Lander, J. P. (2013). *R for Everyone: Advanced Analytics and Graphics*. Addison-Wesley Professional, 1st edition.

Lumley, T. and Zeileis, A. (2015). *sandwich: Robust Covariance Matrix Estimators*. R package version 2.3-4.

Pfaff, B. (2013). *vars: VAR Modelling*. R package version 1.5-2.

R Development Core Team (2008). *R: A Language and Environment for Statistical Computing*. R Foundation for Statistical Computing, Vienna, Austria. ISBN 3-900051-07-0.

Reinhart, A. (2015). *pdfetch: Fetch Economic and Financial Time Series Data from Public Sources*. R package version 0.1.7.

Robinson, D. (2016). *broom: Convert Statistical Analysis Objects into Tidy Data Frames*. R package version 0.4.1.

RStudio Team (2015). *RStudio: Integrated Development Environment for R*. RStudio, Inc., Boston, MA.

Spada, S., Quartagno, M., and Tamburini, M. (2012). *orcutt: Estimate procedure in case of first order autocorrelation*. R package version 1.1.

Trapletti, A. and Hornik, K. (2016). *tseries: Time Series Analysis and Computational Finance*. R package version 0.10-35.

Wickham, H. and Chang, W. (2016a). *devtools: Tools to Make Developing R Packages Easier*. R package version 1.11.1.

Wickham, H. and Chang, W. (2016b). *ggplot2: Create Elegant Data Visualisations Using the Grammar of Graphics*. R package version 2.2.1.

Wickham, H., Francois, R., Henry, L., and Müller, K. (2017). *dplyr: A Grammar of Data Manipulation*. R package version 0.7.0.

Xie, Y. (2016). *bookdown: Authoring Books with R Markdown*. R package version 0.0.71.

Xie, Y. (2017). *knitr: A General-Purpose Package for Dynamic Report Generation in R*. R package version 1.18.

Zeileis, A. (2014). *dynlm: Dynamic Linear Regression*. R package version 0.3-3.

38966793R00167

Made in the USA
Columbia, SC
19 December 2018